VOLVO
Amazon

TITLES IN THE CROWOOD AUTOCLASSICS SERIES

VOLVO

The Complete Story

Richard Dredge

THE CROWOOD PRESS

First published in 2016 by
The Crowood Press Ltd
Ramsbury, Marlborough
Wiltshire SN8 2HR

enquiries@crowood.com

www.crowood.com

This impression 2026

British Library Cataloguing-in-Publication Data
A catalogue record for this book is available from the British Library.

For product safety-related questions contact productsafety@crowood.com

ISBN 978 1 78500 104 8

Acknowledgements
Big thanks are due to several people who helped enormously with the research and
production of this book. These include Rob and Emma Henchoz of Amazon Cars,
who checked the chapter on buying and modifying, offering time and information
freely.

The same goes for Kevin Price, founder of the Volvo Enthusiasts' Club, who
checked the chapters charting the history of the Amazon. Fellow VEC members
Tony and Gillian Whitton are also due a king-sized thank you for letting me loose
with some of their precious Volvo collection for some of the photography within
this book – it's their cars that adorn the front cover.

Also due some appreciation are the folks at Volvo, including Martin Bayntun in the
UK press office and Claes Rydholm of Volvo Heritage – who retired while this book
was being compiled. As a result it was left to Lars Gerdin and Per-Ake Froberg to
trawl through the archives, so many thanks to them for their help.

Thanks are also due to Lillian Bech of the Ole Summer Collection, for sending
through images of the Sommer Coupé, and finally thanks to Crowood for their
patience when I put the book back yet again by several months because of other
commitments. They must have wondered on many occasions whether or not this
book would actually happen – and eventually it did …

Typeset by Jean Cussons Typesetting, Diss, Norfolk

Printed and bound in India by Thomson Press India Pvt. Ltd.

CONTENTS

TIMELINE

- **1956:** In September the Volvo 'Amazon' is first shown to the public as the 121 with a 60bhp B16A engine. Four-door saloon bodywork is available in black, dark blue or red with a light grey roof, or light grey with a black roof. The name Amazon cannot be used beyond Scandinavia, however, because it has already been registered on the continent by the motorcycle manufacturer Kreidler.

  In most export markets, names such as Volvo 121 or Volvo 122S (for one Sport version) are to be the norm for this series. On retiring as managing director, Assar Gabrielsson is appointed chairman of the board. Formerly the head of Volvo Aero, Gunnar Engellau is appointed managing director of AB Volvo.

- **1957:** The Volvo Amazon goes into production and on sale in January, priced at 12,600 Swedish kronor (£868). Anchorages for two-point seatbelts in the front seats become standard in all Volvos this year. Production of the Volvo Sport is stopped, and 1957 is also to be the last model year when the PV444 is made. Volvo's total car output comes to over 50,000 units this year. The company now has a workforce of 13,000 and by December the 5,000th Amazon has been built.

- **1958:** When the Amazon was launched, many thought it would mean the end of the PV models. But not so. In August Volvo presents the PV544, a substantially revised and updated derivative of the PV444. Four versions are made, offering a variety of engines and equipment levels. Seatbelt anchorages for the rear seats now become standard. AB Volvo's turnover exceeds one billion kronor for the first time.

  In March the Amazon 122S is shown at Geneva with an 85bhp B16B engine featuring twin SU carburettors and a redesigned camshaft, plus a standard four-speed gearbox. This is to be the main 'export' model, but the four-speed gearbox is available on the 121 as an alternative in Sweden. The bonnet release is now located inside the car and the suspension is lowered by one inch to improve the car's stance.

  In August the 1959 model-year cars are introduced with standard front seatbelts, then in November dual-circuit, servo-assisted brakes become standard, along with an improved heating system. At the same time, the 122S becomes the first Volvo imported into Britain, by the Brooklands Motor Company, at a basic £932 – which jumps to £1,399 including purchase tax.

The Amazon came with two-tone paintwork as standard when it was launched in 1956.

By 1958, Volvo had built 10,000 examples of the Amazon.

- **1959:** Front-seat three-point seatbelts are made standard in Volvo Amazons and PV544s bound for Scandinavian markets. This makes Volvo the world's first car maker to fit this type of belt as standard equipment. Volvo purchases four million square metres of land in Gothenburg (Hisingen) and starts building roads to the site where the Torslanda plant will take shape. New registrations of Volvo cars in Sweden this year come to 39,016 units – the highest total any single brand has achieved by this stage.

  In April 1959 the 122S is launched in the USA at the New York Automobile Show; at the same time, Danish Volvo agent Sommer builds an Amazon hardtop coupé but it remains a one-off.

- **1960:** Early in the year, the two-seater P1800 sports coupé is presented at the motor show in Brussels. The substantially revised Volvo Duett becomes the Volvo P210. It now has a curved windscreen of the same type as introduced with the first PV544, a four-speed gearbox and a new dashboard. An insurance company called Volvia is set up to offer ongoing cover to Volvo owners after their initial accident damage warranties expire. The company is now making over 80,000 cars a year.

  In August Volvo announces the 1961 model-year Amazon, with new designs of three- (fully synchronized) and four-speed gearboxes – the three-speeder is also offered with optional Laycock de Normanville electric overdrive on second and third. Improved front seats now give better support when cornering.

- **1961:** The P1800 sports car goes into production. It has a brand-new twin-carb engine, the B18B. The powerful new B18 engine (which is actually half of a B36 V8 truck engine) is to be used in the PV544 and Amazon too. For the PV544 there are also new three- and four-speed gearboxes with full synchromesh.

  In August a new engine is fitted to the 120 series, now retitled 130. It's the B18 with a five-bearing crankshaft and new cylinder head that allows fuel to be supplied to each cylinder individually, instead of in pairs. In B18A form it gives 75bhp at 4500rpm with a single Zenith; in B18D form there's 90bhp at 5000rpm with two SUs. The sporty engine merits front disc brakes, while both receive 12-volt electrics, tougher front suspension and an enlarged grille with a red B18 motif in it. No more two-tones from now on.

  A two-door version of the Amazon, the 121, is introduced in October on the same wheelbase. It comes only in black with beige upholstery and 'nougat' trim; and it's sold only in Scandinavia, for a bargain 500 kronor less.

In 1961 a two-door saloon joined the range.

The Amazon estate, introduced in 1962, was even more practical than the spacious four-door saloon.

The Volvo Canadian was the same as a regular Amazon – but it was built in Canada rather than Sweden.

- **1962:** A four-door estate model is added to the Amazon line-up in February. Its rear end is totally new, with an American-style, horizontally split tailgate. Called the 220 Combi estate, it features redesigned suspension and a six-feet-long loading area. A four-speed gearbox is standard and it's priced at 14,475 kronor.

  In the same month, the 100,000th Volvo Amazon is built, then in August the saloon's rear wheel arches are strengthened to cope with buckling in the event of an accident. Also, reversing lights are now fitted. The C version of the PV544 now has the B18 engine – a welcome boost for a model which has been overshadowed by the Volvo Amazon.

- **1963:** Local assembly and local component incentives lead to Volvo opening its first foreign assembly plant, in Halifax, Canada, in June. Its output will be a few thousand vehicles per annum, with cars badged as the Volvo Canadian. The USA is now the company's biggest export market by far, and Volvo is the fourth-largest imported brand there. The Volvo Group now has a turnover in excess of two billion kronor and over 20,000 employees.

  From August an Amazon with two doors and twin carburettors is on sale for the first time, while the four-door saloon is now available with a three-speed Borg-Warner automatic gearbox. All models now come with low-profile tyres and a boot handle incorporating the number plate light. At the same time, the Amazon estate finally arrives in the UK, priced at £1,277.

• **1964:** The new plant at Torslanda is opened officially by King Gustav Adolf of Sweden on 24 April. It has been built for a capacity of up to 200,000 cars per annum under a two-shift system. Several product improvements are introduced, in line with the company's focus on safety. All Amazon models now have disc brakes at the front, and the Amazon estate gets servo-assisted brakes for the first time.

Another key innovation is enlisting the aid of medical experts in designing the front seats for Volvos. And the first prototype of a rear-facing child seat is tested in Volvos this year. Total production this year is 118,464 vehicles, including 8,040 CKD kits for foreign assembly. The company builds its one-millionth car, a Volvo Amazon. Volvo is now the biggest company in Sweden.

The opening of the Torslanda plant in 1964 meant Volvo could ramp up Amazon production significantly.

In August the 1965 model-year Amazon is revealed, and it features a trend-setting orthopaedic seat design, with variable lumbar support control. Upholstery is a new textile-reinforced vinyl. From here on the car's sills are galvanized, and the estate gains a gas strut to support the upper portion of its tailgate.

• **1965:** Finished in black, the last PV544 rolls off the production line at the Lundby plant on 20 October. At an outdoor ceremony that same day, 26 Volvo employees who have won a white PV544 each in a prize draw are presented with the papers to their new cars – a splendid way of rounding off production of the model that made such a difference to Volvo's future. Total production of the PV444 and 544 ends at 440,000 units, 160,000 of which were exported. The official opening ceremony for the assembly plant in Ghent, Belgium, takes place on 3 November. This means that Volvo now has a production plant inside the Common Market.

From August the B18A engine's compression ratio increases from 8.5:1 to 8.7:1. The B18D sports engine gets a 5bhp power increase because of an increased compression ratio and a high-lift camshaft.

In October the Amazon Favorit is launched. It's a reduced-spec, cheaper version of the 75bhp two-door Amazon with a three-speed gearbox, minimal trim and no passenger sun visor. Black paint with red seats is the only colour scheme available.

• **1966:** The Volvo 144 makes its debut in August, marking a great step forward in the safety sphere. It has disc brakes all round, a collapsible steering column, and its three-point seatbelts have a new type of buckle. Its body has energy-absorbing crumple zones front and back, and its braking system has a unique new configuration: the L-split. Two engines are used in the first 144s, of 85 and 115bhp. The more powerful version is called the 144S. The new Volvo receives widespread acclaim and is soon voted Car of the Year in Sweden.

But there's still life in the Amazon, with the 123GT being introduced in August. It uses the two-door bodyshell but with the 115bhp engine from the P1800 coupé and a four-speed gearbox. There are new wheel trims, a rev counter plus fog and spot lamps to single it out. The 121's B18A engine gains a Volvo 140-type Zenith-Stromberg carb to give 85 instead of 75bhp. The 122S has the power of its B18D engine upped to 100 from 95bhp, but is denied standard overdrive.

The arrival of the 140-Series in 1966 meant the Amazon's days were numbered – although it would soldier on for another four years.

- **1967:** Volvo presents the world's first rear-facing child seat, and seatbelts are introduced for the rear seats of the company's cars. The Volvo 144 is soon a success in export markets too. It proves to be able to comply with the next set of safety standards in the USA even though these had not been published when it was developed. The two-door Volvo 142S is launched in June, and the 145 estate model arrives later in the year.

  From August the Amazon gets servo-assisted brakes across the range (they'd been optional up to this point), a collapsible steering column, and a new safety steering wheel that will collapse in the event of a collision. An emission control system is introduced for twin-carburettor models exported to the USA. But the writing is on the wall for the Amazon, with production of the four-door model ceasing in December – it's replaced by the 140.

- **1968:** The exclusive 6-cylinder Volvo 164 is launched, offering refinements like power steering and automatic transmission. The 140 series achieves record sales, becoming Sweden's bestselling car of all time. Head restraints are introduced for the front seats. A new Volvo assembly plant opens in Malaysia, with a capacity of 2,500 cars per annum.

  From August the Amazon is fitted with the new B20 engine with an emission control system. Displacing 1998cc, the B20A gives 90bhp, the B20B 118bhp. At the same time, the 123GT is discontinued.

- **1969:** Planning begins for a new proving ground in Hällered outside Gothenburg, on a six-million-square-metre site. Volvo becomes the owner of Svenska Stålpressnings AB in Olofström, a company that has made bodies and body parts for the brand since 1927.

  The last P210 is made in February, superseded by the Volvo 145 Express, an estate model with an extra-high roof. The Amazon estate is discontinued; from here on, a rationalized range consists of only the two-door Amazon with either engine option. Rear seatbelts are included, as are front seat head restraints. Inertia-reel seatbelts are introduced for the front seats.

- **1970:** Amazon production ends on 3 July, with the final tally coming out at 234,208 examples of the four-door saloon, 359,918 copies of the two-door saloon and 73,197 estates.

CHAPTER ONE

BEFORE THE AMAZON

It was in 1924 that Assar Gabrielsson and Gustaf Larson first discussed the possibility of setting up a company to manufacture cars. In that year, just 15,000 cars found buyers in Sweden and, of those, just one in twenty was sourced from outside North America. The pair resolved to build a car better suited to Sweden's poorly surfaced roads – one that would prove more durable.

In the early days, before the company even had a name, Gabrielsson and Larson worked two evenings a week on their new project, retaining their full-time jobs. They worked in Larson's home to produce a set of designs with which they could source enough capital to go into limited production with a simple and rugged 4-cylinder car.

The person commissioned to design the first cars was Helmer MasOlle, a landscape and portrait artist who had a fascination with cars. His own car was a 1914 Voisin, a make noted for its innovation, and from the outset MasOlle decided that his first design for Volvo would share something of this approach. Larson also enlisted the help of young engineer Jan Smith to ensure any designs were as usable as possible.

By 1925 Volvo had taken on its first employee; 23-year old Henry Westerberg, who was tasked with completing the drawings for the first prototypes. Coachbuilder Freyschuss of Stockholm was com-missioned to produce the first ten bodies, nine of which would be open tourers with the final one being a closed four-door saloon. By June 1926 the first running prototype was ready for testing, and by spring 1927 the first batch of production cars would have to be ready. The deadline was hit, as on 14 April 1927 the first car was driven off the production line, in Volvo's Lundby factory. Apart from the fact that the car moved off in reverse, thanks to the rear axle having been incorrectly assembled, it had all gone to plan – now Volvo had to go out and sell some cars.

On offer was the OV4 (OppenVagn or Open Car, four cylinders) and PV4 (PersonVagn or Passenger Car, four cylinders), both powered by a 28bhp 1944cc engine mated to a three-speed manual gearbox. The tourer cost SKr4,800 (around £270 or $1,300), while the saloon was SKr1,000 more.

Volvo's first car was the open-topped OV4 – which proved unpopular because of Sweden's harsh winters.

Even at this early stage Gustaf Larson had set down the strategy that Volvo would follow – a high level of quality would always be more important than a low price. But since the 1950s the quality with which Volvo has been most often associated is the production of safe cars. As far back as 1936 Volvo was actively promoting safety. In its sales manuals (reputedly written by Assar Gabrielsson), given to all Volvo salesmen and first produced in 1936, the references to safety are clear:

> *An automobile conveys and is driven by people. The fundamental principle of all design work is, and must be, safety. Each individual supporting part and component in the car must be dimensioned in such a way that it will withstand all forms of stresses and strains which it can be expected to be subjected to, apart from collisions and similar types of impact. This applies chiefly to all supporting and driving parts.*

A MOVE TO SIX CYLINDERS

By 1929 it was clear the 4-cylinder cars were underpowered, especially considering their high price. Even before the first OV4 had been built, Larson was considering a 6-cylinder car. When the OV4 was introduced, America's car makers were building cars with just 4-cylinder engines; it was only a couple of years before they generally moved over to six, at least as an option. And as Volvo was competing with the major American car producers, it had to offer a 6-cylinder engine. But whereas with the American car makers the larger engines were seen as an option to sell alongside the smaller ones, with Volvo the 6-cylinder powerplants superseded the 4-cylinder ones. Throughout the 1930s all Volvos had these bigger engines and it wasn't until after the war, when the PV444 was launched, that there would be a return to 4-cylinder power for any of the company's products.

ASSAR GABRIELSSON

Born in Korsberga on 13 August 1891, Assar Gabrielsson was 20 when he graduated from the Stockholm School of Economics. One of the first-year intake of the new course, his tutors were legends of their time and Gabrielsson did incredibly well with his academic studies. He gained top marks in English, Russian and economics – skills that were to prove invaluable when he set up Volvo with Gustaf Larson.

In 1916 he joined one of Sweden's largest industrial empires, Svenska Kullagerfabriken (SKF), where he went on – at the age of 32 – to become sales manager for the entire group. While there he got to know about Gustaf Larson and his great skills as an engineer, so, while Larson set about sorting out the engineering for the new car-producing company they were trying to establish, Gabrielsson ensured that the sums added up.

The venture soon became a great success, with Volvo going from strength to strength throughout Gabrielsson's time as managing director of the company. Although Larson's great talents were key to the company's success, if it hadn't been for Gabrielsson's banking connections the capital to set up the company simply wouldn't have been there. Gabrielsson retired in 1956 but continued as chairman of the board for another six years, until his death on 28 May 1962.

Assar Gabrielsson may have been incredibly conservative, but then so were most of Volvo's customers.

GUSTAF LARSON

Gustaf Larson was born in Vintrosa on 8 July 1887, one of eight children. By the time he was 24 he'd moved to Coventry to work for engine manufacturers White & Poppe, having had a fascination for automotive engineering since an early age. He was briefed with helping to design a new engine for Morris but within two years of arriving in England he had returned to Sweden, where he studied the internal combustion engine at Stockholm's Royal Institute of Technology.

Larson graduated in 1917, which was the year he joined SKF, where he first met Assar Gabrielsson, but it wasn't until 1924 that they started to plan establishing a new car manufacturer for Sweden.

It was while he was in England that Larson came up with the idea of building a car from parts manufactured by outside suppliers, and one of his principles was that it was cheaper to do the job properly the first time rather than skimp on design or manufacture and have to do it again. As a result, his perfectionism earned him a lot of respect throughout the car industry – one of his skills was instantly to be able to identify weaknesses in design before progressing to the manufacturing stage, something that helped to reinforce Volvo's reputation for quality from the outset.

In July 1952 Larson retired, having been in charge of the company's technical development until his departure. But he continued to be a board member until 1958 and he acted as a consultant to the company until his death on 4 July 1968.

Gustaf Larson's attention to detail was what gave Volvos an edge, compared with cheaper American rivals.

Volvo's first 6-cylinder car was the PV651, seen here during development testing.

The first car to use this larger, more powerful engine was the PV651, launched in April 1929 and based on the type PV650 chassis. Its 3010cc 6-cylinder side-valve engine, badged the DB, had nearly double the power of its predecessor, with 55bhp on tap. Although the exterior design of the new car marked a clear advance over the PV4, the transatlantic influences were clear. It also remained resolutely conservative, to remain appealing to the middle-class buyers at whom the car was aimed.

The Wall Street Crash of 1929 meant tough times for Volvo, which had chosen just the wrong time to move upmarket. But while car sales were hard to come by, Volvo moved into profitability thanks to the popularity of its trucks – especially once the 6-cylinder engine was available. Despite the cars' reputation for reliability, their staid design and conservative engineering encouraged buyers to spend their money on cheaper American alternatives, which were reliable enough for most people. Indeed, by the mid-1930s only one in fourteen new-car buyers was choosing a Volvo, the other thirteen invariably opting for something from across the Atlantic. That added up to around a thousand sales a year for the company, so to significantly increase its market share the company had either to add more cars to its range or make its existing cars more affordable. The decision was made to take the former route.

As Volvo already had a reputation for reliability, it made sense to target Sweden's taxi drivers with specially made cars that would suit their needs better than the standard PV651. By targeting taxi drivers, Volvo reckoned it could increase market share significantly, so, instead of just producing a single version, urban and rural taxi drivers got their own derivatives. But it wasn't only taxi drivers who were targeted by Volvo – any group that had a high profile was fair game as the company tried to break into the fleet market. That's why police forces and car hire companies were soon driving Volvos – something which could only reflect well on the company's products.

Although the cars were to prove popular, they were already lagging behind their (mainly American) competitors, which were often equipped with hydraulic brakes all round. Volvo was still using mechanical brakes on all four wheels, so the change to a hydraulic system for the launch of the PV652 in 1930 couldn't come soon enough. The new car also featured an interior that was more luxuriously trimmed and equipped. Instead of replacing the PV651, the new car was sold alongside it and although car production continued at just a trickle, at least Volvo was profitable.

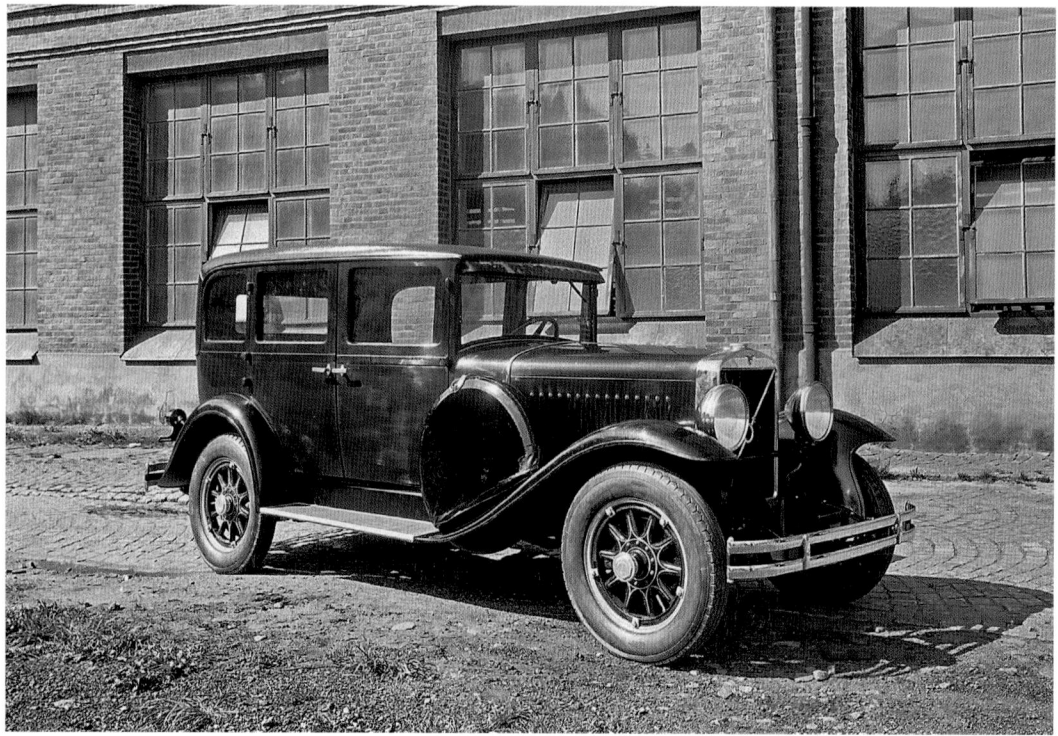

Volvo needed a 6-cylinder car in its range, to compete with its American rivals.

It had been SKF's hope that by the end of the 1920s there would be 8,000 vehicles rolling off Volvo's production lines each year, but in 1930 fewer than 2,000 vehicles were produced, most of which were trucks. But things weren't going badly overall and by 1931 Volvo was on a roll. Its trucks were incredibly popular, taxi ranks were full of cars bearing the 'Mars' logo (see box overleaf) and its cars had a name for ruggedness which meant buyers were opting for a Volvo in place of competing marques.

One of the reasons for the cars' popularity was the attention to detail in the manufacturing process. Because only small numbers of cars were being built, the factory workers could afford to devote a lot of time and attention to each one. There was even a nine-man 'adjusting department' on hand to inspect each chassis and give it a test run both before and after the bodywork had been fitted.

Having already been bench-tested by Pentaverken, Volvo's engine supplier, before it had even left the factory, each powerplant would be fired up from cold once installed in the chassis. The bare chassis would then be run on a tortuous twelve-mile route and the engine tested once up to temperature. Once the body had been fitted the whole process would be repeated, so if anything was amiss the rigorous testing would highlight it before the car reached the customer.

In autumn 1933 the PV653 and PV654 arrived. They replaced the PV651 and PV652, with the PV654 having the higher specification of the two cars. But despite the cars being well built and able to compete on equal terms with their competitors, sales slumped. This was the period of the Great Depression and all

The Venus Bilo concept was so daring, that initially, Volvo didn't claim to have any involvement with it.

Despite Volvo's customers being very conservative in their tastes, the company introduced the radically styled Carioca. It was a sales disaster.

manufacturing industries were feeling the pinch – and makers of luxury cars felt it more than most. As a result fewer than 600 of the PV653 and PV654 were built before the last of the conservatively styled pre-war cars went on sale, the PV658 and PV659.

As a result of sales barely picking up throughout the early 1930s, in 1935 Volvo came up with something more radical – the PV36, nicknamed Carioca after a popular dance of the period. Inspired by Chrysler's daring Airflow of 1934, the Carioca (like the Airflow) proved a flop because people thought it was so ugly. For such a conservative company, Volvo took rather a gamble with the Carioca – its Venus Bilo concept had proved a resounding flop when it was shown as a concept in 1933, so to put something similar into production just two years later was either foolhardy or incredibly optimistic.

The aim was to produce an initial batch of 500 cars and see how popular they were – a decision which was to prove a good one as in the event they took a long time to shift. Buyers weren't ready for a car with such advanced styling and it wasn't until well into 1938 that the last examples were sold.

VOLVO GOES PUBLIC

In 1935 Volvo achieved a major milestone: it was publicly quoted on the stock exchange for the first time. Now that it was nearly a decade old, SKF felt that its baby was capable of standing by itself, even though output was still below that projected. It had hoped to build 3,500 vehicles in 1935 but just 3,079 were produced – just under half being cars. The answer to expansion plans lay in producing something smaller and cheaper, as the company's dealers were crying out for a car to compete with the large numbers of Fords, Opels and DKWs that were now flooding the Swedish market.

The answer arrived at the end of 1936, in the form of the PV51. Less radical than the PV36, and significantly cheaper, the car was greeted with intense interest by the buying public. The PV51 was still more expensive than its rivals, but the Volvo badge meant it was worth paying for the extra quality. The engine was the same as the Carioca's and the gearbox was a three-speed unit with synchromesh on second and third gears. But although the PV51 had much in common with previous Volvos there was one significant difference – this was the first time that a car had been

WHY THE VOLVO NAME AND LOGO?

The company that made the initial investment which allowed Gabrielsson and Larson to commence series production of cars was the company that employed them both: SKF. This industrial giant was known first and foremost for its design and manufacture of bearings, and in 1915 SKF had registered the name AB Volvo but not used it.

Volvo is Latin for 'I roll', a reference to the fact that bearings are known for their rolling properties. As SKF helped to find premises for car production as well as providing SKr200,000 to start production, it was only natural that the company would have a hand in coming up with a name for the fledgling car maker. As a result, Larson's company was allowed to use the name registered by his backer – until they offered him the name he was set to put his own surname on the cars' badges.

The logo chosen for the car was a diagonal line incorporating a circle which enclosed a diagonal-facing arrow. This is the Swedish symbol for iron, known as the Mars symbol. The diagonal line itself wasn't supposed to become a design theme, but the Mars symbol had to be affixed to the radiator in some way. The stripe that was used to locate the trademark logo has probably become a more powerful symbol of Volvo than the logo itself.

Volvo is still using the Mars symbol, although it has passed through several iterations since this early badge.

produced by the company which was built entirely of sheet steel pressings.

To keep costs down, the interior was less plush than the Carioca's and, with a weight of around 29.5cwt, performance was much better than with previous Volvos, thanks to the 85bhp engine. But the car was so incredibly spartan that many buyers were put off – Volvo had skimped to the point that there was only one windscreen wiper and three of the four doors had no armrest. The answer lay in the PV52, introduced in the spring of 1937. This was nothing more than a PV51 with more generous equipment levels, but it did the trick as car sales for 1937 were nearly double those of the previous year – although of the 1,804 cars built, just fifty-six were sold outside Sweden. In March 1938, to try to appeal to even more buyers, Special versions of the PV51 and PV52 were launched, with the spare wheel mounted in the boot instead of on the boot lid.

The PV51 and PV52 (the latter seen here) were the first cars from Volvo designed for mass production.

To eke out the lives of the PV51 and PV52 in both standard and Special forms, they received minor facelifts and changes in name. So in 1938 the PV53 arrived to replace the PV51 while the PV54 replaced the PV51 Special. The PV55 superseded the PV52, and to take over the PV52 Special's place in the pecking order there was the PV56. There was also a PV57, which was merely a rolling chassis for bespoke bodywork. But the whole series was only a stopgap until the arrival of a significantly new model, which was scheduled for launch in February 1940.

When war broke out in Europe in September 1939 this project was severely disrupted, but it wasn't put on hold altogether. Work continued on the car, with further prototypes being built in 1942 and 1943 ready for its introduction when the war was over. So when hostilities ended in 1945, the PV60 was ready to go on sale, although production didn't begin until December 1946. That was more than two years after the car had first been shown. By the

The PV60's design was clearly inspired by American rivals, but it proved tough and reliable.

time the car reached the showroom, it was already out of date; no surprise, as the project had been started nearly a decade before. Its styling was based very heavily on US designs, but American car makers had changed the look of their cars radically since the war. Despite this, the car sold well, with Volvo's traditionally conservative buyers not too bothered by the fact that their car didn't look especially modern.

Under the skin the car was just as old-fashioned, as it was powered by the familiar side-valve 6-cylinder engine, albeit in a slightly more developed form. Despite the car's conservatism, 3,006 examples were sold between 1946 and 1950, which was good going in the years of austerity that followed the Second World War.

VOLVO EMBARKS ON A PEOPLE'S CAR

By 1943 the management at Volvo were looking to the end of the war, and the types of car which would become popular. It was clear that luxury cars would not only be unaffordable to most people, but the costs of producing them would be inordinately high. The answer was to produce something relatively small that was simple and rugged – and most of all affordable for Mr and Mrs Average.

A team of forty designers and engineers was assigned to the project in May 1943, and a consultant by the name of Helmer Petterson (see separate panel) was hired to oversee the group. It had already been decided that the first cars would be shown in the autumn of the following year, so time was tight.

A skilled engineer named Erik Jern was one of the senior members of the team, and he discussed with Petterson the possibilities open to them in terms of engine, transmission and body design. Having looked at some of the DKWs being produced at that time, the two decided that more and more car manufacturers would follow the front-wheel-drive route taken by the German car maker. But having decided to explore the front-wheel-drive option, it became clear that this would be inherently less reliable than a more conventional layout, and Volvo would have to produce more components in-house than was desirable. It was clear that a more conventional, rear-wheel-drive configuration was the way to go. If the engineering was conventional, so too was the styling, which was heavily influenced by contemporary American designs.

HELMER PETTERSON

Helmer Petterson wasn't a Volvo employee as such – but he did advise the company on a variety of topics.

Helmer Petterson's background was in motorcycle racing and engineering, having started with Chicago-based Excelsior, one of the most innovative motorcycle makers of the time. Extrovert and outspoken, Petterson began working with Ford to manufacture gas-producer units in the wake of the outbreak of war, which had cut off fuel supplies.

Volvo began working on similar projects and Assar Gabrielsson began consulting Petterson on the subject. Before long Petterson was being consulted on all sorts of things and it was only a matter of time before he became an official adviser to Volvo.

It was probably Petterson who was behind Volvo's acquisition of a Hanomag – a car which was analysed very closely during the design of Volvo's PV444. He reckoned that, in the wake of the war, fuel taxes would be increased and motoring would become much less affordable. Economy cars would be the only way of turning a profit, he said, and sure enough this turned out to be the case.

The PV-series that resulted from this project was a massive success and Petterson was also involved in coming up with a successor to it. But his PV454 was too similar to the earlier PV-series and in the end it was Jan Wilsgaard's Amazon design that went into production.

When the PV444 was unveiled it caused a storm of interest. This new, more affordable family car was just what Volvo needed.

Despite the new Volvo's conservative design and specification, when it was first displayed in September 1944, no fewer than 2,300 people signed up to take delivery of one. By now the car had a name – PV444 – but the first examples weren't delivered to their owners until 1947.

While there was nothing revolutionary about the PV444, for Volvo it marked several firsts, notably a semi-monocoque construction and an overhead-valve engine. Compared with the UK and America, the car was innovative, with its coil-sprung suspension, but compared with France and Germany it was less advanced.

With production fully under way the PV444 was gradually improved, attention being paid to refinement and reliability as much as possible. All the hard work had certainly paid off as in one of its first post-war tests

Proving that lifestyle marketing is nothing new, from the outset Volvo portrayed the PV444 as the ideal companion for leisure trips.

ABOVE: **The PV444's monocoque construction meant the construction of bespoke bodywork was tricky, so it introduced the separate-chassis PV445.**

LEFT: **Volvo is now synonymous with estate cars, and this is where it all began, with the launch of the Duett way back in 1953.**

Motor commented that the PV444 was sprightly enough, remarkably economical and very comfortable to ride in – as well as rewarding to drive.

The PV444's monocoque construction meant producing one-off bodies for special customers was difficult, if not impossible, so a PV444 with a separate chassis was introduced. It wasn't really a complete PV444 but the engine, electrics, transmission, brakes and front suspension were carried over. The rear suspension was changed to semi-elliptic leaf springs and double-acting hydraulic dampers, all of which was attached directly to the chassis to make bespoke bodywork much easier to fit.

Known as the PV445, this development allowed new variants to be developed very quickly, easily and cheaply – the first of which were light commercial vehicles. The first of these was shown by Volvo in 1949, but it wasn't long before ambulances, hearses and even convertibles were being built by independent coachbuilders. One of the most popular conversions was an estate, built by Gripkarosser, and this was the catalyst that prompted Volvo to develop its own estate car and van, which would be introduced in 1953.

Called the Duett, these more practical PVs allowed customers to buy the cars they wanted, as the independent coachbuilders couldn't keep up with demand. The Duett was a vehicle that combined commercial carrying capabilities with those of transporting a family – a true dual-purpose car (hence the name). Buyers could choose between a van with no side windows (the 445DS), a van with a vestigial rear seat and small side windows (the 445DH) or an estate with a folding rear seat and full-length side windows, known as the 445PH.

Many of the Duett's developments mirrored those of the PV444 on which it was based, although they sometimes lagged behind by a year or two. So when the PV444 was superseded by the PV544 in 1958, the Duett didn't receive the single-piece windscreen until 1960. Two years later the B18 engine replaced the B16 unit (which had been introduced in 1958), then in 1969 the car was taken out of production.

CRACKING AMERICA

The year 1955 marked a major milestone for Volvo, as it was in that year that the first car from the company was exported to America – the start of a huge success story for the maker. The first Volvo sent to America had been the prototype PV444 in 1947, but as Assar Gabrielsson neared retirement in 1955, a concerted effort to export cars to the USA started to gather momentum. The first dealership was set up in Fort Worth, Texas, by Nils Sefeldt, who was an aeronautical engineer with a passion for cars. He borrowed heavily and travelled to New York to collect the first car, driving it back to Texas, where he set up his dealership. His first five cars to sell arrived soon after, but they proved

GUNNAR ENGELLAU

Although the Amazon had been developed before Gunnar Engellau took the helm of Volvo on 13 August 1956, it was due to his efforts and leadership that the company went from strength to strength throughout the fifteen years that he led the car maker.

One of the main reasons was his focus on the American market, the first US sales having taken place just the year before he took over at Volvo. But although just fifty cars had been shipped over in 1955, he increased this to 5,000 in 1956 and 10,300 in 1957. Each year the numbers increased and it was because of this that, during his time as CEO of Volvo AB, Engellau saw turnover rise from SKr600m to SKr6,000m, with car production increasing from 31,000 to 205,000.

He handed over the reins to Pehr Gyllenhammar in 1971 but remained as chairman of the board until 1978. He died on 5 January 1980, aged 80.

The Amazon was already in production when Gunnar Engellau took over the reins at Volvo – but he allowed the company to flourish.

difficult to shift. He did manage to sell them but the next five proved just as difficult. He was on the verge of giving up when things started to pick up in spring 1956, and from then on the sales network expanded with the USA quickly becoming Volvo's biggest market.

The PV444 continued to be developed and in January 1957 the 1.4-litre engine was replaced by the 1582cc B16A unit, which was exactly the same engine as used in the new Amazon. Within a year there would be more significant changes though, when the PV544 superseded the PV444. Using virtually the same bodyshell as its predecessor, the new car had a larger engine and room for five people instead of just four – hence the 544 tag.

By this point, Volvo had started to raise its profile in a big way through its cars' success in motorsport. The rate at which its cars were notching up victories in the hands of

Volvo had always been up against American-built rivals – now the Swedish company intended to give the US car makers a taste of their own medicine.

legendary drivers such as Tom Trana and Gunnar Andersson didn't do the cars' sales any harm at all. As well as the positive publicity generated by this competition success, sales of the PV444 had been increased significantly by offering buyers more choice: Volvo offered no fewer than four different versions of the PV544 including an 85bhp Sport edition. The

A GREEN VOLVO

While Volvo may most frequently be associated with safety, the other overriding quality associated with the brand is that of environmental awareness. Although environmentalism was a bandwagon that relatively few jumped onto until the 1980s or later, Volvo realized much earlier that protecting the environment was incredibly important in all areas of manufacturing.

Volvo had already demonstrated its commitment to the environment by the end of the 1960s by looking at the impact its manufacturing plants had on their immediate surroundings. In 1970 the company was asked to take part in a film called *Environment 70*. It was made for European Environment Conservation Year in 1971, and Volvo was chosen because of its work in emissions control, largely prompted by American legislation.

When the UN Environment Conference took place in Stockholm in 1972, it was only natural that Volvo would do something to mark the occasion. The result was Volvo's first environmental declaration, drawn up by Pehr Gyllenhammar, which stated that the car should not be seen as something to be used at all costs – but with an important part to play in mobilizing society, its benefits shouldn't be underestimated, as it had become an indispensable means of transport. The key word in the declaration was responsibility – something which Volvo had promoted for many years, whether it was in a safety context or an environmental one.

When legislation was passed throughout much of America that dictated vehicle emissions would have to be drastically reduced, some car makers protested loudly and claimed the targets couldn't be met – at least not with their cars remaining affordable. The most ambitious state was California, which decreed that by 1977 emissions would have to be reduced dramatically – as a result, some manufacturers reckoned they would have to shut up shop because the targets weren't achievable.

success of the PV-series was partly accounted for by the fact that Volvo had gone to great trouble to tailor the car for each export market. As a result there were over 100 different versions of the car available around the world, although they only varied from each other in detail.

Sales of the PV544 peaked in 1959, when more than 50,000 cars were delivered. From then on it was a gradual decline until the car was phased out in October 1965, nearly a decade after the introduction of the Amazon. Considering the Amazon had been introduced in 1956 to supersede the PV range, it's a testament to the PV544's popularity that it lived on for so long.

Volvo proved everybody wrong with the introduction of the lambdasond in 1977. This allowed exhaust emissions to be cut by 90 per cent thanks to the use of a three-way catalyst working in conjunction with an oxygen-sensing control box. It wasn't long before all US-market Volvos had this system, but it couldn't be fitted outside America because of an unwillingness on the part of the fuel companies to sell unleaded petrol. Lead damaged the catalytic converter, so until unleaded fuel became the norm – as it was in America – there was no way the technology could be used outside the USA.

But Volvo wasn't just doing its bit for the environment by building cleaner cars – producing its cars more cleanly was also important. By 1981 Volvo was addressing the emissions produced by its main factory at Torslanda, switching to water-based paints in place of the solvent-based chemicals previously used as well as reducing, by more than half, the energy used in some of the production processes within the factory. But despite Volvo's efforts to prove itself environmentally aware, it came in for a lot of criticism during the 1980s, with environmental groups claiming that the company had no regard for the damage it was doing to the environment. So in 1986 the company employed an environmental auditor to report on how green the company was with all of its factories around the world and to make sure that when any new legislation was introduced Volvo was already complying with it.

Several years before catalytic converters became the norm for new European cars, in 1988 Volvo introduced retro-fit systems that could be fitted to cars built as far back as 1975. A year later all plastic parts used in the construction of Volvo cars were being marked ready for recycling – again, a move that pre-empted other car makers by years. By the mid-1990s all of Volvo's cars would be free of asbestos, CFCs and mercury, which would ensure that the annual environmental audits would return results that were ahead of just about any other car maker in the world.

Many car makers took a long time to build their eco credentials – not Volvo, though, which was environmentally aware as far back as the 1960s.

CHAPTER TWO

DEVELOPMENT OF THE AMAZON

By the early 1950s Volvo had to start to think about a replacement for the PV-series, knowing that it would take several years to design and engineer something that would maintain the Volvo reputation for longevity and dependability. More complex in its design and construction, and more costly to build as a result, the new model would take Volvo upmarket from the PV. What wouldn't change was the design in terms of its accessibility; Volvo didn't want to create a car that was brash, aggressive or attention-seeking. Instead, the PV's successor would be stylish, curvy and have a friendly face at a time when rivals were going for an abundance of chrome and sharp-edged designs that were likely to date quickly.

This new car would also have a vitally important job to do in that it would introduce American consumers to Volvo – along with a raft of other consumers around the globe who so far had been denied official imports of the PV and

its predecessors. Volkswagen had done a sterling job of getting car buyers in the USA to take European imports seriously (something later undone by an array of British, French and Italian marques), and with affluence growing every year, Volvo was keen to draw on the increased demand for new cars.

Although Volvo had produced its first car as long ago as 1927, it wasn't until 1950 that the company would formally set up a design department. American designer Edward K. Lindberg had been responsible for the look of many of Volvo's earlier models; in 1950 Lindberg was tasked with setting up a design studio with full-time staff.

Lindberg's first recruit was Jan Wilsgaard, and it was he who was given the job of coming up with a car which could supersede the PV544 and which would compete with the Opel Kapitän along with some of the smaller Mercedes models. Set to be called the Volvo 1200, to replace the 1100 model (otherwise known as the PV444), production of the new model would start at some point in 1956.

Working alongside Wilsgaard were Rustan Lange (interior designer), Stig and Gunnar Falck (two brothers), and Einar Reikeras, a skilled modeller who also happened to be Wilsgaard's brother-in-law. In those early days, Volvo's design centre consisted of a single room, into which a full-size scale model would just about fit with enough room to walk around it. It was so small that there was no chance of standing back and getting a good look from a few feet away — something that seems unthinkable now!

The Amazon may have been conservatively styled, but compared with the PV444 it was positively space age.

JAN WILSGAARD

One of the potential recruits to the design department who showed a lot of promise was 20-year-old Jan Wilsgaard, who was studying sculpture at art college in Gothenburg. Until this point his focus had been sketching people and designing furniture – he'd not worked within an automotive sphere at all. Wilsgaard also still had a year to go before his course would be complete, but instead of graduating he seized the chance to become Volvo's first full-time exterior designer when Lindberg decided he was the man for the job.

Almost as soon as Wilsgaard started working for Volvo he was given the task of coming up with a new large car for the company and the result was the Philip, which remained a one-off. As an encore to the Philip, in 1952 Wilsgaard came up with the PV179, which would also fail to reach production, while the 55 of 1953 would remain a prototype too. You'd think that having designed three stillborn cars in three years Wilsgaard may have been somewhat dispirited, but in 1953 he created his fourth study, and this would go on to become a hugely important car for Volvo – it was the Amazon.

In his early days Wilsgaard was often having to compete with independent styling houses, as there wasn't great confidence in Volvo's in-house styling department because it wasn't well enough established. It was for this reason that Wilsgaard came up with an unusual way of working – to do it behind closed doors, often in Italy, and generally at Coggiola. When his designs were due to be shown he'd then swoop in with them, nobody at Volvo having caught sight of them in the development stages. It was certainly an unconventional approach, but one that was generally successful for Wilsgaard – more often than not, it was his proposals that were adopted, rather than those of outside rivals.

Thanks to this approach, it didn't take long to establish confidence in Volvo's in-house design studio; by 1966 Wilsgaard had been appointed head of the design department and he'd go on to design many of Volvo's concepts such as the VESC (Volvo Experimental Safety Car) (1972), New York Taxi (1976) and Volvo Concept Car (1980). He also designed the 144, 164, 200-series and 700-series.

The last car that was designed with the involvement of Wilsgaard was the 850, launched in 1991. Continuing the boxy theme started in the 1960s with the 140, it was the last of the old-school Volvos before Peter Horbury arrived to inject some aesthetic appeal into the marque. And although Wilsgaard's angular styling may be disliked by many, his name lives on at Volvo as there's an annual scholarship awarded to hopeful students studying at the Gothenburg Institute of Arts and Crafts – and it's known as the Wilsgaard scholarship.

Jan Wilsgaard was Volvo's first design chief; he'd work for Volvo for more than four decades.

GETTING GOING

Wilsgaard's first task was to come up with a pair of designs, to replace the PV544 and the PV60. The latter was Volvo's largest model, and one that was made in small numbers: just 3,006 were built between 1946 and 1950. The styling of the larger car would be inspired by then-fashionable American design, but the resulting car – the Philip (see separate panel) – would be too costly to manufacture in significant numbers.

With this larger car now stillborn, Wilsgaard turned his attention to designing a successor to the PV444 – something that wasn't as easy as it might have been. The biggest stumbling block was Volvo's two founders, Assar Gabrielsson and Gustaf Larson, who had to okay any proposal – and they were incredibly conservative. There would be no cutting-edge styling affectations here; simplicity would always win through and they'd already made it clear that they wanted the PV's successor to continue with a fastback silhouette.

When Wilsgaard started the project he commented:

> A rectangle is the ideal shape for a car that is standing still. It offers the maximum space and it is very practical. But when the car is moving, the ideal shape is a circle. The designer's skill is in finding a synthesis between rectangle and circle.

To spice things up a bit – Gabrielsson and Larson weren't convinced that 20-year-old Wilsgaard was up to the job – it was decided that there would be a competition to come up with the design for the new car. Wilsgaard would have to take on his colleague Rustan Lange along with Helmer Petterson, the latter being the consultant who had been brought in to style the PV444 in the early 1940s.

Wilsgaard came up with a design heavily influenced by a unique Michelotti-penned PV444 which had been built by Allemano in Turin specially for the Swedish business-man who commissioned it. Known as the '55' (see separate panel), Wilsgaard's proposal featured the same crowned

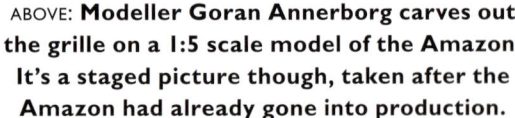

ABOVE: **Modeller Goran Annerborg carves out the grille on a 1:5 scale model of the Amazon. It's a staged picture though, taken after the Amazon had already gone into production.**

LEFT: **Volvo toyed with the idea of giving the Amazon a nose similar to that of the P1900 – a car that proved somewhat unsuccessful, which is perhaps why this idea didn't progress beyond the clay model stage.**

THE PHILIP PROTOTYPE

When the PV444 was first shown in 1944, the American influence in its styling was immediately obvious. So when a replacement model was proposed in the early 1950s it was probably no surprise that the finished prototype wouldn't have looked out of place on the streets of Detroit with its rear wheel spats, heavy chrome bumpers and whitewall tyres. The car was the Philip, so called because its specification was settled on Sweden's Filip day (2 May) in 1950.

Designed by Jan Wilsgaard, the Philip was a proposal to take Volvo upmarket from the PV444, the company's only offering in the post-war years. With styling heavily influenced by the contemporary Kaiser, the natural powerplant for such a car was a V8 engine, mated to an automatic gearbox. But Volvo didn't produce such a thing so a unit had to be produced from scratch. In the event the Philip didn't go into production (only one was built), but a modified version of the V8 developed specially for it did go on to power Volvo trucks.

The V8 engineered by the company had a displacement of 3559cc, with both block and heads being of cast iron. With wedge-type combustion chambers, overhead valves and a compression ratio of 6.8:1, the unit developed 120bhp. In a car weighing more than one and a half tons, that didn't allow for very impressive performance, but at least 100mph was just about possible.

By the time the Philip had been developed enough to make it reliable, Volvo had changed its mind about going too far upmarket. It had taken two years to build the car and in that time things had changed both in the automotive world and within Volvo. The project was canned but the car survives in Volvo's Gothenburg museum.

LEFT: **With its V8 engine and automatic gearbox, the Philip didn't much resemble the Amazon mechanically. Just the one was built.**

RIGHT: **Styled very much along American lines, the Philip looked as though it would have been very costly to build.**

THE '55' – WHAT MIGHT HAVE BEEN

Jan Wilsgaard's 1953 design study was hugely important to Volvo because it was this car which would become the PV544's replacement. Called the '55' in the studio, the car featured a profile very similar to the Amazon's although much of the detail design such as the horse-collar grille was shared with the Elizabeth prototype that had been built in 1953. The car didn't progress beyond a full-size clay model, but elements of it were used in the production Amazon.

wingline that would re-emerge on the Amazon, but we're now jumping ahead.

Lange's design was rejected out of hand because it was too impractical to make; as an interior designer, perhaps he couldn't realistically have been expected to come up with anything suitable. Not so with Helmer Petterson, though; he was expected to deliver, but his proposal was based too heavily on the PV444, although tweaked significantly, so it looked awful from every angle.

Rather than embrace or reject the designs of Wilsgaard and Petterson, Larson and Gabrielsson decided to take elements of both, to come up with Volvo's new car. Such an idea was never going to work and unsurprisingly the project was abandoned altogether soon after, leaving Wilsgaard to get on with an all-new design, the rationale being that it could be sold alongside the PV444 for several years, giving Volvo a two-model range in the process.

THE ELIZABETH I AND II PROTOTYPES

In 1952 a Swedish entrepreneur named Gosta Wennberg was considering the possibility of producing PV444s with exclusive bodywork. To see how viable the project would be he commissioned Vignale to produce a two-door, four-seater car on a PV444 Duett chassis. The car was completed in 1953, and there were strong overtones of contemporary Alfa Romeo in its design.

When the car was despatched to Volvo for them to take a look, there were nods of approval all round. The styling was certainly elegant but the interior packaging was cramped considering the car's external dimensions. So when Volvo commissioned Vignale to produce a successor to the original prototype, the floorpan from a standard PV444 was supplied.

Before Vignale even started building the second prototype the Swedish press had come up with a name for the first – which Wennberg had been parading around to get as much publicity as he could. The press had started calling it the Elizabeth, to connect it to the Philip prototype seen the previous year – this being in the wake of the coronation of Queen Elizabeth that year. As a result, the second prototype was instantly known as the Elizabeth II, as it closely followed the design of the first car.

The second car, completed in 1954, was even more graceful than the first. But it still didn't fit in with Volvo's project plans and it all came to nothing. Wennberg soon realized that building 200 cars at SKr20,000 wasn't viable and everything ground to a halt. But the significance of Wennberg's car shouldn't be underestimated, because Jan Wilsgaard's '55' of 1953 took many of its styling details from it – and that car heavily influenced the Amazon.

It may look like an Alfa Romeo, but this could actually have been the PV444's replacement, instead of the Amazon.

THE PV179

Another potential PV444 replacement was the PV179. Development started in 1952, five years after the PV444 had gone on sale, and introduction was planned for 1954, ten years after the PV444 had first been shown. Another of Jan Wilsgaard's designs, the PV179 was based on the PV444's chassis, which meant the same wheelbase, engine, gearbox and axle had to be used. But the suspension wasn't carried over in its entirety, as some bespoke parts were manufactured for this prototype – although in the event they were nearly identical to those fitted to the Amazon when it was introduced in 1956.

The PV179 looked smart, but developing a four-door model would have been impossible – and the estate would have been very compromised too.

But although the mechanicals were largely familiar, the sheet metal certainly wasn't, as it was all new – Wilsgaard had to retain the PV444's roofline, however. This meant it was difficult to produce a design that looked good from all angles, and the resulting two-door fastback with vestigial fins and narrow grille with recessed headlamps on either side did look slightly clumsy from some viewpoints, although it was not displeasing overall.

But despite the fact that most of the managers within Volvo liked the car very much, Helmer Petterson most certainly didn't. His services had been retained by Volvo as a consultant on design issues and he reckoned the car was too big for the PV444 mechanicals that were planned for it. As a result the project was cancelled and it was then that the Margaret Rose name was conjured up. Pictures of the aborted project were released to the Swedish press and they came up with the Margaret Rose name to maintain the British Royal Family theme which had been started with the Philip and that continued with the Elizabeth cars.

Only one PV179 prototype was built, and it hasn't survived as Raymond Eknor, a Volvo engineer, rolled it and destroyed it in the process.

NOT SO NEW...

While Gabrielsson and Larson rather liked the idea of this two-model range, considering the new model was launched as a more upmarket Volvo than the PV444, rather than the replacement it was originally intended to be, it had rather more in common with its predecessor than you might expect. Not only did both the Amazon and PV444 have a common 102.4-inch (2,600mm) wheelbase (although the new car's bodyshell was shorter, wider and around 50kg heavier), but their engines and gearboxes were also shared. However, the suspension layout for the new car was completely different from the PV444's.

The pushrod 4-cylinder engine was taken from the PV444 but enlarged to 1583cc from 1414cc by increasing the bore from 75mm to 79.4mm – the stroke remained the same, at 80mm, to give a near-square layout. Predictably, while the PV444's powerplant was known as the B14 unit, this larger engine was the B16 and it was to be offered in two states of tune. Those in no hurry could opt for a single-carb engine with 60bhp; those who craved power could instead go for the 85bhp version with its pair of SU carburettors.

While these larger engines offered a useful increase in power and torque over the B14 unit, the gearbox was carried over wholesale – which meant there were just three ratios to choose from. In the mid-1950s this wasn't too impressive – especially as the B16 was hardly over-endowed with torque, even in twin-carb form. The fitment of a three-speed gearbox also didn't do much to reinforce the car's sporting aspirations.

Where the Amazon scored, though, was with its suspension, which was tough and endowed the car with a fabulously comfortable ride, while also providing a decent level of handling. Up front there were coil springs and double wishbones, the steering being by cam and roller. At the rear there were twin radius arms on each side, running almost parallel with the line of the propshaft. As on the PV there was a Panhard rod for sideways location of the axle, but the coil springs were above the axle rather than behind it.

There was, however, a lot more compromise involved in creating this new car than Wilsgaard would have liked. Larson and Gabrielsson had set out some rules that rather stifled Wilsgaard's creativity. For example, one of the initial prerequisites was that this new car would feature a two-piece windscreen, but, desperate to ensure the new model didn't appear outdated as soon as it was unveiled, Wilsgaard managed to convince his bosses that a single-piece windscreen was desirable for a variety of reasons.

ABOVE: **The earliest Amazons were powered by the same B16 engine that was also fitted to the PV444 and PV544.**

LEFT: **Jan Wilsgaard had to fight hard to launch the Amazon with a single-piece windscreen, rather than an outdated two-piece item.**

WHAT'S IN A NAME?

With the run-up to the Amazon's launch in September 1956 being so hectic, nobody had considered that the car would need a name. In rather a hurry, the name 'Amason' was chosen because of its original meaning. If Volvo's iron mark logo was meant to signify masculinity, the word amason did the opposite. According to Greek mythology, the Amazons were female warriors who fought with bows and arrows. Legend has it that they had their right breasts removed in order to be able to better use their deadly weapons; in Greek, *amazos* means breastless.

Although the badge says Amazon, Volvo's new family car was named after the Amasons – and German company Kriedler objected because of its Amazone motorbike.

Unfortunately Volvo's new name didn't go down too well with German motorbike manufacturer Kreidler, which had just launched a moped called the Amazone. The company had registered the name and claimed the sole right to it. A deal struck between Kriedler and Volvo meant the latter was allowed to use the name Amazon in the Nordic markets but nowhere else. The Amazone moped, however, had already disappeared from the market by 1959.

Despite coming up with the name Amason, Volvo soon shifted to Amazon, even though its new car was sold only in the Nordic countries under that name. Volvo 122 was the name of the new model elsewhere, but the designations 12 and 1200 were also used for some markets; the internal designation had been P1200. Consequently, the car line was officially called the 120 with the last digit changed for model variations.

THINGS START TO TAKE SHAPE

By the spring of 1955, Wilsgaard and his small team had come up with the basic shape and proportions for the forth-coming new car, and while they needed some modifications to be approved for production, these were essentially right and needed surprisingly little work. As a result, it was just a matter of weeks before the thumbs up was given to these tweaked designs, and now the serious work could begin on building prototypes and starting the testing work.

Within a year Volvo had a small number of prototypes ready for testing and it quickly became clear that Wilsgaard's initial designs were pretty much spot on – very few changes were required for a safe, comfortable, reliable, practical and spacious family car to go into production. Indeed, compared with the prototypes, the production cars differed only in terms of their detail.

The grilles didn't yet feature any meshing and embossed into the rear bumper were the letters VOLVO – a feature which perhaps Gabrielsson and Larson felt was too showy. Whatever the reason, the feature was ditched and more conventional, less prominent badging was adopted instead. One early prototype also explored the possibility of featuring a single-piece grille, but it looked incredibly fussy with its half-a-dozen chromed slats. It never saw the light of day, with Volvo choosing instead to go with a simple two-piece grille for all cars.

Some of the earlier sketches also featured cars with prominent fins; a popular stylistic feature of the time, but neither Wilsgaard nor Volvo's management were convinced

At first there was no mesh in the grille, but the car looked unfinished without it.

31

The PV444 had always featured just two doors; a four-door configuration made the Amazon much better suited to families.

by their aesthetic qualities. Always thinking of the future, it was clear that the new car would be in production for several years and the chances of such a styling affectation remaining in vogue for the car's lifespan were remote to say the least – which is why from the outset, production Amazons didn't feature fins.

Instead, Wilsgaard came up with a design that looked modern without being fashionably so – and as a result it was unlikely to date quickly. Instead the four-door saloon had a timeless elegance, while offering a spacious cabin, a generously sized boot and, as a result, huge amounts of practicality. Perhaps the only thing that dated the car was Volvo's insistence on using two-tone colour schemes for the early cars; as these fell out of favour, they dropped off the paint charts.

COUNTDOWN TO THE BIG REVEAL

Speculation about the car's specification was rife in the run-up to its launch. Press reports talked about a car which would be powered by a 6-cylinder engine and maybe even a development of the V8 seen in the Philip prototype. Sketchy details were released to the press in February 1956

but that only fuelled the fire. Announcements were made in April 1956 that the prototypes had been completed but the car wouldn't go on sale until the following year.

In the event, the first time the new Volvo was officially shown was at a dealer conference in the town of Skövde, on 3 August 1956. The car was unveiled as the Amason, and suddenly Volvo had a legitimate new product with a name – the fact that this name would soon have to be ditched was something the company didn't yet know about (*see separate panel*).

The car on display bore chassis number 2, featured right-hand drive and two-tone paintwork, and differed from the upcoming production version in a number of ways, both on the outside and on the inside.

Immediately the press started to talk about a 2.5-litre 6-cylinder engine being developed but when the 121 first went on sale it was equipped with a single-carb 1583cc version of the three-bearing B14 engine fitted to the PV444. Badged the B16A and with just 60bhp on tap, performance wasn't exactly startling and part of the problem was the three-speed manual gearbox carried over from the PV444. What was really needed was an extra ratio, but the intended four-speed 'box was not ready at that stage.

At the front there were still coil springs and double wishbones but the set-up was redesigned with shorter upper and longer lower wishbones. There were also changes at the back, with the rear axle now located by longitudinal supports in rubber bushes in place of the angled support arms previously fitted. Torsional stiffness was excellent despite the large doors, and great attention was paid to high-quality rustproofing to ensure the bodyshell stayed in fine shape.

After much positive feedback from dealers, Volvo started to build the Amazon at its Lundby factory – just as Assar Gabrielsson handed over the reins of the company to Gunnar Engellau. His parting shot to Wilsgaard, on the design of the Amazon, was reputed to be: 'It looks fine, but there's too much of the pin-up about it. It would be better if it was ugly rather than too beautiful.' Thankfully he didn't ask for a redesign though…

Early **Amazons** came with an attractive two-tone finish, which set off the car's lines perfectly.

The exterior lines were conservative but tasteful, and the interior followed the same theme.

Durability had always been very important to Volvo, which is why the Amazon was put through a punishing testing regime before it went on sale.

121 WITH B16A ENGINE (1957–61)

Engine
Four cylinders in line, iron block and head

Bore × stroke:	79.4 × 80mm
Capacity:	1583cc
Valvegear:	Overhead valve
Compression ratio:	7.4:1
Fuelling:	Single Zenith carburettor
Maximum power:	66bhp (SAE) at 4,500rpm
Maximum torque:	85lb ft at 2,500rpm

Transmission
Rear-wheel drive
Three-speed synchro on second and third

Final drive ratio:	4.56:1

Overdrive was optional from 1960, as was an all-synchro gearbox. A four-speed all-synchro gearbox was optional from 1958 and for the 1961 model year an automatic transmission was available.

Suspension
Front: Independent with coil springs, telescopic dampers, wishbones, anti-roll bar
Rear: Live axle, coil springs, telescopic dampers, Panhard rod, torque arms

Steering
Cam and roller

Turns lock-to-lock:	3.5
Turning circle:	32 feet 6 inches

Brakes
Front: Drum
Rear: Drum
Servo assistance standard from November 1958

Wheels and tyres
Steel disc wheels with 5.90 × 15 tubeless whitewall tyres

Bodywork
Four-door saloon of unitary construction

Dimensions

Length	14ft 7in (4,450mm)
Wheelbase	8ft 6in (2,600mm)
Track	4ft 4in (1,320mm)
Width	5ft 4in (1,620mm)
Height	4ft 11in (1,510mm)
Weight	2,398lb (1,090kg)

Performance (Autocar)

Max speed (top):	94mph (151km/h)
0–60mph:	14 sec
30–50mph in top:	9.7 sec
50–70mph in top:	12.5 sec

Price including tax when new (June 1958)

Four-door saloon:	SKr12,600 (£868, but not officially imported into the UK)

AMAZON ENGINES – BACKGROUND AND OVERVIEW

All of the cars made by Volvo in the 1930s were fitted with side-valve 6-cylinder engines. Only a handful of cars with special bodies had been fitted with the overhead-valve FE engine, which was the standard unit used in some of Volvo's trucks. By the end of the 1930s, though, there were more and more reasons for Volvo's designers to think about a smaller engine for a smaller car. Sales of brands such as Opel, DKW, Austin and Fiat showed that there was a definite demand for small cars. Volvo was in a strong position with its 6-cylinder cars, but the brand was known more for reliability than low prices. The need for a smaller car was

clear, and the outbreak of war in September 1939 seemed likely to increase this need, eventually. In the wake of a war there tends to be a pent-up desire for higher consumption, but generally not a great deal of money to spare – so a small car seemed the obvious choice.

Work on the new small Volvo was to begin in early 1943. The initiative appears to have started with Helmer Petterson, who had gained valuable experience in the American car and motorcycle industries, and who had also proven to be a capable designer of motor vehicle producer gas units. There were no particular initial constraints in terms of body and engine type or drive layout, so there were some flights of fancy aired to begin with. Someone even arranged a demonstration of an 8-cylinder two-stroke powerplant!

But at this point Gustaf Larson (Volvo's technical director) put his foot down. He declared that the engine would have to feature four cylinders, and that this was not to be a rear-engined car. This was an important step in the decision-making process, but the question of front- versus rear-wheel drive had still not been settled. Both the project manager Erik Jern and Helmer Petterson were very taken with the front-wheel drive DKWs and Adlers that were selling so well in Sweden at the time.

Gustaf Larson intervened again. He said that Volvo's success to date had not been derived from constant experimentation, so he took the decision that the new small Volvo would have to have rear-wheel drive. There were many good reasons for this key decision, including the way that Volvo went about manufacturing its cars. It was a company that designed most of the parts for its own cars, then had these made for it by a large number of external suppliers. If Volvo was to opt for front-wheel drive at this point, it would complicate matters too much for its suppliers.

The small-car project may have got under way early in 1943, but it was to take Volvo until the end of the same year to finalize its engine type and drive configuration. This now meant that the various project groups involved had less than a year in which to build a show car. The reason for the urgency was that the various manufacturing divisions at Volvo had already decided to stage a gigantic exhibition of their products in Stockholm's Royal Tennis Hall in September 1944. A new small Volvo would be an irresistible draw at the show.

As soon as it was settled that the new engine was to have four cylinders, its designers adopted the time-honoured approach of looking at other existing designs, in particular the 4-cylinder units from Opel, Fiat and Hanomag. The engine they developed and started trialling was in no way revolutionary, but it was one which was to prove uncommonly robust and adaptable.

The company estimated at this stage that it might be able to sell 8,000 units of this small-car series – with a little luck, and once the war ended, production could get under

THE AMERICAN INFLUENCE

When the Amazon was revealed there were some who said it looked uncannily like the last of the Willys saloons, while the PV444 and PV544 were clearly inspired by the fastback Fords of the mid-1940s. And why not? Sweden's new-car buyers had long been fed a diet of American machinery, and as a result that's all that was to be found on Swedish roads for many years. It was what Swedes grew up with – what they were immersed in. So it could come as no surprise when Volvo's Swedish designers (especially Jan Wilsgaard and Helmer Petterson) took their inspiration from the models of Ford and General Motors.

That final Willys, which arguably provided the inspiration for the Amazon, was the Aero sedan, launched in 1952 and current in North America until 1955; the marque had been taken over by Kaiser in 1954. Offered in two or four-door saloon forms, the Aero was designed by Phil Wright and engineered by Clyde Paton. Offered with a choice of 6-cylinder engines, once the car had been withdrawn from sale in the North American market it remained on sale in South America until the early 1960s. It was built in Argentina in a joint venture set up by Kaiser, the Argentinian government and private investors.

Perhaps it was no coincidence that the Amazon had a transatlantic look; American cars were popular in Sweden.

way. This was the biggest series Volvo had planned so far, but its early estimates of the total volume were to prove completely wrong. In the end, Volvo was to make 440,000 units of the PV444 and PV544, all with engines derived from a few months' hard work in the spring and summer of 1944!

Not long after the Volvo exhibition of September 1944 (which had attracted nearly 150,000 visitors), a long article appeared in the technical journal of Stockholm's Royal Institute of Technology. It contained descriptions of the new Volvo engine by Gustaf Larson and Erik Jern:

The engine is a four-cylinder one with suspended valves. The bore is 75mm and the stroke 80mm – thus a modern design with a relatively slow piston velocity, namely 10.6 metres per second at 4,000rpm, the speed at which the engine delivers its maximum power. This is 43 horsepower, as can be seen in the diagram showing test data using Motyl 25 fuel.

The B4B engine was introduced in the PV444 and would evolve into the B16 engine in the Amazon.

The crankshaft had three main bearings, and the camshaft was driven from it by bevel gears. The light-alloy pistons were of the very latest type. Trials showed that this engine could also run on 65 octane fuel without engine-knock at a compression ratio of 6.5:1. The shaft of the water pump had ball bearings and the impellor was made of Bakelite. A thermostat in the coolant outlet and a bypass channel in the engine block helped ensure fast warming up and a steady coolant temperature.

A carburettor tuned for economy, thermostatic heat control and vacuum timing control all helped achieve low fuel consumption, even under fractional load. The 6-volt electrical system was made by Bosch, and it included an 84Ah battery and a 90-watt generator that was able to control its own current output.

The engine is mounted on two obliquely aligned rubber blocks at the front and a heavy-duty rubber pad under the gearbox. It is mounted in such a way as to ensure that it oscillates only around its natural centre-of-gravity axis, which means that no engine vibration is transmitted to the car body. With the kingpin support and front suspension, the engine unit is an easily installed unit, attached to the supporting bodywork by a minimal number of bolts.

This was how the engine of the new small Volvo was described when it went into production in February 1947. The new engine was called the B4B and it weighed approximately 145kg.

Despite the rating of 43 horsepower cited by Larson and Jern in the 1944 article, 40 horsepower is the output normally quoted for this first version of the PV444 engine. By altering the camshaft design and valve mechanism, its power was boosted to 44bhp in 1950. After that there were no significant changes made in this engine until autumn 1955, when a new camshaft, cylinder head, valve springs, pushrods and other changes helped increase its power to 51bhp.

The engine in the PV444 was neither powerful nor especially exciting, but it was unusually durable and reliable. The same could be said about the PV444 itself, which, apart from the large taxi models, was for a time the only car made by Volvo. As the middle of the 1950s approached, it became increasingly clear that Volvo needed a new model series to take it onward and upward in the Swedish new-car registration statistics. The race for supremacy in the Swedish market was between Volkswagen and Volvo, but the home brand was winning even before the Volvo Amazon (120 series) was launched.

For several years, Volvo had been evaluating possible additions to its line-up or replacements for the PV444, which was now around ten years old. All of them had one thing in common – they all featured the same 102-inch (2,600mm) wheelbase of the PV444. Some of the prototypes had features in common with the PV444, but eventually the decision-makers agreed upon developing one of Jan Wilsgaard's two design proposals: Volvo was to develop a stylish four-door car, while reusing as much of its existing technology as possible. No money was to be wasted on whims of fashion!

What Volvo was up to was a matter of national interest in Sweden, so discussion of the next car from this company was by no means confined to the motoring magazines. There was much speculation in the mainstream press about the precise nature of what Volvo should make next, and, in particular, what kind of engine it should have. There were many who predicted a straight-six, while others hoped for a small V8. Little did they realize how tightly the purse strings were held at Volvo!

When, in August 1956, Volvo finally presented its new model at a conference for dealers in Skövde, it had a new engine under its nicely sculpted bonnet. Admittedly, its 60bhp (DIN) output was an improvement on the 51bhp of the PV444, but many were disappointed that the B16A engine was really just a souped-up version of the B4B from the PV444. Although you would not have thought so when reading the brochure:

> *The newly designed four-cylinder ohv engine gives the Amazon good acceleration, good torque at low revs and a high top speed. It is remarkably economical – squeezing the maximum power out of every drop of petrol. As standard equipment it has a so-called full-flow oil filter – so oil changes are needed only once every 5,000 kilometres.*

Boring out the cylinders from 75mm to 79.37mm had given a cubic capacity of 1583 cc, hence the '16' in the engine name. Its peak power output was at 4,500rpm and its compression ratio was 7.5:1. The compression ratings of Volvo engines were on their way up.

Volvo's engineers had worked hard to make the engine as discreet as they could. New engine mounts, an efficient intake silencer and good soundproofing of the engine bulkhead all helped to make it very quiet inside the cabin. In the event, the Amazon's refinement levels would always be one of its many strong points.

The B16 Engine

Four forward gears, 85bhp, a five-year manufacturer's warranty and 0 to 100km/h in 16 seconds – a pretty impressive set of figures in the late 1950s. Those are what the B16 engine offered as fitted to the Amazon 122S when it was introduced in 1958.

'The economical Sport engine delivers exhilarating acceleration and a high top speed. That means quick and risk-free overtaking.' In engineering and performance terms, this was fully in line with buyer expectations in 1958. The 1583cc displacement of the Sport engine was identical to that of the standard engine in the Volvo Amazon and PV444 models. One key difference between them, though, was the compression ratio – 8.2:1 in the Sport engine, instead of 7.5:1, although you could hardly call this 85bhp unit a high-compression engine.

The Sport engine's camshaft design also made for longer valve opening times. The tempered crankshaft had lead–bronze big-end and main bearings, and the upper compression rings were chromium-plated. And the proud owner of a car with this Sport engine had some more cards up his sleeve when he opened the bonnet: a chrome-plated rocker cover and twin SU carburettors. Motoring buffs loved the sporty look and performance of British SU carbs like this.

This engine's peak output of 85bhp (SAE) was at 5,500rpm, and its maximum torque of about 120Nm (88lb ft) was achieved at 3,500 revs, at around 100km/h (62mph) in top gear.

The Sport version of the PV544 was presented together with the Amazon Sport in August 1958. Motoring journalists were effusive in their praise, and of the engine in particular. The reviewer in the Swedish magazine *Teknikens Värld* wrote:

> *The chance to drive this and to use its resources to the full is an experience in itself. In combination with the well-dimensioned M4 gearbox, it gives the car acceleration in the best sports car league. Even at speeds around 120–130km/h, it has plenty of acceleration left.*

85 BHP

The VOLVO 122S is powered by the B16B four-cylinder, overhead-valve engine. Here again Scandinavian precision engineering has produced this robust, powerful and compact unit combining the essential qualities of durability and dependability with an outstandingly flexible performance and economical operation. The twin SU carburetters are vital factors in the sustained highspeed performance of the car as well as its quiet and efficient lowspeed characteristics. The absolute accessibility of the power unit and all other equipment under the hood is a well-appreciated quality as far as routine servicing is concerned.

Many hoped for an all-new engine for the Amazon. Instead they got an evolution of the PV444 powerplant.

Interestingly, this writer managed to improve on the official Volvo 0–100km/h acceleration time by two seconds, paring it down to 14 seconds.

Buyers in the United States had been able to buy the last of the PV444s sold there with an 85bhp engine and the earlier standard three-speed gearbox, but, for technical reasons to do with customs duties, this engine was not offered in Volvo's home market. So it was exciting news for performance-conscious Volvo fans when the PV544 was launched with a new gearbox. *Road & Track* magazine in the USA was very enthusiastic about the combination of the 85bhp engine and the new four-speed gearbox, and impressed by the fact that the car's acceleration was just as lively in second gear as in first. The reviewer thought the step up to third was a bit much, but once in top gear found its acceleration positive and stable again.

This writer experienced a little of the same roughness he had noticed in earlier test drives, but decided it was not as marked as before. 'This is one of the most free-revving rocker-arm engines we've seen,' he wrote.

With its lively 85bhp engine, the PV544 Sport in particular proved a great commercial success. In fact, roughly one in six of all the PV544s sold in the first few years had the Sport badge, despite their higher price.

The B18 Engine

Volvo's first overhead-valve engine had proved to be very tough and also quite easy to tune. Both of the traits made it appealing, especially the latter, because 51bhp was not a lot to offer, even in the mid-1950s. And besides, when it

The Volvo B 18 engine is a strong and durable unit with the performance of a sports engine. It is available in two versions for the 120 series: 85 b.h.p. (SAE) and 100 b.h.p. (SAE).

The B 18 engine has a high torque value over a wide range of engine speed. This gives it excellent pulling power. It is also extremely economical. High output and a high degree of efficiency have been obtained by the use of twin horizontal carburetters (only on 100 b.h.p. motor), separate induction ports for each cylinder, a high compression ratio, fully machined combustion chambers and a twin exhaust system from the flywheel housing rearwards.

The B 18 engine can stand up to extreme stresses arising from sustained hard driving because of its five-bearing crankshaft and throw-away full-flow oil filter. A sealed cooling system ensures effective cooling — and heating — under all conditions of operation.

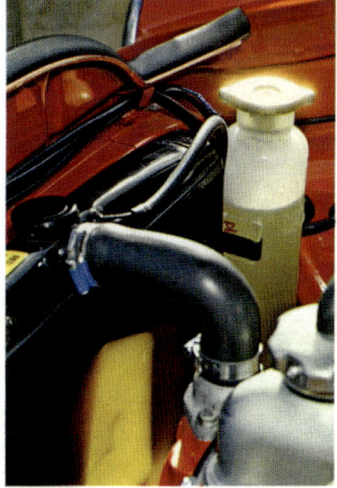

Sealed cooling system

The B18 engine was offered with single or twin carburettors; in the 1966 brochure it was shown in the latter form.

39

was introduced the 70bhp Sport engine was not available to buyers in Sweden. A few were used in Swedish police cars, however.

With the arrival of the 60bhp B16 engine and the 85bhp Sport version, sales were soon improving, at home and in Volvo's export markets too. But it was clear that buyers were prepared to pay for more power. A larger engine was already in the pipeline, and by 1960 it was undergoing comprehensive trials.

The new engine was also of a pushrod design, but that was the only major resemblance it bore to the previous generation. This engine, known as the B18 on account of its displacement, had barely a single component in common with the B16 engines. But as it was effectively half of a B36 V8 truck engine, complete with carried-over cylinder head, it wasn't as completely new as Volvo wanted people to think. But what no one – neither Volvo's engineers nor anyone else – knew yet was that Sweden and Volvo's fifty or so export markets were about to have an instant classic. Simple, compact, robust – and ready to respond to all types of use.

The first car to use the new 4-cylinder engine was a brand-new model, the Volvo P1800 coupé, which went into production in May 1961. Its power was impressive: 100bhp, the most powerful production Volvo up to then. The P1800 was probably beyond the means of the average car buyer at the time, but couldn't its engine be put into a PV544 or a Volvo Amazon? Of course! Proof of that arrived in August 1961, when the B18 engine was introduced into both the PV544 and the Amazon. They were not to have the 100bhp version, though, as 75 or 90bhp had to suffice for them, so P1800 owners could feel they'd got something exclusive with their stylish new sports car.

When Volvo stopped making its big taxis in 1958, it was left with only one engine type for its car models. Quite a responsibility for the people designing the B18, in other words, but one which the new engine in its first three forms was soon to prove more than a match for. There was a long list of requirements for the engineers. The engine block would have to be more stable than before, to give less vibration and lower noise levels. It needed better low-end torque than its predecessor had offered, and better fuel economy too. In the end, all of these items on the wish list were ticked off, a fact that motoring magazines around the world were happy to confirm.

The displacement of all versions of the B18 engine was 1778cc, thanks to a bore of 84.14mm and an 80mm stroke.

As such it was a short-stroke engine, such designs being renowned for their high-end revving ability.

One of the most significant differences in this engine's design was the fact that it had a crankshaft with five main bearings; all of Volvo's previous 4-cylinder engines had featured just three. The reason for the change – aside from improved longevity – was not more power, but improved torque. Volvo's engineers did, in fact, give the B18 engine greater power too, but then it did have a bigger displacement. In terms of specific power (horsepower per litre), the B18 was broadly similar to its predecessor, but its torque was better. The 75bhp (SAE) B18A engine had a maximum torque of 140Nm (103lb ft) at 2,800rpm, and the B18D generated torque of 145Nm (107lb ft) at 3,500rpm.

The engines used in the Amazon and PV544 had a compression ratio of 8.5:1, compared with 9.5:1 for the 100bhp engine in the P1800. The latter engine had an oil cooler, but the Amazon and PV544 versions of the same engine had to do without such technology. There were many other differences too, such as the fact that the camshaft gave less lift in the ordinary saloon engines than in the sports car engine.

Other key differences were to be found in the new engine's gas flow. These changes were made to minimize noise and give better economy. In the earlier engines there were two inlet ports in the cylinder head, but in the B18 there was an inlet port for each cylinder. The 75bhp engine had a single Zenith carburettor of downdraught type, but the Sport engine, like Volvo's earlier high-performance engines, had twin SU carbs.

The B18 engine went through a long testing period – several years – before the decision was taken to put it into production at the Skövde plant (Penta). It was to prove very useful for marine applications too, and was launched by Penta in 1959 in its Aquamatic marine propulsion system.

The amount of capital invested in the Skövde engine plant gives an indication of the importance of this new engine to Volvo. Remodelling the plant to produce the B18 cost 27 million kronor, although that sum did cover the cost of developing the engine too.

The power output of the B18A engine was increased slightly in autumn 1965, although by so little that it wasn't even mentioned in the marketing. But the power boost for the B18D Sport engine was made widely known – from 90 to 95bhp. It was achieved by raising the compression ratio and increasing the valve lift. A year later Volvo was to present not only the peppy 115bhp Amazon 123GT, but also the brand-new Volvo 144 with its choice of 85 and 115 horse-

The B18 was offered in an array of forms over the years. Here it's fitted to a 1968 Amazon 221 estate in single-carb form.

power engines. And for the first two years of the Volvo 142's life (1967–68), the two-door model was given the same practically indestructible B18 engine.

The B20 Engine

Long before an engine series reaches the end of its useful life in production – sometimes even before it has been launched – the engineers will be hard at work on its replacement. Arriving in 1961, Volvo's B18 engine was an undeniable success, but it could not be expected to live for ever. The outline of a new generation of engines had been on Volvo drawing boards since the mid-1960s. The engineers involved could perhaps have started by looking in their own archives, as the B18 was originally planned as a two-litre engine. But in

the end a displacement of 1.8 litres was deemed big enough for the cars it would be fitted to.

So it was that, by the end of the 1960s, the B18 series engines were thought to have done their bit for Volvo and all the trials and testing of their successor had been completed. Everything was ready for its introduction into three Volvo model series: the Amazon, the P1800 and the 140. There was good news for Volvo fans everywhere in the autumn of 1968: new engines in all models. Sceptics might have assumed this would be merely a bored-out version of the B18, but not so. The new engine was much more than just 200cc bigger (or 198cc, to be precise).

The basic version, known as the B20A, had a single Zenith-Stromberg carburettor and developed 82bhp (DIN) at 4,700rpm. The B20B had twin SU carbs – by now something of a Volvo classic – and produced 100bhp (DIN) at

5,500rpm. The B20B was a good choice for the environmentally conscious motorist. It had the same type of emission control as Volvos bound for the American market had

2-litre engine with exhaust emission control

The Volvo 121/122 S is fitted with the Volvo two-litre B 20 engine. Tough, durable and utterly reliable. Exhilarating acceleration for safety-fast overtaking. The powerful torque gives excellent performance even from low engine speeds. This engine also features the Volvo exhaust emission control system which, in combination with positive crankcase ventilation provides highly-

effective combustion and considerably cleaner exhaust gases. An added advantage is even better fuel economy. The newly designed air cleaner on the 118 b.h.p. engine cuts induction roar considerably.

The Volvo 121/122 S now feature thermostatically controlled preheating of induction air. No matter how cold the ambient temperature is, the air reaching

the carburetters via the induction preheater holds a constant temperature of approximately +30°C (86°F). No stalling. And smooth running immediately after a cold start.

The B 20 engine is available in two versions. 90 b.h.p. or 118 b.h.p. SAE.

The sports version has twin carburetters.

The B20 was the largest engine offered in the Amazon. Again there were single- or twin-carb variations on the theme.

featured since 1967. This was based on preheating the fuel/air mixture in the inlet manifold. So it also meant that anyone buying a Volvo 140 or an Amazon with the B20A engine's preheating and good combustion would have a car capable of complying with the forthcoming emission control standards, just proposed.

Other advances made with the B20 were the introduction of an alternator and a viscous coupling for the radiator fan. The less powerful engine was used for only a few years in most markets before it was superseded by the 90bhp B20D. This had twin SU carburettors of a new type. Its torque curve extended through a greater range of engine speeds than the B version had.

The B20E had Bosch electronic fuel injection and developed 120bhp (DIN). It was used only in the Volvo 142 GL (Grand Luxe) and the P1800 E. In the latter car, it produced 130bhp. In 1974 the electronic injection system was replaced by a system called Continuous Injection (a mechanical, vacuum-controlled system), which had the advantages of a relatively low noise level and clean emissions.

Like the B18 before it, the B20 engine acquired a reputation for reliability, and performance enthusiasts liked it because it was so easy to tune. In certain markets, the B20 was also the standard engine in the 240 series. It continued to be made in 82 and 90bhp versions throughout its long career – right up until 1993.

CHAPTER THREE

THE AMAZON ARRIVES

As soon as the new Amazon was shown to the public on 1 and 2 September 1956, the orders came flooding in. It was priced at SKr12,600, and buyers were asked to pay a SKr4,000 deposit, with the first cars promised for delivery the following spring. Compared with the SKr9,275 that Volvo charged for a PV444L Standard, the Amazon was pretty pricey (it cost almost 36 per cent more).

In the event the initial batch of cars was shipped in February and March 1957 and they were an instant success, despite costing a third more than the PV444L by this time. But problems soon arose, with the first 100 or so cars suffering from an array of issues, including water leaks into the cabin, self-lowering windows and rattling gear levers. Volvo acted swiftly to cure the problems and very soon the car

At a time when many car makers aimed their products at male buyers, Volvo focused on women as much as on men.

The earliest Amazons came with two-tone paint as standard – and looked very smart as a result.

While many two-tone schemes were rather conservative, some of the brighter options really made the Amazon stand out.

However, many Volvo buyers were businessmen, who wanted a car that looked discreet but was of very high quality.

was largely free of such irritations, although curing the water leaks proved to be an ongoing challenge for some owners, as dealers struggled to find effective fixes.

Those initial hiccups don't appear to have done the Amazon any harm, the car proving easy to sell – to the point where the Lundby factory struggled to cope with demand. It was clear another factory would be needed as it wasn't possible to expand the Lundby facility, but the situation was remedied by the building of more factories. The first over-

seas factory was opened in Canada, in June 1963, in Halifax, Nova Scotia. Less than two years later there was a factory in Ghent in Belgium, but the production facility that made the biggest difference to Volvo's capacity was the opening of the Swedish Torslanda factory in 1964 (see separate panel). This allowed up to 200,000 cars to be built each year, although it would be a long time before that many cars would be made there – the first year's production tally was just 118,465 units, around half of which were sold in Sweden.

The Amazon proved such a hit that the Lundby factory struggled to cope.
The Torslanda facility couldn't come on stream soon enough.

The first Amazon brochures claimed that the car was a 'fast and fiery Swedish beauty', with its maker claiming that many would buy it simply for its good looks. There was no denying that the Amazon had a certain charm, with its understated curves and spot-on proportions – at this stage it came only as a four-door saloon. Setting off the lines was an array of two-tone colour schemes; in theory, early adopters of the Amazon couldn't specify a monotone paint job, although some such cars were built. More usual were cars with a black and red colour scheme, topped off by a grey roof. Alternatively, buyers could have a light grey car with a black roof or a dark blue finish with a light grey roof.

Although there was a high degree of automation on the Amazon production line, a lot of work needed to be done by hand.

AN ICONIC FACTORY

Volvo's first car factory was in Lundby in Sweden, and until the late 1950s it had the capacity to build all the cars that Volvo could sell. But as affluence grew in the post-war years, and car ownership increased, Volvo knew it would need far more capacity – not least of all because it was clear that the US market would provide rich pickings.

With the Lundby factory unable to be extended, in March 1959 four million square metres of land was acquired in Sörredsdalen on the island of Hisingen, four miles (7km) west of the old factory. This was the largest ever land purchase in Sweden's history and on 4 November that year construction started on what would become Volvo Car Torslanda.

On 24 April 1964 the new plant was inaugurated. It was a facility of immense proportions by contemporary standards, with a total floor area of 180,000 square metres. The plant building with its three units was more than a kilometre long and the fence surrounding the facility was no less than 4.2 kilometres long.

The production plan was set for 110,000 cars a year in one shift operation, 150,000 cars for two shifts and up to 200,000 cars annually in full-scale operation. The plant could handle 1,600 bodies or cars simultaneously in various stages of production.

The total investment was 240 million kronor and the project was able to be completed largely thanks to close cooperation with the Swedish state. Volvo Cars' special status as a vital Swedish exporter and the company's considerable significance at both regional and national level meant the new plant was a matter of prime importance for the entire nation.

The production facility was state of the art, with two- and four-door saloons built alongside estates.

Here, the bodyshells are being prepared by hand before the process of priming and rustproofing starts.

For many years Volvo Car Torslanda was Sweden's largest single workplace, with up to 11,000 employees. By the time Volvo Car Torslanda celebrated its 50th anniversary on 24 April 2014, the development of new production systems and automation meant the total workforce was about 3,000 people.

At that stage the plant was going through its biggest overhaul ever, which incorporated the inauguration of a new body plant. The investment was for Volvo's then-new SPA (Scalable Product Architecture) platform, which formed the basis for scalable and flexible development and production of Volvo's then-new range.

The Torslanda factory was unbelievably huge – it represented the largest-ever land purchase in Sweden's history.

THE PV SOLDIERS ON

It was reasonable to assume that when the Amazon arrived in 1957, it would replace the PV444. But Volvo had other ideas; within a year of the Amazon's arrival, a heavily updated PV444 was announced: the PV544. Using virtually the same bodyshell as its predecessor, the new car had a larger engine and room for five people instead of just four – hence the 544 tag. The extra space was created by the use of a rear seat more than six inches wider and thinner front seats to allow more legroom.

Although few people expected Volvo to continue producing a car that had already been around for nearly a decade, it all made sense – especially as the car was still incredibly popular. Not only was the body tooling long since paid for, but with a bit of a tweak here and there the car could see service for another decade before finally being put out to pasture. And besides, it allowed Volvo to have a two-car product range rather than just the one.

Most people assumed the Amazon would replace the PV444, but Volvo refreshed the latter and kept it on sale for ten years after the Amazon made its debut.

By updating the old design, Volvo spent just three million kronor on its 'new' car – whereas an all-new model would have cost the company at least 35 million kronor. The car's durability was also well proven and through continuous development of the model the PV was still competitive from a performance and driving point of view. Indeed, in America, the country where the car was at its most popular, the PV was nicer to drive than most of its home-grown rivals. And to cap it all, whereas the typical American car depreciated by 40 per cent in its first year, the Volvo lost just 8 per cent of its value in the same period – it was no wonder Volvo was reluctant to replace the car with an all-new model.

By sticking with a well-established car Volvo could focus on addressing the shortcomings of the existing model, so the cramped interior and poor visibility were the key areas to be tackled. As a result, the most significant change externally was a larger one-piece curved windscreen – all PV444s had featured a split windscreen with flat glass. The rear window was also larger and the tail lights changed in appearance.

But although changes on the outside were slight, there were more significant ones under the skin. The steering box was now more responsive and passenger space was significantly increased. Rear seatbelt mountings were now standard, as was a padded safety dash. In 1969, four years after the PV544 had gone out of production, Volvo's decision to stick with the basic formula of the PV444 would be vindicated, when eleven Volvo dealers smashed up a 1958 example of the PV544 in New York. They were protesting publicly that Volvos were made too well – something that was at odds with their need to make a profit. Owners didn't need to replace their cars as frequently and warranties were rarely called upon because the cars were so reliable. Having turned it over and smashed it up, the car was pretty much wrecked. But one of the dealers decided to see if it would still start, and of course as soon as he turned the key the engine burst into life. Proof, if any were needed, that Volvos were streets ahead of their competitors when it came to durability.

The PV544 sold alongside the Amazon, with many buyers loving the car's strength and proven reliability.

The success of the PV was partly accounted for by the fact that Volvo had gone to great trouble to tailor the car for each export market. As a result there were over 100 different versions of the car available around the world, although they varied from each other only in detail.

In terms of sales, the PV544 was at its peak in 1959, when no fewer than 51,560 cars were delivered. From then on there was a gradual decline and on 20 October 1965, nearly a decade after the introduction of the Amazon, the last PV544 was built. Considering the Amazon had been introduced in 1956 to supersede the PV range, it's a testament to the PV544's popularity that it lived so long.

THE PV WARRANTY

The cat was well and truly put among the pigeons in 1954 when Volvo announced that it was offering a five-year PV Warranty on the PV444 as part of the purchase cost. Although that in itself doesn't sound such a deal, it wasn't a guarantee as such – it was actually a comprehensive insurance cover given away free with each car bought. The car's owner still had to buy third-party insurance cover, but Volvo would pay for the cost of any repairs exceeding SKr200 in the event of any accident – regardless of whose fault it was.

Sweden's insurance industry took exception to such an offer and accused the company of unfair practices. The initial idea had been Assar Gabrielsson's in 1954, so it was he who ended up in the dock in 1956 when Volvo was taken to court over the warranty. But it wasn't until September 1958 that the matter was finally resolved and the case was dismissed by Sweden's Supreme Court. As a result, all Swedish Amazon owners benefited from the scheme from this point on.

Volvo made great capital of the benefits offered to owners, with plenty of case histories of cars written off and replaced for SKr200 featuring in advertisements. And because the warranty was valid for only five years, Volvo set up its own insurance company (named Volvia) to allow owners to buy an insurance policy from their vehicle's maker. It wasn't until shortly after Ford's acquisition of Volvo in 1999 that the insurance scheme was transferred from the ownership of Volvo to its Swedish partner *if*.

SAFETY FIRST

While the Amazon's looks and colour schemes were appealing, it was the car's safety credentials that some found more alluring. As well as a padded dash top and door trims there were mounting points for front seatbelts – although at this point the belts themselves weren't standard. However, by 1959 there were three-point belts fitted by the factory to all Amazons sold in the Nordic markets, making it the first car in the world to offer such life-saving equipment as standard.

Because of the two-point seatbelt's relatively poor protective ability and the fact that it was perceived as awkward, some customers were initially sceptical about the benefits of Volvo's three-point seatbelt – even though it was comfortable and effective.

Ahead of the launch of the three-point belt in global markets, a series of sled tests and trial impacts was first carried

Volvo was the first car maker to fit three-point seatbelts as standard – they featured in the Amazon from 1959.

Even rear-seat passengers could be strapped in; this publicity shot from 1958 shows a three-point seatbelt in use in the back seat.

NILS BOHLIN AND THE SEATBELT

Few people have saved as many lives as Nils Bohlin – the Volvo engineer who in 1959 invented the three-point seatbelt. Providing the most effective protection in the event of an impact, since its introduction Bohlin's belt has saved millions of lives and prevented or reduced the severity of injuries for millions more. So it seems fair to say that the three-point seatbelt must be the single most important safety advance in the history of the car; it's no wonder Bohlin's invention has been identified by German patent registrars as one of the eight patents to have the greatest significance for humanity in the hundred years up to 1985. Bohlin was born in 1920 in Härnösand, Sweden. He started his career in 1942 at Svenska Aeroplan Aktiebolaget (SAAB) as an aircraft engineer and by 1955 he was responsible for the development of catapult seats and for the pilots' other safety equipment. Bohlin was also interested in keeping

It would be hard to imagine cars without three-point seatbelts nowadays, but it was Nils Bohlin who perfected the concept.

out on all the designs of seatbelt available at the time. The results were clear: Volvo's three-point seatbelt provided by far the best level of protection for the car's occupants. Backed by these results, in 1963 Volvo introduced the three-point seatbelt in the USA and in other markets where it was not yet fitted. This meant that all Volvo cars leaving the factory were now fitted as standard with the three-point seatbelts for those in the front.

Convincing front-seat passengers to belt up was a thankless task in the late 1950s, so the idea of getting those in the back to wear a belt was even more fantastic. But, as we now know, seatbelts in the rear are just as important as those in the front and Volvo soon realized the importance of ensuring that all of its cars' occupants were held securely in their seats, which is why work on equipping the rear seats with belts was undertaken in parallel with other safety-related developments. As a result the Amazon featured mounting points for rear seatbelts as early as 1958, but it wasn't until 1967 that Volvo succeeded in convincing the car-buying public that the rear seat's occupants should also use the belts.

Bizarrely, people had previously held the peculiar belief that just sitting in the rear seat provided protection in a collision – they felt that it was those in the front who were in

the human body as safe as possible during extreme retardation – and he soon got the opportunity to develop his ideas.

In 1958 Bohlin was recruited by Volvo to work as a safety engineer by Gunnar Engellau. The latter knew that the two-point seatbelt wasn't safe or practical enough. During the latter half of the 1950s, Volvo developed a number of possible solutions, to prevent occupants coming into contact with the car's interior components or to lessen the severity of the consequences of such impacts in a collision. These included a collapsible steering column, a padded dashboard and attachment points for diagonal two-point belts in the front seats.

Volvo had already been equipping its cars with standard-fit mountings for two-point front seatbelts as far back as 1957, but the so-called 'diagonal belt' didn't have the required potential that Volvo wanted. The belt buckle was positioned at the height of the occupant's ribcage, so it damaged the body's soft organs instead of protecting them. Engellau had a relative who had died in a road accident because of shortcomings in the two-point belt, so he tasked Bohlin with developing a better alternative.

Bohlin soon realized that both the upper and lower body had to be properly secured in place, with one belt across the chest and another across the hips. His biggest challenge was to create a solution that was both simple to use and effective, since the belt had to be able to be put on using just one hand.

In 1958 Bohlin's work resulted in a patent application for his three-point belt. What Bohlin integrated into his design, and which he regarded as most important for

This rear-facing child seat looks clunky now, but this was the face of child safety if you drove an Amazon.

a car safety belt, were four golden rules: the belt consisted of both a hip or lap belt and also a diagonal belt across the upper body, which was positioned correctly from the physiological viewpoint. That is to say across the pelvis and the ribcage, and attached at a low anchorage point beside the seat. The belt geometry formed a V with the peak pointing down towards the floor.

In addition, the belt stayed in position and did not move when it was under load. This is the crucial difference between the effective V-shaped belt according to Bohlin's design and the previous three-point design, or Y-type. Bohlin's belt was in fact an effective demonstration of geometrical perfection rather than a cutting-edge innovation. The solution and the benefits of the three-point design soon spread throughout the world, since Volvo immediately made Bohlin's patent available to all car makers.

Bohlin didn't stop there, though; he was quick to realize the need for side-impact protection, so back in the 1970s he started working on various technical solutions that eventually resulted in what is now the well-known and patented SIPS – Side Impact Protection System – which Volvo was among the world's first car makers to introduce.

After retiring in 1985, Bohlin was consulted by Volvo on numerous occasions regarding particularly complicated safety issues. In 2002, Bohlin died at the age of 82 from the after-effects of a stroke.

danger. They were oblivious to the fact that, in an impact, rear seat occupants could be hurled forward with a force of up to five tonnes, risking serious injury to both themselves and the occupants of the front seats.

While the PV444 had featured an umbrella-style hand-brake under the dashboard, its successor's handbrake lever was sited on the outside of the driver's seat. It was resited for safety reasons, although its new position raised a few eyebrows as such a location was decidedly unconventional. The reasoning was clear though; Volvo knew the Amazon would have to succeed in the USA if the company was to expand significantly. It also knew that US car buyers favoured a bench in the front, so to accommodate this the Amazon's handbrake would have to sit on the outside of the driver's seat, while the gearchange was sited on the dash.

PRESS REACTION

Although Volvo's export drive was well under way by the time the Amazon was launched, it didn't introduce its new four-door saloon into many markets at first. The PV had been slow to be accepted in the USA and it was never offi-cially offered in the UK, which is why there was no rush to introduce the Amazon to these markets.

As was common at the time, chrome hub caps featured as standard, while for some markets there were whitewall tyres.

However, it was clear that by the time the Amazon was unveiled at the 1959 New York Auto Show there was a demand for it and British buyers were also keen to buy Swedish – although they didn't get the chance until 1958, by which point the 122S was available.

As a result, although the original Amazon was in produc-tion for a full year before it started to be developed, the mainstream press outside Sweden didn't bother with this earlier edition – their first taste of the Amazon was of the sportier variation on the theme, launched in spring 1958.

THE AMAZON GETS SPORTY

By the end of 1957, 5,000 Amazons had been built and in March 1958 the next development arrived – the Sport. Developed mainly for export markets where it would be known as the 122S (for Sport), this variant was also some-times known as the Amazon S. First shown at the Geneva motor show, the B16B-engined Sport featured twin SU carbs, revised bearings, valves and valve springs, plus a re-profiled camshaft to raise power to 85bhp – an increase of almost 50 per cent over the standard car. Also part of the mix was a raised compression ratio; that of the standard car was just 7.5:1, but this new powerplant was taken up to 8.2:1.

There was a minimum of decoration on the Amazon. What was there was largely functional.

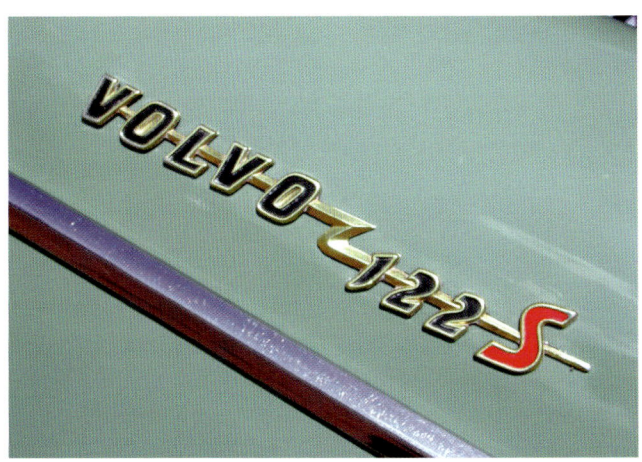

Even the standard Amazon was surprisingly perky; the fitment of twin carburettors to create the 122S made the car even sportier.

While the perkier Amazon was known as the 122S in export markets, in the Swedish market it was sold as the Sport.

The three-speed gearbox fitted as standard until now was replaced with an all-synchromesh four-speed transmission, which from this point on was also offered as an optional extra on the regular Amazon. While the extra power was very welcome, it was the fitment of this extra cog that really allowed the Amazon to shine; it permitted the ratios to be closed up so the yawning gaps of the three-speed unit could be dispensed with.

However, the fourth gear of this new gearbox was the same ratio as the top gear in the three-speed unit (it was a direct ratio), and as Volvo didn't increase the back axle ratio for more relaxed cruising, things got rather busy when the 122S was sitting at high speeds. While raising the rear axle ratio would have increased acceleration times, there were some who felt this was preferable to keeping things as they were.

Other than the new gearbox and the engine modifications, the 122S was pretty much the same as the earlier model, although the ride height was also lowered by an inch to improve the handling. There was also a new colour option of dark blue with a light grey roof – other than this, it was business as usual in terms of styling inside and out.

Within six months of the appearance of the 122S, seatbelts were fitted as standard to all 120-series cars, the first time that such a move was made by any car maker in the world. By the end of the year all 120-series cars were also equipped with dual-circuit, servo-assisted brakes. Safety has always been high on Volvo's list of priorities – now it was the thing that Volvo was seen to stand for more than anything.

122S WITH B16B ENGINE (MARCH 1958 TO 1961)

As 121 except:

Engine
Compression ratio:	8.2:1
Fuelling:	Twin SU carburettors
Maximum power:	85bhp (SAE) at 5,500rpm
Maximum torque:	87lb ft at 3,000rpm

Transmission
Four-speed all-synchro manual gearbox
Weight:	2,352lb (1,068kg)

Performance (Motor)
Max speed:	94mph (151km/h)
Third:	76mph (122km/h)
Second:	51mph (82km/h)
First:	33mph (53km/h)
0–60mph	14.0 sec
30–50mph in top:	12.4 sec
50–70mph in top:	18.3 sec
Fuel consumption:	22.5–36mpg (7.9–12.6ltr/100km)

Price including tax when new (January 1959)
Four-door saloon	£1,399

LEFT OR RIGHT?

Less than one per cent of Amazon buyers in Sweden chose to buy a car with right-hand drive, despite the fact that the country drove on the left – until 3 September 1967. Until 1948 (when Volvo became the biggest-selling brand), the most popular cars in Sweden were Chevrolets. These were offered with left-hand drive only – it made no commercial sense to re-engineer them with right-hand drive for such a tiny market. Adopting an 'if-you-can't-beat-them-join-them' approach, Volvo also focused on left-hand-drive cars for its home market, as explained by Assar Gabrielsson in his 1936 sales handbook:

American cars were always delivered with their steering wheels on the left side, and for such a small market as Sweden they were reluctant to change their cars to right-hand drive. Consequently, salesmen of American cars in Sweden often exaggerated the importance of the left shoulder. Through this, the Swedish people have become used to having the steering wheel on the left side, in spite of Sweden having left-hand traffic.

In most other countries, the steering wheel is located at the right side when the traffic is left-hand, or at the left when traffic is right-hand. We at Volvo are fully convinced that taking the road standard into consideration, the left shoulder is of little or no importance. It is much more important to have a clear view of the road ahead when overtaking. Therefore, the most logical thing would be that Volvos were made with right-hand drive. In spite of this, we have kept left-hand drive because we do not feel that we have to be pioneers in this area. We believe that we would only meet resistance from our customers and create extra work for our dealers if we only delivered right-hand-drive Volvos. We will therefore continue to sell left-hand-drive cars. Volvo trucks and buses, however, can be delivered with left-hand drive or right-hand drive at customer request.

Maybe Bryan Hanrahan was correct when he wrote in Australia's *Modern Motor* in September 1961:

The Swedes drive on the left-hand side of the road in cars that have LEFT-HAND DRIVE. Presumably this is to make absolutely sure that the front passenger cops it in a prang instead of the driver.

Or perhaps Volvo could also see what was coming; it must have appeared inevitable back then that traffic in Sweden would start to drive on the right at some point. After all, its neighbours did so and having to switch sides when moving between countries was fraught with danger.

The matter was regularly discussed in Sweden's parliament, but when a referendum was held in 1955, a massive 83 per cent of voters opted to keep things as they were. However, by 1963 the Swedish parliament had opted to move to the right, with the change set for 1967.

On 3 September, at 4.50am, all Swedish traffic was directed over to the right-hand side of the road and stopped. Everything remained still for 10 minutes, then at 05.00, when it started again, all road users in Sweden from heavy trucks to cyclists were already on the right side of the road, where they've remained ever since.

Roads, junctions, roundabouts and flyovers had already been redesigned while 360,000 road signs were changed during the night. Predictably, a massive campaign across Sweden informed everyone of what was about to take place, with 130,000 notices springing up across the country to remind everyone. These featured a large H (for Höger, which is right in Swedish) while many cars now featured an H sticker on the dashboard to remind drivers that they needed to switch sides.

In a bid to minimize the chances of casualties, there was also a speed limit of 30km/h in built-up areas and 50km/h on all other roads on that first day (3 September), which was a Sunday. In total, just 150 or so minor collisions were reported on that first day, with another 125 on Monday 4 September – compared with a typical 160 or so. In the event, 1967 would see fewer people killed or seriously injured on Sweden's roads than previously, but as drivers became more complacent those figures would start to creep up once more.

Changing sides of the road meant a huge amount of preparation – but it paid off as the switch went smoothly.

ABOVE: **The Amazon 122S was the perfect sporting saloon; fast, comfortable, refined and spacious. It made a perfect tow car too.**

LEFT: **The 122S was the ideal getaway car – it could take you wherever you wanted to go.**

This braking system upgrade in November 1958 coincided with the first official Volvo imports into the UK. It was the Brooklands Motor Company that handled the process (it would later become Volvo concessionaire for the UK market), but a £932 pre-tax price translated into a very hefty £1,399 by the time duties had been paid. You had to want one very badly to pay that sort of money, when an Austin A95 De Luxe was pegged at £1,079 and a Ford Zodiac MkII saloon was just £1,013.

With such sporting credentials, it's no wonder the 122S became so popular with police forces, keen to equip their traffic officers with something that could keep up with criminals keen to evade justice. By the end of 1958 the

Swedish police had ordered a fleet of Amazon Sports and in time the British police would follow suit.

Amazon 122S Press Reaction

By the time the 122S was launched, the Amazon had become widely available around the globe and magazines were keen to put the new model through its paces. For most readers, this was the first opportunity to read about what the new saloon was like – aside from the odd small new piece when the car had originally been unveiled.

In the UK, *Motor* tested a 122S and was astonished at how

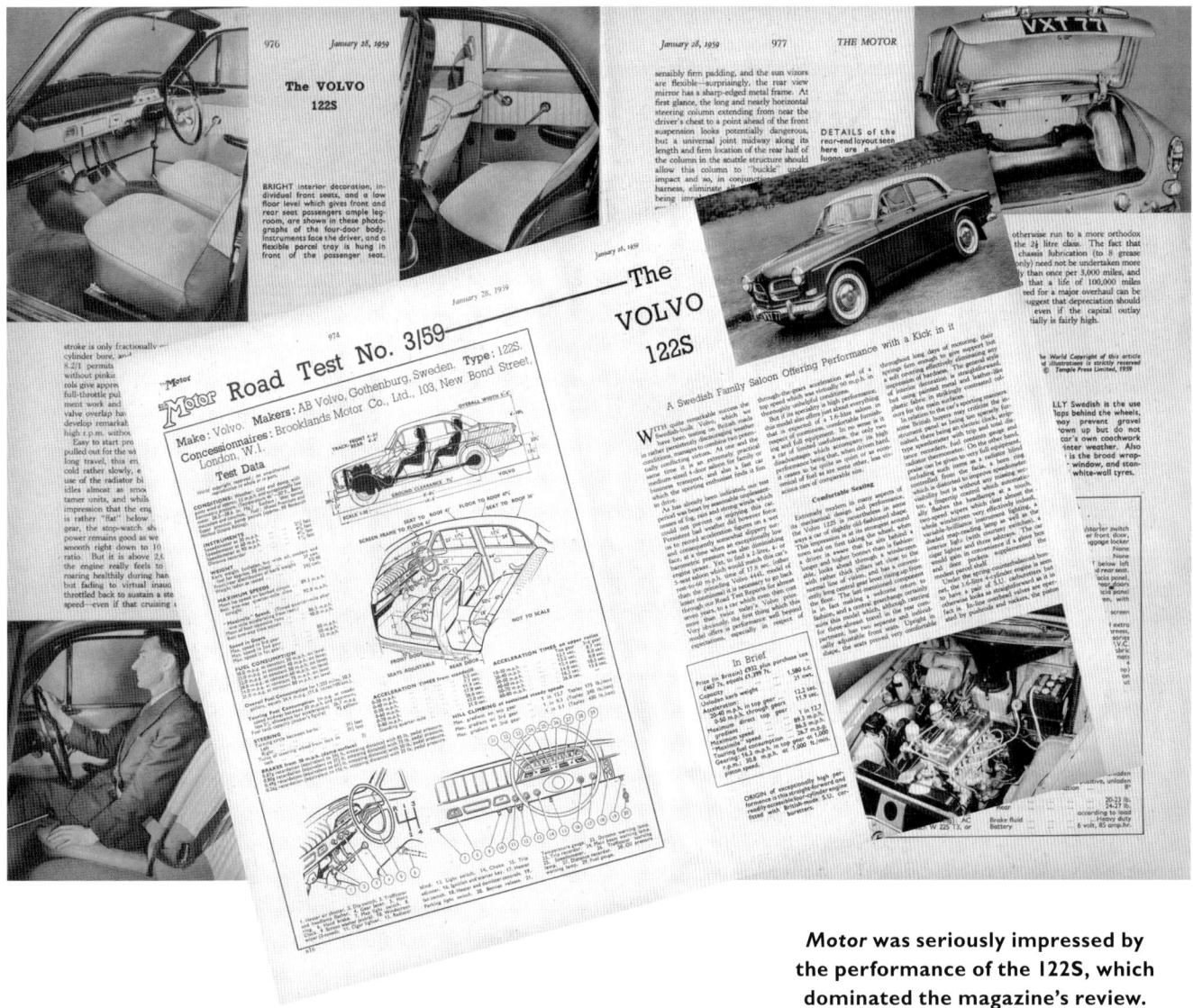

Motor **was seriously impressed by the performance of the 122S, which dominated the magazine's review.**

The pleasing proportions are evident in this side view of the 122-S.

ROAD TEST **VOLVO 122-S**

A newer and more attractive product of superb Swedish engineering

THE VOLVO 122-S, called the Amazon in Europe, has been built and sold in Sweden for over two years, but it is new to the U.S. market.

And a refreshing new car it is, too: pleasant looking, easy (and fun) to drive, economical and durable in the extreme. It is also refreshing to find a company that actually does something to make its product safe for the occupants, and does it without making asinine statements that the public won't buy safety.

The safety-conscious Swedes have inaugurated many features we've long advocated for cars and would like to see incorporated, in some form, in all passenger vehicles. Here we have the padded instrument panel, a dished steering wheel that is attached to a column built to collapse under pressure, and a plastic package shelf on the passenger's side which folds under impact. The sun visors are of thick foam rubber construction, and seat belts (diagonal straps that extend from the floor in the center across the passenger to the door post) are available on order.

You can, of course, put safety belts in any car, and many vehicles have padded instrument panels to protect the passenger, but most manufacturers install a row of projecting knobs, handles or switches below the padding which nullifies its effectiveness. If no deterrents to the effectiveness of the Volvo's padded panel were the two radio control knobs.

The newest import is a handsome car in a reserved way, with no evident ostentation or gaudiness. Its excellent over-all proportions carry it well past the average medium-sized sedan in appearance. From some angles, notably the side and rear, it resembles the smaller Simca Aronde (nothing wrong with that). It is quite easily lost in the traffic shuffle, not being an outstanding example of something new in the styling department. This, of course, will keep the car from getting old as quickly as some other contemporary vehicles, so it can mean money for its owner at trade-in time.

A close examination of the car, along with many miles behind the wheel, brought favorable comments from every tester and rider. Design, construction and general quality are obviously excellent, and there is a pervasive feeling of durability. Yet there is no indication of the luxury that we expected of a 4-cyl sedan in this price bracket.

With 3 less horsepower, the same gear ratios, and over-all size and frontal area similar to those of the PV-544, the performance would be expected to be about the same on both models, and so it is. The 122-S weighs

Under the hood, a fine 4-cyl, ohv engine and a fine heater, so necessary for Sweden's cold climate.

COLOR PHOTO BY RAY HALIN

PHOTOS BY POOLE

65 lb more, and acceleration is reduced proportionately. It is our feeling that the last Volvo we tested (the PV-444, October 1958) was in slightly better tune. If so, the difference in performance was a little more than would be indicated by the two cars' specifications:

	PV-444	122-S
Weight	2160 lb	2225 lb
BHP	85 @ 5500	88 @ 5500
Torque	90 @ 3500	90 @ 3500
Gear ratio (over all)	4.55:1	4.55:1
0–30 mph	4.2 sec	4.7 sec
0–60 mph	13.0 sec	16.2 sec
Top speed	93.5 mph	91.9 mph

Road & Track has not tested a 159 PV-544 because of its similarity to the 444, but the above figures can be assumed to be accurate for this year's model.

The 1600-cc, 4-cyl engine is extremely flexible and, as we've said before, one of the most free-revving rocker-arm engines we've seen. It also seemed to run smoother than other Volvo engines.

Even low gear is synchronized in the 4-speed transmission. Still controlled by a long floor-mounted lever, as in more familiar Volvo models, it operated magnificently every time. There is still too much gap between the ratios of 2nd and 3rd, but the bright side of this is that the car starts easily in 2nd gear. Those who shift more traditionally will find that the shift lever has so strong a spring that it wants to go directly from low gear to 4th instead of 2nd. Yet the engine is so amenable that it pulls

A pleasant but unexciting interior is functional.

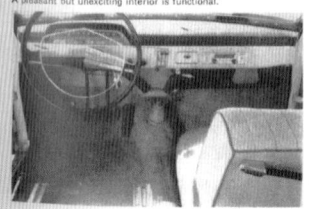

calmly (albeit with little power) from about 15 mph on up.

Both the sturdily vinyl-covered seats and the suspension of the 122-S appear at first to be a little too stiff for comfort. Longer excursions in the car emphasize the wisdom of fairly firm seat cushions (ultra-soft seats are fine on a sofa, but not in a car) but also point up the need for a more bucket-like treatment of the seats themselves; the backs are fine. The suspension grows to feel a little softer. Bad bumps, however, catch it napping.

Foot room for both front- and rear-seat passengers is good, but the knee room of rear-seat passengers is somewhat limited when the front seats are in a position from the center of travel on back. The front-seat adjustment handle itself is the biggest single annoyance in the entire car. It seems mechanically sound, but it's the poorest we've seen for safety. We strongly advise purchasers of the car to exercise extreme caution when adjusting the seat (especially rearward), lest their cut or pinched fingers require medical aid. The rear door window handles are difficult to use when the front seats are back.

The emergency brake is handily located on the driver's left and a clever protective ring prevents its accidental release. Several times during the test we were moved to wonder why they didn't mount it on the driver's right, between the front seats.

Visibility is excellent, due to the well placed window areas (not overly large) and the high seating position. After several years in cars with low builds, the seating

The neat luggage compartment is easily accessible . . .

18   19

Despite (or maybe because of) its compact dimensions compared with most American rivals, US magazine *Road & Track* rather liked the Amazon.

fast it was considering it packed just a 1.6-litre engine. A 0–60mph time of 17.8 seconds may seem sluggish by modern standards, but at the time it was remarkable for a large saloon. In fact the first thing about the Amazon that made an impression on the road tester was its performance – after that it was fairly ordinary in most respects. The driving position was seen as old-fashioned, and once up to speed it lost some of the refinement that gave it an edge at lower velocities. Fuel consumption was also not especially competitive but at least the car was comfortable, solidly built and very well equipped. That first test by *Motor* marked the introduction of official UK sales with right-hand drive cars. Although the company didn't have an especially strong image in Britain, its cars had received some coverage in British car magazines and it wasn't long before sales steadily increased.

In September 1959, *Road & Track* compared a 122S with a PV444, a car which was at that time obsolete, but in many ways little changed from the PV544 that had superseded it. Considering this was the year of greatest excess when it came to American car design, *Road & Track*'s testers found the 122S refreshingly understated. There were no outrageous fins or huge slabs of chrome plastered across the car, merely clean lines and useful safety features. This was something that wasn't lost on the magazine's reporters, who clearly felt that what Volvo was doing was far more worthwhile than the tactics of many American car producers. Interestingly, the 122S was a far more compact car than its competitors in the American marketplace, yet when positioned alongside its European rivals the car was very much comparable in size – but despite this the Amazon compared favourably in every market in which it was being sold.

Despite the Amazon's high price, sales would have been helped by Mike Hawthorn's review of the car, which appeared in an edition of the *Sunday Express* shortly before his death. In it he extolled the virtues of the 122S, saying that its staid looks and conservative Swedish image could all be forgiven when the car was opened up and given its head. Or as he put it:

> Have you ever gulped at your glass of honest, sober ginger ale to discover that you have picked up someone's neat Scotch by mistake? Well that's the shock I got when I tested a Volvo 122S the other day.

A standing quarter-mile time of 19 seconds was fast and Hawthorn reckoned the Volvo was 'as fast and vivid as a rocket burst', adding that: 'The Volvo is a sensation of a car, and about as typical of its background as a battleship called *Buttercup*.'

Indeed, the performance of the 122S was something that was at odds with its staid looks, as when *Motor* tested one in 1959 it described the car as a 'Swedish family saloon offering performance with a kick in it'.

CONQUERING AMERICA

Although Volvo had made its first car in 1927, it would be another three decades before it officially sold its wares in the USA. Blazing the trail was the PV444, which had been shown in prototype form as early as 1947. However, it wasn't until 1955 that US importer Nils Sefeldt was appointed – and at first he received just five cars, which he struggled to sell. He then received another five cars and they were no easier to shift, but, just as he was on the point of giving up, sales started to pick up in the spring of 1956.

Meanwhile, Los Angeles-based businessman Leo Hirsch visited Sweden in 1955 and took a trip in a Volvo taxi. Unfamiliar with the marque and impressed by the PV444's virtues he reckoned he could shift some of the cars so he also took on a contract to import Volvos to America's western states. It didn't take long for the cars to prove a hit, despite the fact that the PV444 was quirky and rather dated.

So when the all-new Amazon made its debut at the New York Auto Show in April 1959, there was a definite appetite for it among American buyers. However, although the car was very warmly received, when the first examples were sold soon after it was clear that all was not well. The camshafts

fitted to some engines had been badly made and very quickly everyone knew about it. Common practice at that time was for car makers to deny everything and hope the problems went away, but Volvo chose to announce very openly that a mistake had been made and the company would put everything right without any owners losing out – the event did much to bolster Volvo's caring image.

While Volvo wasted no time building a reputation for looking after its customers, the company had a mountain to climb in terms of competing with US-built products, which were invariably bigger, with larger engines and more spacious cabins. The fact that the Amazon was more efficient didn't cut much ice with many American buyers; cars and fuel were both cheap, so something home-built and inefficient was the obvious way to go.

The Amazon's Adversaries in the USA

Across the Atlantic, Volvo had a far from insignificant problem; that of convincing buyers its Amazon was a suitable alternative to larger home-built models that weren't necessarily much more costly to buy and didn't necessarily cost a lot more to run – but which offered more space and lazy cruising potential thanks to bigger engines and (invariably) an automatic gearbox.

When *Road & Track* tested one of the first examples of the 122S, it was listed at $2,895 – by 1965 the same car cost $3,015. A $120 increase in six years, representing just 4 per cent, is pretty impressive – especially when you consider that the earlier car featured a four-speed manual gearbox while the later one was a three-speed auto. And with the auto carrying a $180 premium over its manual counterpart in 1965, that meant the 122S had actually gone down in price between 1959 and 1965.

But the 122S needed to go down in price even further if it was to compete on equal terms with US-built products, as you could buy a Chevrolet Corvair, Ford Falcon, Rambler American, Chrysler Valiant or Dodge Dart for less money. These were all available in 6-cylinder form for less than $2,700 and even the V8 editions were generally less than $3,000 – many were priced at under $2,800. With the Amazon coming in 4-cylinder form only, it had to work hard to tempt buyers away from home-grown models.

It also didn't help that the Amazon was rather more compact than its US-built rivals. Some buyers saw that as a good thing; urban dwellers found the Amazon more

The first Volvos landed in America in 1955 and weren't easy to sell. But the Amazon
really took Volvo places in the world's biggest new-car market.

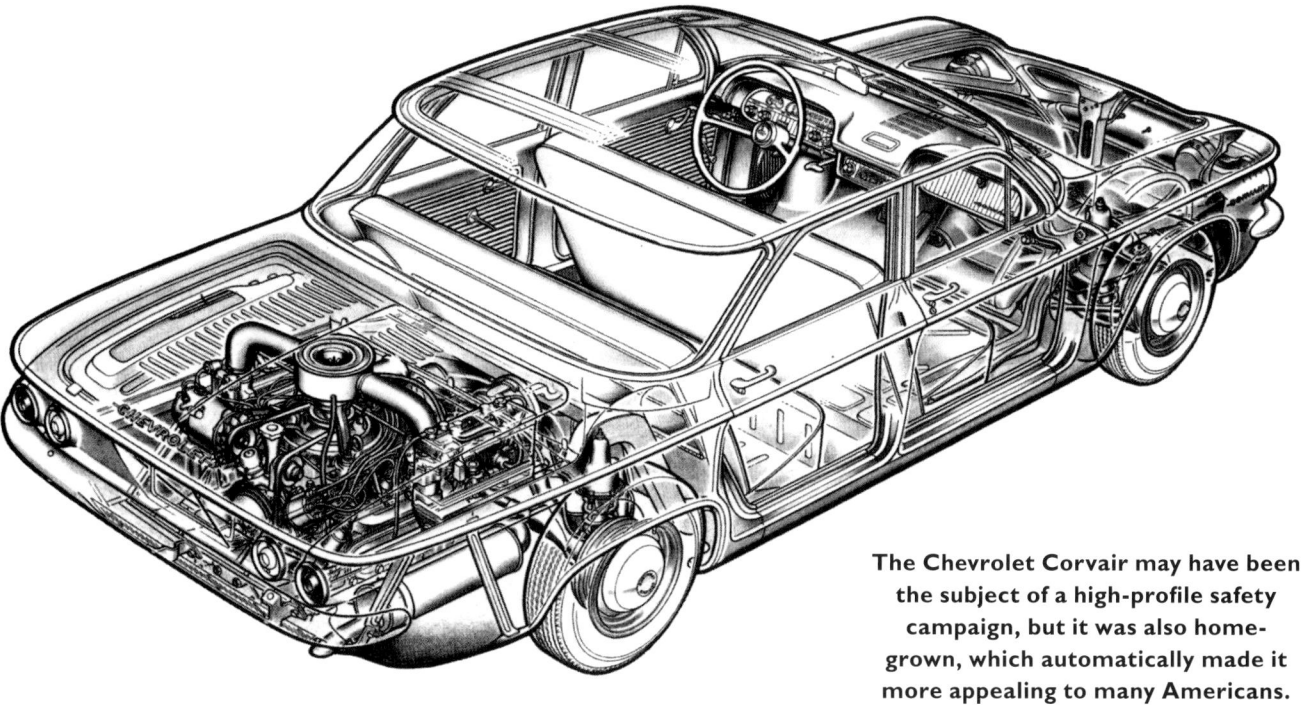

The Chevrolet Corvair may have been the subject of a high-profile safety campaign, but it was also home-grown, which automatically made it more appealing to many Americans.

As in the UK, the marketing muscle of Ford US ensured the Falcon would be at the forefront of the minds of many new-car buyers in America.

**Much less conservatively designed, more spacious and with larger engines too,
the Dodge Dart was very tempting for car buyers in the USA.**

manoeuvrable than the bigger alternatives, but with most American models at least a foot longer – and in some cases close to two feet longer – the Volvo looked like poor value to many. With a length of 175 inches (4,445mm) and a width of just under 64 inches (1,625mm), the Amazon seemed tiny when most American adversaries were closer to 200 inches long and 75 inches wide.

While American cars weren't always the most cleverly packaged, their extra length and width invariably had a beneficial effect on cabin space; many of the products from Ford, Chrysler, AMC and GM could accommodate six adults in comfort while it was a squeeze for five in the Volvo. The Swede also couldn't compete when it came to boot space, and there was no air-conditioning option either – at a time when it was becoming a standard fitment for many mid-priced and mid-sized US cars. Volvo also didn't offer an automatic transmission option at first – in a country where most drivers didn't know how to use a 'stick-shift'. Such a move may seem like commercial suicide, but it didn't make as much of a difference as you might think.

But while the Amazon didn't always fare too well against its American-made rivals on paper, many car buyers looked beyond the bald figures and saw the Amazon for what it was – a high-quality compact family car that would just keep going. Most American alternatives were built very much down to a price and didn't have the durability of the Volvo. They also didn't have the safety features, the economy or the driving characteristics – some who drove the Amazon reckoned it was more like a sports car than a family saloon. But what swung it for many was the fact that the Volvo was different, and thankfully there will always be a proportion of discerning buyers for whom that alone is almost enough.

Buying Swedish – Quality Built In

For example, someone looking to buy a new car in the summer of 1961 could buy a Volvo 122S for $2,495, or for $2,529 they could have a Buick Special. The Swede was realistically a four-seater only, featured an 85bhp 1586cc (96.6 cubic inch) 4-cylinder engine and could manage all of 90mph (145km/h) along with 0–60mph in 16.6 seconds. Compare that with the 185bhp Buick, with its 3524cc (215 cubic inch) V8 that gave 110mph (177km/h) along with 0–60mph in ten seconds dead, and suddenly that $34 seemed like money very well spent.

Of course the pay-off came with the fuel economy; the Volvo was pegged at 27mpg (10.5 ltr/100km) while the Buick was officially rated at 21mpg (13.5 ltr/100km). The problem was, with fuel at 30 cents per gallon, anybody driving 10,000 miles per year would spend just $31.80 more to keep the Buick going ($142.86 compared with $111.06), and with so much more effortless performance on tap, such a small premium was worth every dime.

Thankfully, some new-car buyers looked beyond mere price and performance though. Instead they looked at the quality of the fit and finish, they appreciated greater economy (or simply wanted to drive something more compact) and they wanted something that handled with more precision; surprisingly, the Volvo's kerb weight wasn't far off that of the Buick's as they were rated at 2400lb and 2560lb respectively. But the Volvo was one of the biggest new cars imported to the USA, and the Buick was one of the smaller home-built products…

Despite the on-paper advantage that the home-built products had, Volvo didn't just survive – it prospered. By 1961 there were long waiting lists in the USA for a new Volvo, with Amazons becoming seriously hot property. Which just goes to prove that car buyers in 1960s America were rather more discerning than is sometimes assumed.

Despite the fact that most US-built rivals were bigger, cheaper and featured 6- or 8-cylinder engines, the Amazon wasn't hard to sell in America.

THE AMAZON'S ADVERSARIES IN THE UK

In the 1960s, the family saloon was king. Any car maker worth its salt offered at least one – the bigger outfits tended to offer a multitude of them. But when it comes to working out what the Amazon's rivals were, things aren't quite as clear-cut as they might seem. The Amazon's price fluctuated significantly, depending on the country of sale (because of import taxes), while the market also dictated which cars were alongside the Amazon in the price lists. In mainland Europe there were numerous models offered that didn't make it to the UK, while in the USA there was a whole raft of marques which weren't imported to Europe.

The Rover P6 was a tough adversary because it managed to scoop the inaugural Car of the Year award, thanks to its cutting-edge design.

Those wanting a sporty drive could opt for the Alfa Romeo Giulietta TI saloon, with its zesty 1290cc twin-cam engine – despite its diminutive size, this powerplant provided plenty of fun thanks to the Alfa's low kerb weight. However, in 1961 it was priced at £1,641 in the UK compared with £1,240 for the 122S in B16 form, or £1,372 with a B18 engine. However, the addition of overdrive increased this by a hefty £87, pushing the cost up to £1,459.

Things were distorted in the UK, as buyers paid differing rates of purchase tax depending on whether the car was made in the EEC (European Economic Community), a country that was a member of EFTA (the European Free Trade Association) or somewhere else altogether such as the USA or Japan. The EEC was set up in 1957 and initially consisted of Belgium, France, Italy, Luxembourg, the Netherlands and West Germany, while EFTA was the result of a collaboration between Austria, Denmark, Norway, Portugal, Sweden, Switzerland and the UK. In time the EEC would become the much larger EU (European Union) while EFTA would shrink to encompass just Iceland, Liechtenstein, Norway and Switzerland.

When EFTA was first set up, UK car buyers paid around half the level of import tax that they would if they chose something made from an EEC country. As a result, the Amazon was taxed rather less heavily than models made by French, Italian or German marques – it also helped that soon after the Amazon made its debut on the UK market, purchase tax on cars was cut from 60 per cent to 50 per cent. The result was a huge increase in car sales; 820,000 were sold in 1960, compared with 650,000 the year before. Imports were also on the up: while just 27,000 foreign cars were sold in the UK in 1959, within a year this had jumped to 57,309. Then the chancellor increased the purchase tax rate to 55 per cent in 1961 and it all slowed down again, only for the rate to drop to 45 per cent in 1962 – and then again to just 25 per cent. So it was no surprise when the UK market grew to more than a million for the first time ever, in 1963.

It was in 1963 that one of the Amazon's keenest rivals was launched, the Rover P6. The first ever Car of the Year, the P6 packed in innovations including in-board rear brakes, multi-function light stalks and a height-adjustable steering column; cutting-edge stuff in 1963. At a time when cross-ply tyres were still the norm, the P6 was the first car designed

While Volvo didn't offer a 6-cylinder engine in the Amazon, the Triumph 2000 came with one as standard.

to wear radials, while the steering rack was also placed much further back than usual, to improve crash safety. By positioning it just ahead of the bulkhead, the P6 didn't need the collapsible steering column usually required to pass US crash tests. You could put a Rover 2000 on your drive for £1,264, at a time when the Amazon's price had shrunk to £1,098 in 122S form or just £997 for a 121. Those taxation changes made a big difference.

If you were keen to buy British and the Rover was a bit too radical (or costly) there was always the Triumph 2000, which at £1,094 was just £4 short of the Amazon's price. Unlike the Volvo, the Triumph came with a smooth 6-cylinder engine and felt every inch the luxury car; it was also available in saloon or estate forms and you could choose an automatic gearbox if you didn't want to have to swap cogs yourself.

Alongside the Rover and Triumph was a raft of other British metal that you could put in your garage, including the Humber Hawk (£1,057), Ford Zodiac MkIII (£970), Vauxhall Cresta (£943), Wolseley 6/110 (£1,112) and Austin A110 Westminster saloon (£1,051). All these relatively mainstream alternatives offered space and style with 6-cylinder smoothness (apart from the 2.3-litre four-pot Humber).

If you weren't bothered about buying British, though, you could opt for a Peugeot 404, which in 72bhp 1.6-litre form was just £6 less than the 122S in 1964. Slower and without the feeling of invulnerability, the Peugeot was nevertheless spacious, comfortable and more refined.

Alternatively there were the Fiat 1300 and 1500 saloons, priced at £910 and £949, but what anyone wanting to stand out from the crowd in the mid-sixties would be aiming for would be a Citroen DS or ID. You'd need to have pretty deep pockets to buy one, though, because in 1964 the ID was priced at a hefty £1,307 – and if you wanted a DS you'd have to find a rather strong £1,568 to secure it. That was exactly the same price as the Daimler V8 250 and only £73 less than the wonderfully stately Rover 3-Litre saloon.

The Zodiac was always going to be a tough rival to take on, thanks to the marketing might of Ford.

It was no surprise that the Peugeot 404 looked like the BMC Farina range – they were both designed by Pininfarina.

CHAPTER FOUR

THE AMAZON EVOLVES

Within a year of the Amazon's arrival in the USA in 1959, Volvo set to work on upgrading its smart family saloon. Wholesale changes were unnecessary, but it was clear that there was room for improvement. As a result, from August 1960 there was a revised Amazon available, with completely redesigned seats, which offered much better support during cornering. The seat backrests could also be adjusted to three different angles, in a bid to allow occupants to find the optimum position.

One of the few significant criticisms levelled at the Amazon by the Swedish motoring press was a lack of rear seat legroom, and in a bid to tackle this the front seats were sculpted in such a way that extra space was freed up behind. Volvo didn't stop there though; it also moved the back seats down and rearwards to increase head- and legroom for those sitting in them. The changes made a useful difference but Volvo wasn't convinced it had gone far enough, so it looked at raising the roof height or fitting thinner seats, in a bid to free up even more space. In the end it was reckoned that such changes would be too costly and were probably unnecessary anyway.

While the extra rear seat space was welcome, for many

For 1960 there was a new rear design for the interior – and for the exterior there was still two-tone paintwork on offer.

buyers the adoption of new gearboxes was of more interest. Alongside a new three-speed transmission was a four-speed unit, the former offered with an electrically operated Laycock de Normanville overdrive to cut engine revs and, in the process, fuel consumption too.

A HOTTER AMAZON

Ever since its inception in 1927, Volvo had stood for safe, solid family transport. The marque didn't do sexy, adventurous or overtly sporty, so when the stylish 1800 coupé was revealed in 1959 it came as something of a surprise. Such a move wasn't unprecedented, though. After all, the ill-fated P1900 of 1954 was a two-seater sports car, but just sixty-seven of those were built (along with four or five prototypes), so revisiting that market seemed like an odd thing to do.

This wasn't the first time there had been a 122S as part of the range – but it was the first time it had been offered with a 1.8-litre engine.

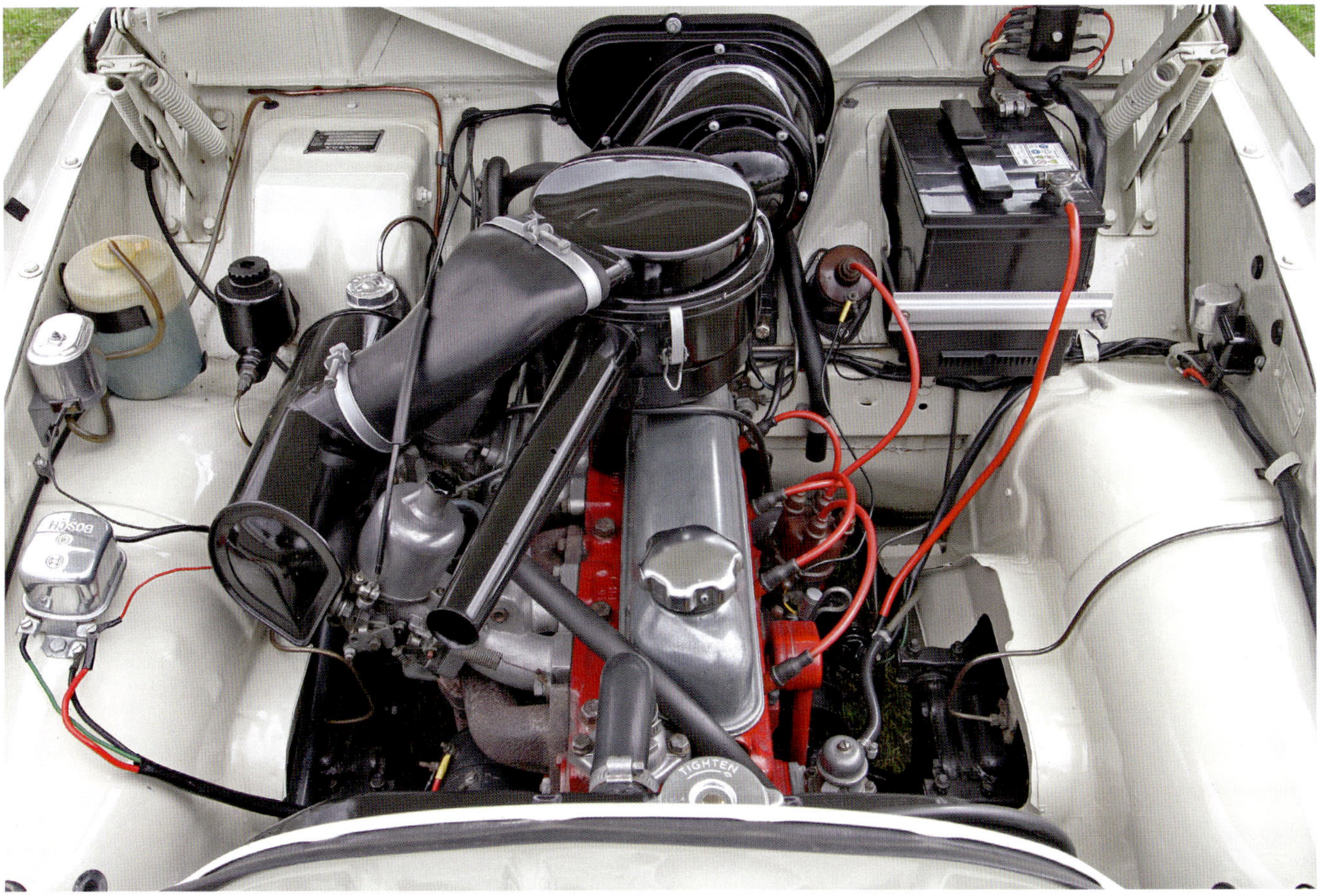

The key to the extra power on tap was the fitment of a pair of **SU** carburettors, which set off the engine bay nicely.

121, 131, 221 WITH B18A ENGINE (1961–68)

Engine
Four cylinders in line, iron block and iron head

Bore × stroke:	84 × 80mm
Capacity:	1778cc
Valvegear:	Overhead valve
Compression ratio:	8.5:1
Fuelling:	Single Zenith carburettor
Maximum power:	75bhp (net) at 4,500rpm (85bhp from August 1966)
Maximum torque:	101lb ft at 2,800rpm

Transmission
Rear-wheel drive
Four-speed all-synchro manual gearbox

Saloon final drive ratio:	4.1:1
Estate final drive ratio:	4.56:1

Suspension
Front: Independent with coil springs, telescopic dampers, wishbones, anti-roll bar
Rear: Live axle, coil springs, telescopic dampers, Panhard rod

Steering
Cam and roller

Turns lock-to-lock:	3.25

Brakes
Front: Disc
Rear: Drum
Servo assistance optional until 1967, when it became standard

Wheels and tyres
Pressed-steel wheels with 5.90 × 15 or 165 × 15 tyres

Weight
Two-door saloon	2,357lb (1,070kg)
Four-door saloon	2,400lb (1,090kg)
Estate	2,621lb (1,190kg)

Performance (Autocar)
Max speed:	90mph (145km/h)
0–60mph:	17.6 sec
30–50mph in top:	10.1 sec
50–70mph in top:	14.7 sec

Price including tax when new (April 1965):
Four-door saloon:	£1,022

That's exactly what Volvo did, however, and with the introduction of the P1800 in 1959 – it would be another two years before the first customer cars were delivered – Volvo decided to have another go at the sports car market. The P1800 was equipped with an uprated version of the B18 engine, the B18B boasting a healthy 100bhp. Surely the company wouldn't restrict use of this powerplant solely to the P1800?

Buyers' prayers were answered when in August 1961 Volvo revealed an uprated 122S, also sold in some markets as the 130. Offered with a choice of either 75bhp B18A or 90bhp B18D engines, this was the first time the 1.8-litre engine was available in the Amazon, and instead of simply being a development of the earlier 1.6-litre unit, it was a new design with a five-bearing crankshaft for greater reliability.

In standard (75bhp) form there was a single Zenith carburettor, while those who wanted extra power could opt for the same engine but with a pair of SU carbs. Even in this guise there was just 90bhp on tap – compared with the 100bhp of the P1800 – but thanks to the fitment of a new design of cylinder head it was easy to increase the power output without spending a fortune. While previous Volvo engines had fuel supplied to the combustion chambers two at a time, this new design had the petrol going to each cylinder individually, and it was this aspect which ensured that the new powerplant was so much easier to tune. Knowing that some owners would be tempted to do exactly that, and to ensure greater reliability with standard cars, Volvo fitted an oil cooler as standard to the 130.

At the same time there was also a move to 12-volt electrics and buyers who opted for the 90bhp Sports engine benefited from Girling disc brakes at the front. There was also a simpler radiator grille, which was larger but which featured fewer bars, while there was no longer a two-tone paint option. To promote the fact that there was a new powerplant under the bonnet there was now a 'B18' badge on the grille and in place of the previous single-colour indicator lenses there were now orange and clear (for indicators and sidelights respectively) lenses.

Amazon 122S B18: Press Reaction

Sports Car Graphic tested the upgraded 122S in March 1962 and was immediately impressed by it, stating that: 'Power alone is not the only improvement but detail changes have been made all down the line to make an already desirable package even more so.'

It was clear that Jerry Titus at *Sports Car Graphic* was no xenophobe, his review going on to say:

The construction technique, gauge of metal and quality of workmanship are that of the PV544 on which the firm built its reputation. Extra monies spent on finish materials and sound deadening make it one of the most solid-feeling units we've ever sat in – not completely quiet, but most certainly solid.

On the back of a 1,000-mile drive, *Sports Car Graphic* came out in favour of pretty much everything the 122S had to

Sports Car Graphic reckoned that while the 122S Amazon's performance was a high spot, this was no one-trick pony as it was comfortable and practical too.

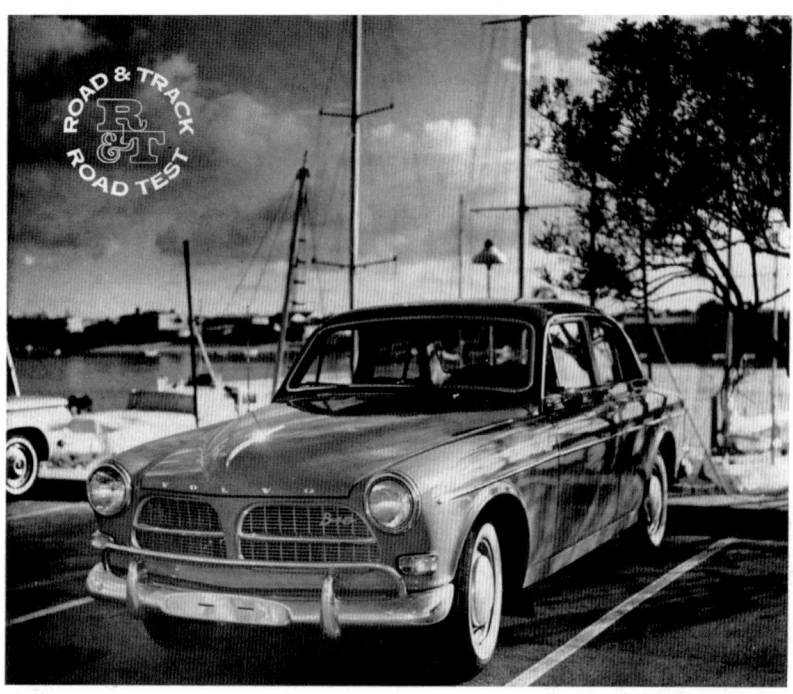

offer. The ride, ergonomics, seats, visibility, fuel economy, price, performance, heating, quality, brakes – all got the thumbs up. The only flies in the ointment were a minor lack of refinement and rear seat space being tight for five – if you could live with these, the Volvo was the car for you.

A month later, when *Car & Driver* reviewed the 122S, the magazine was equally positive about it. Its testers criticized the instruments ('the instrumentation is poor for a car of this class, with non-precision gauges and warning lights instead of proper dials'), but was far more upbeat about just about every other aspect.

Intriguingly, the magazine also highlighted the fitment of standard seatbelts as of great benefit – but not necessarily for safety reasons:

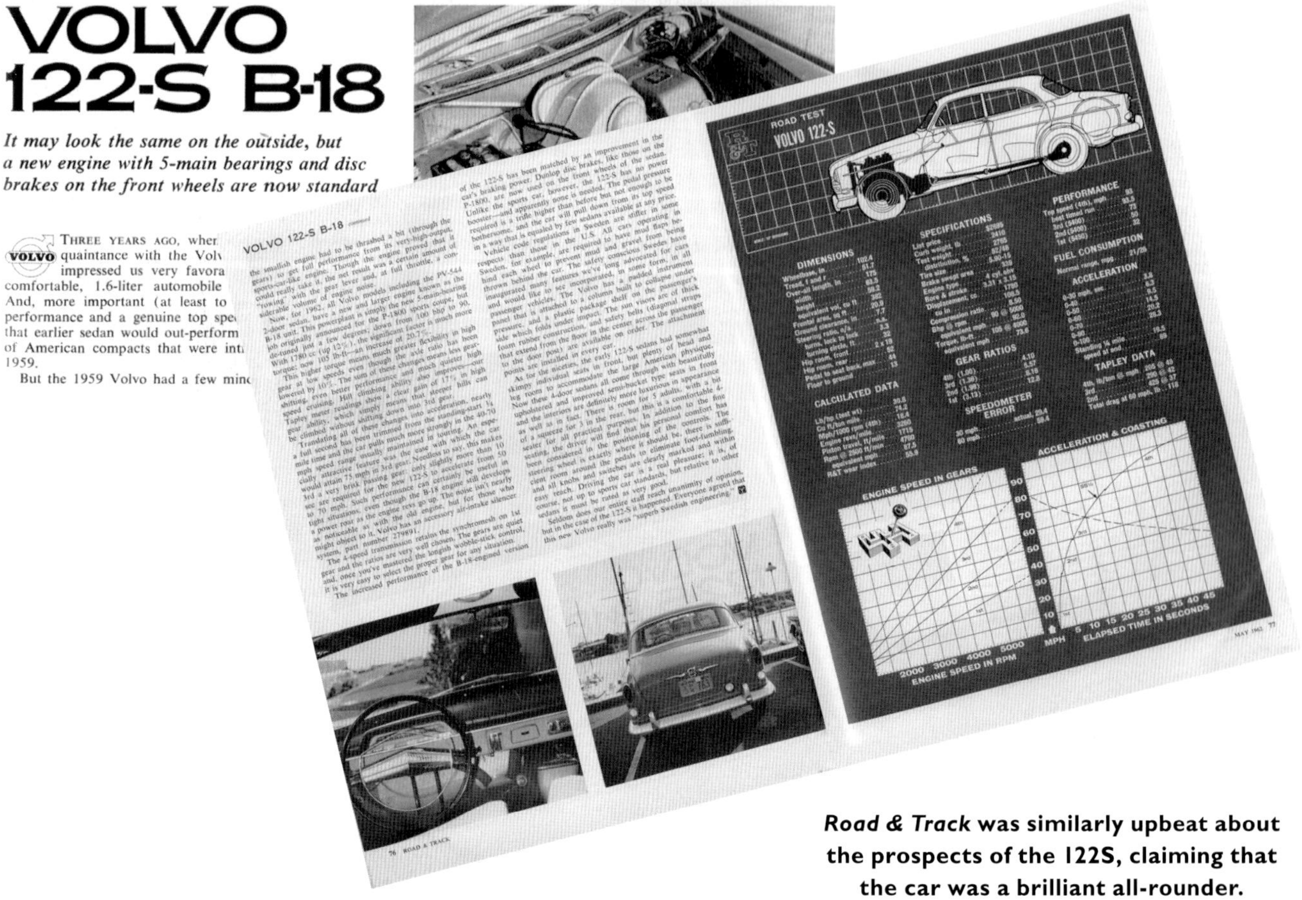
VOLVO 122-S B-18

It may look the same on the outside, but a new engine with 5-main bearings and disc brakes on the front wheels are now standard

THREE YEARS AGO, wher... quaintance with the Volv... impressed us very favora... comfortable, 1.6-liter automobile... And, more important (at least to... performance and a genuine top spe... that earlier sedan would out-perform... of American compacts that were int... 1959.

But the 1959 Volvo had a few min...

Road & Track was similarly upbeat about the prospects of the 122S, claiming that the car was a brilliant all-rounder.

These belts are really comfortable, so that if you would not wear them for reasons of safety, you would put them on because they keep you in your seat during hard cornering yet give your arms complete freedom of movement.

Everyone else who tested the newly upgraded 122S came out just as enthusiastic. *Road & Track* said:

Seldom does our entire staff reach unanimity of opinion, but in the case of the 122S it happened. Everyone agreed that this new Volvo really was superb Swedish engineering.

Meanwhile, in the UK, *Autocar* had gone with:

Without being flashy the Volvo combines a high degree of quality, good workmanship and much attention to detail, with clear-cut functional serviceability. Throughout the interior of the car the care taken to protect passengers in the event of a violent stop is gratifying, and the bodyshell gives the impression of being extremely robust. With no sacrifice in flexibility or smoothness, the engine gives an impressive performance with surprising economy. The basic 'inventory' is comprehensive for a medium-priced family saloon, and the car provides comfortable, effortless travel for its four occupants.

TESTING THE WATERS

From the moment the Amazon project began, it was clear it wasn't intended to ever go through any major facelifts if at all possible. It would evolve with the odd nip and tuck here and there, but there would be no huge changes in panelwork or interior design. But once the Amazon had been launched it was obvious that Volvo couldn't just keep churning them out with no thought given to updates or improvements.

As you can read in this and the previous chapters, Volvo introduced a succession of changes throughout the Amazon's life to keep things fresh, but in many cases this was simply to compete with rival car makers. What it didn't tend to do was redesign significant aspects of the car – despite a production run of well over a decade.

That's not to say Volvo didn't look at the possibility of overhauling the design of the interior, even if attempts to tweak the exterior design appear to have been on the low-key side. As well as a squared-off steering wheel (several years before the Austin Allegro featured one), Volvo also experimented with the idea of introducing a vertically stacked strip speedometer as well as fitting a P1800-inspired facia. But neither of these ideas were carried through to production, Volvo preferring instead to stick with the original design throughout the lifetime of the Amazon.

One of the key features of the Amazon was always its split grille, so this single-piece alternative doesn't quite work.

The same car as in the previous picture, this two-door Amazon looks pretty radical compared with the production car, with those emphasized fins.

ABOVE: **Volvo also explored the idea of an Amazon estate with the single-piece grille, plus a rather complex roof design.**

LEFT: **In the prototype car, the retractable roof section over the load bay was an idea taken straight from US design – and sadly far too radical for conservative Volvo.**

There was still a two-piece tailgate though, as on the production car. The
hinges for the lower portion can be seen clearly here.

It's no secret that many Volvos took their inspiration from American cars, but while the company was never afraid to use the same proportions and basic styling cues of models from Chevrolet or GM, it tended to chicken out when it came to the details. This is rather a shame because it came up with a couple of proposals that didn't see the light of day in production form.

The design study pictured appears to be a clay model only, going by the blacked-out windows. It doesn't look especially revolutionary, with its single-piece grille incorporating a large 'V' within a central bar. More interesting is the roof treatment, which consists of an array of what appear to be glass or plastic panels to let the light in.

The prototype pictured is much more interesting, though, as it features a single-piece tailgate with a window which retracted into the lower half. More intriguingly, the roof sec-

tion also retracted, into the panel over the rear seat. At the time it was something that had never been seen before, but it proved too radical for Volvo to offer in production form – and not reliable enough either. It couldn't seal the tailgate effectively, thanks to that retractable roof panel – but that didn't stop Studebaker from using the same idea in its 1963 Lark Wagonaire.

THEN THERE WERE TWO...

The next major change for the Amazon range came in October 1961, when a two-door edition was introduced. Known as the 121, at first it was available only in Sweden, Norway and Denmark. It was at this point that the Amazon name was also dropped – except, confusingly, right up until the end of production Volvo referred to the car as the Amazon in its advertisements.

Offered only with black paint and beige trim, the 121 featured a rear seat that was redesigned to increase the available space for occupants. In a bid to maximize room for those in the back the armrests were built into the trim panels, and to improve ventilation the rear side windows could be popped outwards. There was no denying this new two-door Amazon wasn't as practical as its four-door sibling, but as it was priced at 500 kronor below its four-door equivalent, there was a useful saving to be made.

The two-door Amazon looked every bit as stylish as its four-door counterpart – some would say even more so.

ABOVE: **Most Amazons were finished in sober hues, but a coat of red paint really set off the two-door model's stylish lines.**

RIGHT: **Volvo clearly decided to make use of the company plane for this marketing shot, showing a two-door 122S at the airfield.**

Rear seat space was the same as in the four-door car – but that space wasn't quite as accessible.

In place of the wind-down rear windows was this hinged glazing, with a neat two-stage catch that allowed the glass to be opened to different degrees.

Amazon Two-Door: Press Reaction

Perhaps it should come as no surprise that nobody was in a hurry to test the two-door Amazon; it's usually mechanical improvements that get road testers salivating, rather than changes in body style. So when Canada's *Track & Traffic* magazine got behind the wheel of an Amazon in July 1962, it was almost incidental that it featured just the one pair of doors.

Of more interest to the magazine was the fact that Volvo had christened this car the Canadian, in a bid to bolster its tough image. After all, if it could survive the harsh realities of the Canadian winter, it could survive anything. And of course it could survive Canadian winters because it was developed to survive Scandinavian winters…

Not unreasonably, *Track & Traffic* reckoned its review of the Canadian (in 90bhp 1.8-litre form) was the longest, most extensive road test ever conducted by a North American publication up to that point – more than 7,000 miles were notched up in two weeks of driving. In that time the car impressed with its handling, brakes, visibility, cabin, steering, seating and exterior design – and its performance too. The testers were so moved by the car they claimed: 'In the faster corners the Volvo Canadian handles as though it were sired by a Grand Prix racing car.'

Reliability proved a major plus point too:

> Driving a new car over such a long distance can be expected to produce some faults, and a few repairs were anticipated. Nevertheless we were pleased that only three loose bolts marred an otherwise perfect run. None were of a nature to prevent the car from continuing, and all three loosened-up before we reached Vancouver. The final 4,000 miles were trouble-free.

British car buyers wouldn't get to read a two-door Amazon review until *Autocar* tested one as late as April 1965: a 75bhp 131. Once again the focus was on the mechanical specification rather than the fact that this particular Amazon featured two doors fewer than usual. However, the fitment of just two doors was noteworthy as the magazine had always tested four-door derivatives before.

Offering approval for the Amazon's styling, *Autocar* wrote:

> Two-door bodywork always has some advantages, other than the sporty style. There are two fewer doors to produce rattles and two fewer sources of draughts; small children can be carried safely without fear of the door being opened by inquisitive, tiny fingers.

Although the two-door Amazon looked sportier than the four-door alternative, *Autocar* focused more on the practicalities of the new arrival.

(continued overleaf)

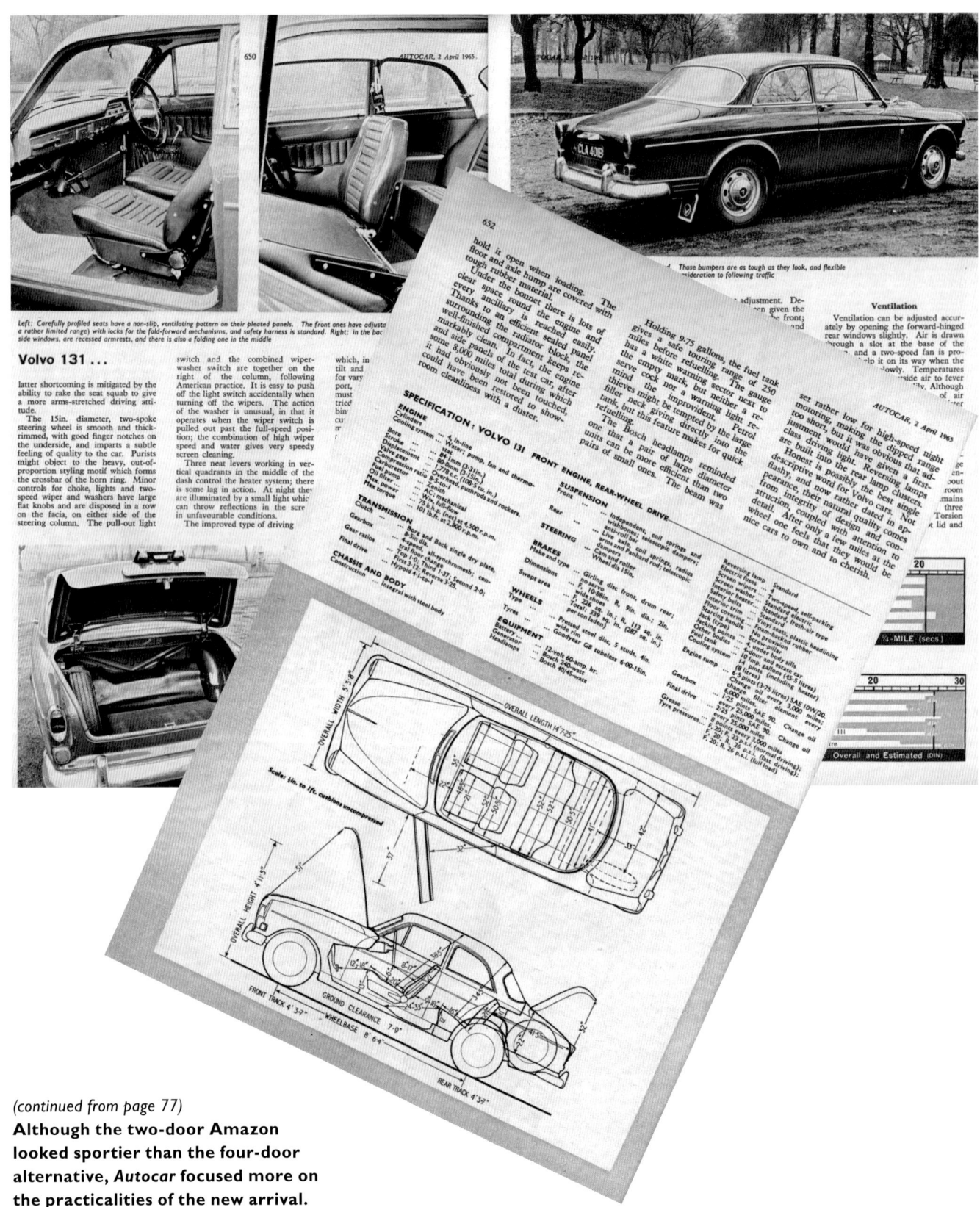

Left: Carefully profiled seats have a non-slip, ventilating pattern on their pleated panels. The front ones have adjusta a rather limited range) with locks for the fold-forward mechanisms, and safety harness is standard. Right: in the bac side windows, are recessed armrests, and there is also a folding one in the middle

Volvo 131 ...

latter shortcoming is mitigated by the ability to rake the seat squab to give a more arms-stretched driving attitude.

The 15in. diameter, two-spoke steering wheel is smooth and thickrimmed, with good finger notches on the underside, and imparts a subtle feeling of quality to the car. Purists might object to the heavy, out-ofproportion styling motif which forms the crossbar of the horn ring. Minor controls for choke, lights and twospeed wiper and washers have large flat knobs and are disposed in a row on the facia, on either side of the steering column. The pull-out light

switch and the combined wiperwasher switch are together on the right of the column, following American practice. It is easy to push off the light switch accidentally when turning off the wipers. The action of the washer is unusual, in that it operates when the wiper switch is pulled out past the full-speed position; the combination of high wiper speed and water gives very speedy screen cleaning.

Three neat levers working in vertical quadrants in the middle of the dash control the heater system; there is some lag in action. At night they are illuminated by a small light which can throw reflections in the scre in unfavourable conditions.

The improved type of driving

Those bumpers are as tough as they look, and flexible siideration to following traffic

hold it open when loading. The floor and axle hump are covered with tough rubber material.

Under the bonnet there is lots of clear space round the engine and every ancillary is reached easily. Thanks to an efficient sealed panel surrounding the radiator block, the well-finished compartment keeps remarkably clean. In fact, the engine panels of the test car, after some 8,000 miles total during which it had obviously not been touched, could have been restored to showroom cleanliness with a duster.

Holding 9.75 gallons, the fuel tank gives a safe touring range of 250 miles before refuelling. The gauge has a white warning sector but neither the empty mark, nor a warning light reserve cock giving the improvident. Petrol mind thieves might be tempted by the large filler neck giving directly into the tank but this feature makes for quick refuelling.

The Bosch headlamps reminded one that a pair of large diameter units can be more efficient than two pairs of small ones. The beam was

adjustment. De... ... ...given the ...the front; ...and

Ventilation

Ventilation can be adjusted accurately by opening the forward-hinged rear windows slightly. Air is drawn ...rough a slot at the base of the ...and a two-speed fan is pro... help it on its way when the ...slowly. Temperatures ...side air to fever ...v. Although ...of air

ser rather low for high-speed night motoring, making the dipped range too short, but it was possible that adjustment would have given a firstclass driving light. Reversing lamps are built into the rear lamp clusters.

Honest is possibly the best single descriptive word for Volvo cars. Not flashy, and now rather dated in appearance, their natural quality comes from integrity of design and construction, coupled with attention to detail. After only a few miles at the wheel one feels that they would be nice cars to own and to cherish.

SPECIFICATION: VOLVO 131 FRONT ENGINE, REAR-WHEEL DRIVE

ENGINE	
Cylinders	... 4, in-line
Cooling system	... Water; pump, fan and thermostat
Bore	... 84·1mm (3·31in.)
Stroke	... 80·0mm (3·15in.)
Displacement	... 1,778 c.c. (108·5 cu. in.)
Valve gear	... Overhead, pushrods and rockers.
Compression ratio	... 8·5 to 1
Carburettor	... Zenith
Fuel pump	... 2·5-s.u.
Oil filter	... Full-flow
Max. power	... 90 b.h.p. (net) at 4,500 r.p.m.
Max. torque	... 101 lb.ft. at 2,800 r.p.m.

TRANSMISSION	
Clutch	... 8½in.
Gearbox	... Bars and Back single dry plate
	... 4-speed, all-synchromesh; cen...
Gear ratios	... Top 1·0; Third 1·37; Second 2·0;
	... First 3·13; Reverse 3·25
Final drive	... Hypoid 4·1 to 1

CHASSIS AND BODY	
Construction	... Integral with steel body

SUSPENSION	
Front	... Independant, coil springs and
Rear	... Live axle, coil springs, Panhard rod telescopic dampers;

STEERING	
Make and type	... Cam and roller
Dimensions	... Wheel dia 15in.

BRAKES	
Type	... Girling disc front, drum rear;
Swept area	... 226 sq. in.; R. 113 sq. in. Total: per ton laden

WHEELS	
Tyres	... Pressed steel disc, 5 studs, 4in. wide rim
	... Goodyear GB tubeless 6·00-15in.

EQUIPMENT	
Battery	... 12-volt 60-amp. hr.
Headlamps	... Bosch 240-watt
	... Bosch 40/45-watt

(specification continues, partly obscured)

OVERALL WIDTH 5' 3-0"
OVERALL LENGTH 14' 7·25"
OVERALL HEIGHT 4' 11·5"
Scale: ½in. to 1ft. cushions uncompressed
FRONT TRACK 4' 3·7"
GROUND CLEARANCE
WHEELBASE 8' 6·4"
REAR TRACK 4' 3·7"

(continued from page 77)

Although the two-door Amazon looked sportier than the four-door alternative, *Autocar* focused more on the practicalities of the new arrival.

THE AMAZON ESTATE

For those whose priority was practicality, the next introduction was just the ticket – a five-door estate model, initially offered to buyers in Sweden only. Launched in February 1962 at the Stockholm motor show, there shouldn't have been any references to the term Amazon, but when Volvo announced the impending arrival in a press release published on 15 February 1962, it crowed:

> A new Volvo estate car. An exclusive estate car, designed for European conditions enters the Swedish market. It will be shown for the first time at the Stockholm Motor Show. It is Volvo's much longed for Amazon estate.

The release continued:

> The new estate is a new Volvo model, for which the existing components of the Amazon have been used to the largest possible degree. The result is a fast and roomy passenger car with an extremely good load capacity. Four doors and a split tailgate enhance the positive character just as the design, the quality, the road manners and the overall economy. The aim has been to create a spacious family car for long-distance travelling and leisure needs – a functional car which can also be used professionally. It is called the Volvo 221 Amazon.

The new arrival generally became known as the Amazon P220 Combi. It had taken five or six years for the estate to appear, but this wasn't because of drawn-out development. It was simply a matter of production capacity, as Volvo didn't have enough to build a two-door saloon alongside a four-door version as well as a five-door split-tailgate model.

It wasn't as though the Amazon estate was just a saloon with a tweaked rear end. Although the saloon and estate were identical up to the B-pillars, the rear doors were changed and the whole of the back of the car was new – even under the skin. The redesigned suspension was strengthened and lowered to allow a low floor that could hold nearly half a ton without giving problems.

The horizontally split tailgate was a clever feature that made loading and unloading very easy. The lower part rested on the rubber-covered flat tops of the bumper overriders, while the tailgate was horizontally split in two. In the lower half, the number plate holder rested on hinges, which meant that it folded down and became visible from behind when the lower part was open – the same idea that was used for the first Minis. Using this facility it was possible to carry an 8ft × 4ft sheet of wood – something which may not have been necessary very often, but which usually nothing else smaller than a van could do.

The two-piece tailgate added to the estate's practicality, as the rear window could be opened separately from the lower portion.

LEFT: **Rear seat space was the same as in the saloon's, but to boost usability the backrest folded flat to give a huge load bay.**

BELOW: **An idea probably borrowed from the 1959 Mini, the lower portion of the tailgate featured a drop-down number plate that was visible when carrying large loads.**

The Amazon estate carried over the metalwork forward of the B-pillars, so it looked every bit as smart.

**When the Amazon estate was launched in 1962, most car makers still hadn't embraced
the idea of offering an estate car as part of their mainstream model range.**

In this position, the tailgate was supported by the upper parts of the bumper overriders, which also served as footsteps when reaching up to the roof rack – a popular standard accessory – or something inside the car with the lower tailgate section closed. The luggage compartment was 72 inches (1830mm) long and 50 inches (1260mm) across with the rear seat folded down. Load capacity was 490kg, which was just 10kg less than the Duett.

Keen to ensure that buyers didn't defect from Volvo, the popular and even more capacious Duett continued to be offered alongside the Amazon for another seven years. For the family with children, the more modern Amazon made life much easier, while the travelling salesman could travel in more style and the craftsman had much better access to the luggage compartment through the rear doors and the split tailgate.

When the Amazon had gone on sale way back in 1962, estate cars weren't commonly offered by car makers. Those that were generally were seen as workhorses and in some cases (such as Vauxhall and Ford) the cars were converted from saloons by third parties, so the styling wasn't especially cohesive.

Volvo – forward-thinking as ever – made great play of the lifestyle opportunities afforded by buying an Amazon estate. The company highlighted the fact that the passenger compartment could be turned into a sleeping compartment, but the word 'comfort' was mentioned before the phrase 'luggage compartment' as the Amazon was the first Volvo estate that was based on a passenger car rather than a delivery van with a separate frame.

Volvo had worked both cleverly and cost-effectively. The elegant lines of the Amazon sedan had been retained and transferred in a stylish and efficient way to the estate. The roomy rear section of the body had been created without altering the exterior dimensions, largely thanks to the efforts of Jan Wilsgaard, who had designed the Amazon in the first place. Halfway along the long roof, at B-pillar height, there was a reinforcement pressing to maintain rigidity. The upper sections of the rear doors were straight and followed the roofline, with only the window frames having to be redesigned. The doors themselves were the same as those on the four-door saloon.

Volvo was keen to ensure that the estate shouldn't be seen as the poor relation in any way, so it put a lot of effort into ensuring that the load-lugger's performance, handling and ride were similar to those of the saloon. To prove just how efficient the estate's design was, Volvo claimed that it was capable of achieving more than 140km/h (88mph) with a 75bhp single-carburettor engine and a kerb weight of 1,250kg (2,750lb).

The only colour offered for the estate during the first year, 1962, was mist green, but by 1963 this was already obsolete; most early Amazons are instead finished in white, beige or blue. Whitewall tyres were never available for the estate, although some early publicity photos show them. Those opting for the entry-level car with the 75bhp engine would have to find SKr14,475 plus tax, which represented a premium of about SKr1,000 over an equivalent saloon.

Although most car makers – and buyers for that matter – saw estates as workhorses, there were some who wanted more than a minimum of performance. It was these buyers who Volvo had in mind when it introduced a twin-carb 122S edition in 1963.

With 90bhp on tap (from 5,500rpm) from the 1780cc four-pot, there was a decent turn of speed and no obvious handling penalty compared with the saloon. Indeed, when *Car & Driver* tested the Amazon 122S estate against the contemporary Peugeot 404 estate, it was moved to write:

> *With a normal load, the 122S wagon is indistinguishable from the sedan under most driving conditions; if there is a difference it is a bit more harshness in the wagon.*

The estate's cabin was identical to the saloon's.

Volvo was already well known for its **Duett**, which had planted the idea of a **Swedish** estate in buyers' minds. The **Amazon** estate was the logical next step.

The estate's driving characteristics were also very similar to the saloon's, which meant it was swift, comfortable and composed.

At a time when estate cars were seen as utilitarian workhorses, the load-lugging Amazon was every bit as desirable as its saloon counterpart.

Taking the two cars together, the *Car & Driver* verdict ran:

> *A buyer would be hard put to find any other station wagons on the market that were anywhere near as responsive and fun to drive.*

So once again Volvo had come up trumps with a car that was agile, quick and frugal. The twin SU H6 carburettors pushed torque up to 105lb ft from 3,500rpm – enough to give 0–60mph in 14.6 seconds and a top speed of 97mph (156km/h). The performance estate was born, and, as you can read in Chapter 7, there were plenty of companies who would be happy to take things even further.

Amazon Estate: Press Reaction

It took more than a year for the Amazon estate to reach British shores; when it did, it was priced at £1,227 and 5 shillings including taxes. First to try out the car was *Autocar*, which reckoned the Volvo was quite costly, but refinements such as electric screen washers, seatbelts and a heater plus a radiator blind compensated somewhat. Strong performance (the top speed was 88mph (142km/h)) also helped – along with 'safe handling'.

With just 68bhp available from its single-carburettor 1780cc engine, the 121 driven by *Autocar* was designed more for economy than outright performance. Over a 1,300-mile test route the Volvo averaged a commendable 28mpg (10.1ltr/100km) – along with 1.25 pints (0.7 litres) of oil. Acknowledging that its testers may have worn lead-lined boots for some of those miles, *Autocar* conceded that by sticking to a 70mph cruise it was possible to get closer to a 32mpg (8.8 ltr/100km) average; it seems that the car had been driven everywhere at 80mph…

With stiffer rear suspension than the saloon, it was reckoned that the estate handled and rode better with a couple of people in the back. The clutch was light and the

It seemed that Volvo could do no wrong with the Amazon as far as *Autocar* was concerned, the estate receiving yet more glowing praise.

**SUPPLEMENT
TO ROAD TEST No. 28/66**

See previous pages

Volvo 221 estate car

OUR test of the Volvo 132S coupé described on the preceding pages was associated with a test of the 221 estate car which is fitted with the less powerful 68 b.h.p. engine (estate cars with the high power engine are not available in the U.K.). Driving this car after the coupé, a strong family resemblance is at once apparent. The facia and driving position are very similar, as is the handling. A servo makes the estate car brakes lighter but a little unprogressive in the middle of the pedal pressure range. More surprisingly the steering is also lighter, but this may be due to the slight rearward weight bias of the estate car compared with the coupé. In addition, the 221's engine is far less noisy.

The estate car has a large carrying capacity, even with the rear seat in its normal position, and is trimmed at the back with a tough, practical cloth—it is often so easy to tear carpets or trim with the corners of the sort of heavy object which needs to be carried in estate cars. There are also a number of thoughtful details. For example, the rear doors are arranged so that one folds up and the other folds down to increase the load space, and the door that lifts upwards is automatically opened and held open by a strut incorporating a spring of compressed gas. Similarly a rubber-covered step on the rear bumper facilitates access to the special Volvo roof rack that can be fitted.

M

Performance

Test Data: World copyright reserved; no unauthorised reproduction in whole or in part.

Weight

Kerb weight (unladen with fuel for approximately 50 miles)	23.1 cwt.
Front/rear distribution	48/52
Weight laden as tested	26.9 cwt.
Mean lap speed banked circuit . .	88.0 m.p.h.
Best one-way ¼-mile	90.9 m.p.h.
Maximile speed—Mean	84.9 m.p.h.
Best	88.3 m.p.h.

Acceleration times

m.p.h.		sec.
0-30		4.2
0-40		7.3
0-50		11.2
0-60		16.6
0-70		25.3
0-80		40.1

m.p.h.	Top sec.	3rd sec.
10-30	—	7.2
20-40	9.6	6.6
30-50	10.3	7.3
40-60	11.7	9.6
50-70	15.1	13.0
60-80	21.8	—

Fuel consumption

m.p.h.		m.p.g.
30		42.6
40		37.5
50		33.4
60		28.9
70		27.9

Touring (consumption midway between 30 m.p.h. and maximum less 5% allowance for acceleration) . . . . 28.0 m.p.g.
Overall . . . . 23.9 m.p.g.
(= 11.8 litres/100 km.)

Estate car body has clean lines. Upper door is automatically raised when lower door is opened and held by a strut with a spring of compressed gas.

Rear luggage space is large with seat folded forward.

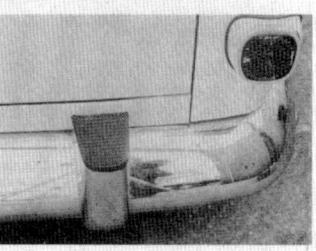

Thoughtful detail: step in bumper for access to roof to which special Volvo roof rack can be fitted.

Motor also tested the Amazon estate, but with its review stretching to all of one page, it wasn't an especially comprehensive test.

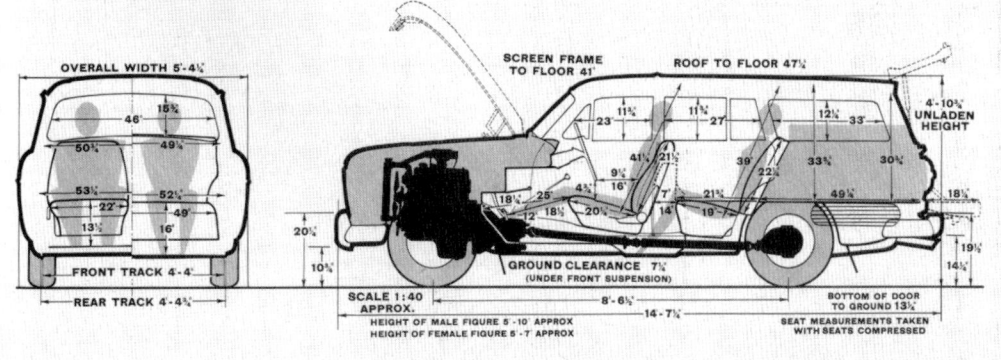

transmission free from backlash – but the gearchange was criticized for its notchy action. Most intriguing, though, was the magazine's analysis of the brakes:

> The braking system is a curious international cock-tail of components, the master cylinder being German Schaeffer, the wheel cylinders British Girling, the shoes American Wagner and the drums Volvo. Despite the care taken in selecting parts, the result is a system which is progressive only at moderate pedal loads, retardation building up rapidly as loads increase, until the brakes grab quite sharply.

The idea of pinning down where individual components were made for a twenty-first-century car review would be unthinkable!

Naturally, safety featured highly in this estate, just as it did in the saloons:

> The edge of the scuttle has a firmly padded, black, plastic-covered roll along its edge, which would give good protection in a collision. All the switches have flat knobs and the steering wheel has two broad spokes. Soft, padded sun visors, a plastic-framed driving mirror and a firm but collapsible parcel shelf with a padded edge complete the list of safety features.

As had become the norm with these things, Autocar signed off with another glowing summary:

> Outwardly an ordinary quantity-produced car, the Volvo has the quality that comes from careful selective assembly and great attention to detail. Combined with good performance and handling, its assets make it an attractive vehicle for the sporting-minded family man, and for the country dweller. For what it can do, the engine is surprisingly economical and there is no need of extras with this Volvo.

AMAZON GOES AUTOMATIC

For August 1962 there were new rear lights along with reversing lights that illuminated automatically when reverse gear was selected. Intriguingly, even though it was now five years since the first customer cars were delivered, Volvo corrected a defect in the original Amazon design. It had become clear that when a car drove into the back of an Amazon, the latter would crumple a bit too much for Volvo's liking. The answer lay in reinforcing the tunnel that housed the rear axle, in a bid to reduce the amount of intrusion into the cabin in a severe impact.

Although the two-door Amazon had initially been offered only in Sweden when it was introduced in October 1961, buyers couldn't buy a sporty edition until August 1963. That's when the 122S was finally launched on the home market, alongside an edition aimed at the other end of the spectrum – an automatic.

This wasn't the first time that a two-pedal Amazon had been offered, though; the 122S was available in some markets as a semi-automatic from March 1961. It wasn't a conventional auto however; it was a three-speed manual gearbox with an electrically operated clutch. Opt for one of these and you automatically got a bench front seat along with a column change for the gears, and while this technology wasn't unique to Volvo, it was unusual enough to make buyers wary. The result was minimal sales, and within months the option had been withdrawn from Amazon price lists.

For years, US dealers had been crying out for an automatic Amazon, but Volvo had refused to add such a product to the model mix. Then, finally, years after the Amazon had made its debut, the company relented and started to offer a three-speed Borg-Warner Type 35 transmission. At first it was available only with the two- or four-door saloons, but by 1967 estate buyers could choose it too. It proved unpopular with estate buyers, though, and was offered for just a year.

Having tested the Hobbs Mechamatic transmission at length, Volvo decided to look elsewhere. It also opted not to develop a passenger car version of its own Volvomatic gearbox, as fitted to Volvo buses. The solution, reckoned Volvo, was to work with Borg-Warner to develop a gearbox that would do the Amazon's torquey, flexible engine justice. Matching the gearbox to the engine proved hugely beneficial, as neither Rootes nor Ford had been so fastidious. The result for them had been a transmission that wasn't especially accomplished – whereas in the Volvo it did about as good a job as anybody could have expected. Which wasn't all that good according to some.

There were further refinements for the 122S for the 1964 model year: Volvo fitted low-profile tyres as standard, and a modified boot lid handle along with revised number

THE VOLVO 122 S SERIES

Intriguingly, while the automatic transmission was usually mentioned almost in passing in the technical specifications, Amazon brochures didn't overtly promote the two-pedal option, such as in this 1966 US-market brochure.

T&T ROAD TEST

VOLVO CANADIAN AUTOMATIC

This seems to be the year for European cars to shift into the automatic transmission market . . . and Volvo is one of the early birds. The company has selected its rugged, popular Canadian (122S) four-door sedan to launch this venture. We have tested this car before but feel it is worth reviewing as an automatic, particularly because it indeed makes a gentleman of this hardy competitor. The transmission used in the Volvo is the Borg Warner model 35. Basically a hydraulically controlled unit with three forward speeds and reverse it is driven by a torque converter. Somehow we miss the traditional Volvo floor shift but the automatic does provide a quick, smooth run through various gear ratios. It is also designed to lock in first and second gears, which makes it very handy for hard accelerating and braking. We found a slight tendency to over rev the engine, but this can be corrected as the feel of the transmission becomes more familiar. The addition of the automatic undoubtedly will help enhance Volvo's sales picture.

coachwork

Simplicity of design and a superb, durable finish are two outstanding features of the Volvo Canadian. The long hood and set-back rear hump combine to give it a sporting appearance while preserving its conventional sedan qualities. The grille and bumper attachments are substantial but conservative. Whitewalls and mud guards are standard equipment. In brief, its styling is well suited to its character: tough but polished, with plenty of muscle and a minimum of frills.

...d lasts an

Volvo out-accelerates 6...
average of 11 years in Swe...

101

Canada's *Track & Traffic* magazine reckoned the Amazon auto was just what dealers needed to give the model a sales boost.

plate lighting. Gone was the fabric headlining, to be replaced by a plastic alternative, and the interior trim now came in a choice of either grey or red finishes. Meanwhile, the exterior finishes were also updated, the previous brown and green replaced by yellow and blue-green hues.

Amazon Auto: Press Reaction

Canada's *Track & Traffic* magazine tried out the automatic 122S in April 1964, and it reckoned the new transmission was just what Volvo needed to boost sales in North America and Canada. Reviewing every aspect of the tweaked saloon, *Track & Traffic* was as enthusiastic as ever about all of the Amazon's virtues:

> With or without the automatic, we're sold on the Volvo. It is difficult to pick holes in the machine, except for some picayune [trivial – Ed.] matters such as dashboard readings, lack of locked glove compartment, a bit of heavy handling at slow speed.

When it came to the fitment of the Borg-Warner gearbox, the review was just as positive:

> The progression through various gear ratios is accomplished with fluid power and just a hint of hesitation along the way. The performance is particularly good at highway speeds and the Canadian will cruise almost nonchalantly at 80 to 85mph. Acceleration is slingshot quick, perhaps even a shade faster than the conventional gearshift leap ahead. Addition of the automatic transmission should win more support for Volvo Canadians from the distaff side of the family.

When *Car & Driver* tested the 122S auto the following month its verdict was that the lack of an automatic option for so many years didn't seem to have held back Volvo sales. But it did concede that an automatic option was a good thing – not least of all because Volvo had taken the time to develop a decent transmission rather than stick in the first thing it came across in the corner of the workshop.

However, *Car & Driver* wasn't convinced by the Amazon's performance:

> The efficiency of the Type 35 Borg-Warner torque converter is substantially less than that of the Daim-

ler-Benz hydraulic coupling as used on the 1.9-liter sedan. We are disappointed that Volvo didn't choose to ignore hydraulic transmissions altogether and concentrate on the Mechamatic, if indeed any alternative to their own excellent four-speed all-synchro gearbox is needed.

The review continued:

> The lively 122S loses not only some of its performance by using the Borg-Warner automatic, but also its sporting personality to an alarming extent … the effervescent performance which comes effortlessly with the stick-shift calls for concentrated planning (and prayer) with the automatic.

Perhaps the figures don't tell the whole story, as *Car & Driver* captioned its picture of a Type 35 transmission thus: 'Borg-Warner's type 35 is light, compact, inexpensive and does not require any maintenance. But it just kills the Volvo's performance.' Despite this, it knocked off just 2–3mph from the top speed and added about three seconds to the 0–60mph time – which now stood at somewhere between 17 and 18 seconds, compared with the manual car's 14.6 seconds. Meanwhile, the standing quarter-mile time was increased from 19.9 seconds to 21.0 seconds, so the two-pedal Amazon's performance was hardly a disaster.

Despite this, *Car & Driver* concluded:

> All in all, the automatic 122S is as much a no-nonsense car as its manually shifted counterpart. The transmission of their choice has proved completely reliable, and it will no doubt win many friends who think a certain loss of performance is a small price to pay for two-pedal control.

Just to reinforce the fact that three pedals are better than two when it comes to Amazons, *Road & Track* also gave the 122S auto a thumbs down. Came the verdict:

> From the enthusiastic driver's point of view there's simply too big a gap between the three gears, the shifts are relatively slow and, when this transmission is used with a typically small-displacement, low-torque European engine, there is an annoying lurch and a noticeable loss of steerage way after each shift.

Car & Driver was less enthusiastic, though. It felt the Amazon auto was a good car, but the gearbox didn't make it any more appealing.

efficiency of the Type 35
verter is substantially less
Benz hydraulic coupling as
We are disappointed that Vo
hydraulic transmissions alto
the MechaMatic, if indeed a
excellent four-speed all-syn
The lively 122-S loses not
ance by using the Borg-Wai
sporting personality to an al
fortunately has enough pow
mission fluid around *and* dr
vescent performance which
stick-shift calls for concent:
er) with the automatic. The
throttle makes it difficult to
aration for a turn or a hill
that the transmission takes
gine, to be broken only by a
down beyond the full throt:
The transmission is set t
between 5 and 37 mph acce
and from 2nd to 3rd betwee
shifts from 3rd to 2nd can be
up to 56 mph by kickdown,
mph. The selector is on a col
As usual with other PRNI
will give first-gear starts v
hold switch for first. Selectir
et second or first, accordi
ening.
On our acceleration runs,
en 17 and 18 seconds, an
covered in about 21 sec
ck-shift 122-S, we ave
mph runs and did the
conds with a termina
the top speed of th
om experience that
mph off the top e
tting there consid
of it all, we are
stay with the
ay from the tr
the next inter
be people wh
a Volvo bu
esign, its ma
who migh
over 3-lite

e well-
th lots
afety fe
int se:
incre
eas
ed,
l i

love
, as the Volv
ijusting. Even th
aretors just seem to sta
All-in-all, the automatic
nonsense car as its manually
transmission of their choic
reliable, and it will no doul
think a certain loss of perf
to pay for two-pedal contro

VOLVO 122-S AUTO

The familiar Swedish sedan is now available with

VOLVO 122-S AUTOMATIC

Now Volvo offers a car
for senior citizens too. But
ever live to retire

105

Road & Track was also in the 'no' camp, claiming
that the three-speed automatic gearbox wasn't
sporty enough to be appealing to the enthusiast
buyers that Volvo courted with the Amazon.

But accepting that Volvo had created an automatic Amazon for pragmatic reasons rather than for the hell of it, *Road & Track* concluded:

> *We realize that the manufacturer didn't add the automatic transmission to the options list expecting that the experienced enthusiast would become rapturous over it. The automatic is offered because there is an ever-growing segment of the auto driving public that has never learned to use a manual transmission and isn't going to learn. So the manufacturer sells cars that he would not have been able to sell otherwise. It's good business.*

THE DEVELOPMENT CONTINUES

Despite the Amazon's advancing years, Volvo reckoned there was still plenty of life left in it yet. There were further enhancements for the 1965 model year, announced in August 1964. The most significant of these changes was the introduction of front disc brakes as standard for all models – for the estate there was also servo assistance – while the sills were now partly galvanized to improve durability.

While Volvo had always been dismissive of the built-in obsolescence so favoured by its rivals, this time round it decided to join in by titivating the Amazon's aesthetics with

some redesigned wheels: new chrome-plated stainless-steel hub caps along with a fresh radiator grille – hardly revolutionary stuff, but all things that marked out the revised Amazon from its predecessor.

Having led the way with standard front seatbelts the next step was to redesign the seats to ensure that passengers sat properly. Medical experts were consulted and as a result there were new fabrics, new designs and new construction techniques, to make sure that accidents didn't happen because drivers weren't sitting comfortably or that injuries sustained weren't more severe than they might have been because passengers weren't properly located.

Volvo paid attention to every aspect of the new seat design: the foam, the springing, the shape and the materials too. The result was an ultra-modern set of chairs that supported all occupants far better than ever before, especially when cornering at speed. The seat base angle could be adjusted to provide optimum thigh support while the backrest angle could also be adjusted to suit. More impressive, though, was the adoption of an adjustable lumbar support for the driver, at a time when most rivals didn't even know what this was. Adjusted via a screwdriver, this ensured that the driver of a post-1964 Amazon was among the most comfortable on the road.

Proving that Volvo still paid attention to the small things, it also added a gas strut to the tailgate of the estate, a dash-mounted grab handle for the front seat passenger and a duct to channel hot air to the rear seat when the heater was

Volvo was the first car maker to put serious effort into designing the best possible seats for the occupants of its cars. In 1964 it introduced adjustable lumbar support in the Amazon – a world first.

RIGHT: **The new orthopaedically designed front seats being fitted on the production line.**

BELOW: **Volvo was never a fan of built-in obsolescence. This 1965 Amazon looks barely different from the car first seen in 1956.**

As with the exterior, the Amazon's cabin has a timeless elegance. The owner of this car has created a dash-top mat to cut down on reflections in the windscreen.

switched on. From this point on there was also an armrest fitted to the centre of the rear seat – something which had been fitted to the first cars, but which had quietly been deleted from the standard equipment list for most Amazon derivatives from 1960.

A MORE AFFORDABLE AMAZON

For 1966, the big news was the introduction of a more affordable Amazon. Known as the Favorit, the car was launched despite a similar attempt made with the PV444

Volvo decided to offer a cheaper Amazon from 1966, in the form of the Favorit.

122S WITH B18D ENGINE (1961–68)

As 121 with B18 engine except:

Engine

Compression ratio:	8.4:1
Fuelling:	Twin SU HS6 carburettors
Maximum power:	90bhp (gross) at 5,000rpm
Maximum torque:	105lb ft at 3,500rpm

Transmission

Optional Laycock de Normanville overdrive

Weight

Four-door saloon	2,394lb (1,085kg)

Performance (*Autocar*)

Max speed (overdrive top):	95mph (153km/h)
In top:	91mph (146km/h)
In third:	68mph (109km/h)
In second:	47mph (76km/h)
In first:	29mph (47km/h)
0–60mph:	14.4 sec
30–50mph in top:	8.9 sec
50–70mph in top:	11.4 sec

Price including tax when new (May 1962):

Four-door saloon:	£1,293 10s 0d

having flopped and the car being withdrawn after just two seasons. That's probably because the Favorit wasn't nearly as stripped out as the PV444 Export had been, with equipment reductions confined to the external brightwork being removed, and the deletion of the cigarette lighter and passenger sun visor, while there was now a three-speed all-synchromesh gearbox in place of the four-speed unit normally fitted.

The rationale behind the Favorit was that some buyers wanted a Volvo but didn't have very deep pockets, and they couldn't afford a regular Amazon. With the final PV544 being built on 20 October 1965, there was no longer a cheap option for those wanting a Volvo; the Favorit was aimed to fill the gap as much as possible. Initially it came only with

black paintwork and a red interior, but in time a white paint finish would also be offered.

Volvo couldn't resist tinkering with the regular Amazon's oily bits too, and for the 1966 model year the B18A engine's compression ratio was increased by fitting the thinner head gasket more usually seen in the B18B powerplant. This took the compression ratio from 8.5:1 to 8.7:1, the result of which was extra power – but Volvo didn't disclose how much as it felt the changes weren't significant enough to warrant it. However, the B18D engine was also breathed on at the same time, again by raising the compression ratio, but this time in tandem with a revised camshaft that provided more valve lift. The result of this was an increase in power from 90bhp to 95bhp, with a consequent 5km/h (3mph) more on the top speed.

To go with the engine upgrades there was a useful change for the braking system too. From this point on the rear brakes incorporated a pressure-reduction valve to prevent the rear wheels from locking up too readily during severe retardation. Meanwhile, the front suspension and propshaft now incorporated sealed joints so it was no longer necessary for them to be greased every 5,000km (3,000 miles).

THE AMAZON GOES V8

The Philip was the car that might have become the Amazon – but it didn't. It was powered by a V8, and when the Philip died any thoughts of a family car built by Volvo, with a V8 engine, seemed to die with it. Although the engine was developed into a unit to power Volvo's trucks, it never saw the light of day in a passenger car – but Volvo still considered giving the Amazon V8 power. The company developed a V8 codenamed C8B (the Philip engine which evolved into a truck powerplant was the B8B), and five examples were constructed.

In the event, Volvo decided that a V8 wasn't right for its Amazon; considering it was never officially fitted with a 6-cylinder powerplant, jumping from four cylinders to eight would have been a leap too far. While there would be 6-cylinder versions of Volvo's later family cars, it wouldn't be until 2006 that there would be a factory-built V8-powered passenger car. That was the XC90 with the engine developed in conjunction with Yamaha – the same powerplant would also be fitted to the S80 saloon in the same year.

THE 123GT

Towards the end of 1966 the Amazon was still being built in large numbers and it looked as though the car would remain in production for a while yet, despite its successor, the 140, going on sale in autumn 1966. While the 140 ushered in a whole new era for Volvo, it made sense to eke out the Amazon's lifespan for a bit longer if possible. The car still had its devotees, which is why for 1967 there was a round of further tweaks, most of which were too small to be noticed. The first was a new grille, which was joined by new rear light clusters. The air intake ahead of the windscreen was now made of stainless steel and the three-point front seatbelts were of a new design too.

The 123GT may have been the most potent Amazon yet, but in typical Volvo fashion it didn't look any spicier than what had come before.

Out on the road though, it was clear that this was no regular Amazon – the 123GT was a real flier.

There was
no four-door
option for the
123GT, which
is a shame
because that
would have
made a superb
Q-car.

ABOVE: **This was what you were paying for if you bought a 123GT – a 115bhp twin-carb 1.8-litre powerhouse.**

LEFT: **The sporty theme continued inside, with red detailing in strategic places, plus that stick-on rev counter that looks like an afterthought.**

The regular steering wheel was also ditched, to be replaced by this sportier three-spoke alternative.

To the casual observer, there was little to mark out the 123GT as the fastest Amazon yet; eagle-eyed onlookers would have spotted this badge on the bootlid.

There were also discreet badges on the front wings.

While all these adjustments were nice enough, what really got Amazon fans excited was the introduction of a new sporty Amazon derivative, badged the 123GT (or 120GT in some export markets). The new car mated a 115bhp 1.8-litre engine from the 1800S with the two-door bodyshell of the 122. As standard there was a four-speed gearbox with overdrive, and with the car being more practical than the 1800S, as well as more affordable, the car was sure to be a hit.

As well as a more powerful engine the 123GT also featured wing mirrors on both sides; something that was still far from common and which even other Amazon derivatives didn't offer. Throw in a foglight and spotlamp plus unique wheel trims and the 123GT was marked out quite nicely from its lesser siblings. And just to top things off there was also lighting for the engine bay and boot, a sportier steering-wheel design (inspired by the 1800) and a rev counter above the instrument panel.

While the 123GT was the most powerful Amazon yet, its more prosaic siblings were also given a power boost for the 1967 model year. The entry-level car's power output jumped from 76bhp to 85bhp through the fitment of a Zenith-Stromberg carburettor as seen in the new 140, while the Sport now packed a 100bhp punch (previously 95bhp) thanks mainly to revisions in the exhaust design.

By the autumn of 1967, it was all go for Volvo. Sweden was gearing up to change which side of the road it drove on, Volvo was preparing to end production of the four-door Amazon and at the same time it was unveiling another raft of changes for the two-door and estate editions. It made sense for Volvo to kill off the four-door Amazon because the 144 had become a more popular car, although for the first half of the year the 121 was still the bestselling car in Sweden.

With Sweden in the grip of a major publicity drive about the impending H-day (see Chapter 3), Volvo chose to reveal the 1968 model-year changes in Norway and Denmark first. The biggest news was the introduction of a collapsible steering column along with a steering wheel that gave way in an impact. A brake servo was now standard across the range while twin-carb variants for the US market now featured a rather crude exhaust gas purification system.

Amazon 123GT: Press Reaction

By the time the 123GT was introduced, it seems car magazines around the world had lost interest in Volvo's ageing family car. They were no doubt much more interested in its replacement, the 140, which was first shown in 1966. As a result, while most magazines acknowledged the 123GT's introduction with a small news story, few bothered to put one through its paces.

Indeed, it seems that only *Wheels* and *Sports Car World*, both based in Australia, put the 123GT through its paces. The latter slotted it into a four-car group test, pitched against the Alfa Romeo Giulia Super, Lancia Fulvia 1.3 Rallye and Toyota 1600GT. Marked out as the best-value performance saloons of the time, this quartet of enthusiast machines were closely matched in terms of price but varied widely in just about every other respect.

123GT WITH B18 ENGINE (1966–70)

As 121 with B18 engine except:

Engine
Compression ratio:	10.0:1
Fuelling:	Twin SU carburettors
Maximum power:	115bhp (SAE) at 6,000rpm
Maximum torque:	112lb ft at 4,000rpm

Transmission
Four-speed all-synchro with overdrive
Final drive ratio:	4.56:1

Wheels and tyres
4.5J disc wheels from 1800S, with 165 SR15 tyres

Bodywork
Two-door saloon only

Weight:	2,398lb (1,090kg)

Performance (*Wheels*, 1968)
Max speed:	104mph (167km/h)
0–50mph:	7.7 sec
30–50mph in top:	8.0 sec
Fuel consumption:	23.3mpg (12.1ltr/100km)

Sports Car World in Australia was as much of a fan of the Amazon in 123GT form as you'd expect; they reckoned it was the best all-round performance car available.

We drive the . . .

VOLVO 123 GT

The Volvo 123GT is not the cheapest high-performance car in Australia; and it's not the fastest. It may be one of the most economical, it's almost certainly the most durable and it's very likely the best all-rounder . . .

THE man said he thought it was really just a like feeding him a race full of signet rings. But I don't wear any signet rings. But I troys the whole image of flushed face With a quality car tread image of Volvo one With a with composure and dignity you ran at least do it In fact you can defy everything in a Volvo with composure and dignity you ran at least do it diabolical wet-road slide or crossing no more effort or stop for an unexpected obstacle with nonchalantly gazing your own window, with nonchalantly pleasure average man with just rnat level in confidence drive a Volvo 123GT. But the average man does not what he drives a quality car that does sheer shape, and land doesn't. For the man does sheer mundane too, need it might land a versatile man are not total disdain, and its likely hard to say too, the 123GT owner does refer to a crude reference for the manners. After all it speaks for a reason in proof of the 123GT is a car able to be coveted in the tradition of the modern classics.

the push of a button, but winding on six and a half turns of lock to get out of the man's garage will inevitably bring out of the man's garage.

Seven-League Boots

How to get there quickly and comfortably: Go by Boeing 727 or go buy a Volvo 123GT.

We can't blame you if you haven't heard of it. They probably don't want the word to get around in case this stunning new Swedish screamer becomes a habit that's hard to kick.

THESE days, you've got to be on your toes. Volvo concessionaires Swedish Motor Importers snuck the

of course, have expected SMI to be quick off the mark in importing the first of these new hot ones; company chief Max Winkless and service operative Bill Nolan are this year bombing the local rally scene with works Volvos, ably helped by brilliant newcomer John Keran.

It is reasonable to assume that the 123 GT has been born directly from Volvo's extensive rallying experience, even though the company no longer competes in the European championship with a works team. Essentially, it is the 122S series with the

This is one of the toughest, most resilient engines in the world, and will stand an incredible amount of abuse. In fact, it is very probably one of the best production engines ever built. It was originally a 1.4 litre developing 40 bhp, which went up to 80 bhp being enlarged to 1.6 litres and 85 bhp. The P1800 version puts out 115 bhp (SAE) at 6000 rpm on 10 to 1 compression; it will run on straight local super, but prefers

a one-in-three methyl-benzine or benzol mix.

But even at that, its highest production power output, the engine is still not over-developed. Volvo has competition options for the engine that are used to put together special racing versions in Europe and America. These take the power output to around 125 bhp and enable the engine to crank to 7000 rpm. The block can be bored to raise the displacement to 1860 ccs, a higher overlap cam added, and special valve springs and twin-choke Weber carburettors used on a modified head.

The significant thing about this is that even the factory stormers use standard P1800 bearing shells and clutch, and the standard combustion chambers are not touched, as these leave the factory fully machined. About the only thing done to the engine apart from fitting "hot bits" is to lighten the flywheel and do a complete balance job.

So in the engine the basis is there to make the 123GT a first-class fast touring car. And this is what it is. We have never been out-and-out

The 123GT isn't spectacular or sensational as a high performance car — it's simply undramatically efficient. When you race it at a corner hard it doesn't scream for the one and racer behind in it just scream for the one and hang out in lots of sound of that road on its chassis a bit to take up knock without a jar. This is all designed to take up you're driving on a good road handling of the body pretty observant you may not note very fast balance. If road's facing corners you road very fast balance. If down But you'll note it looking out the way you handling going into the front wheels win worth it's further detail its say it this does the a tamer further, the 123S all appear to has a word label; the 123S it this car's been upped to coincide with and a possibly slightly firmer damper settings. So makes for increased spring stability, and appear body roll, and some extra stickiness probably more course that roll-oversteer sensation at the

takes some time to free up. At the end of more than 2000 miles of exceptionally fast motoring we felt that this was one of the fastest and safest point-to-point cars anybody could possibly buy.

All the normal 122S Volvo characteristics are there — the best seats in the world — without exception — ball-joint front suspension with roll bar, live rear axle beautifully located by support arms, torque rods and a track rod, and slung on coils. Girling disc front brakes, drum rear with pressure-limiting valve in the system. That, and the legendary Volvo construction and rust-proofing.

As well, the 123GT comes with laminated windscreen, higher rated dampers, radial ply tyres (Cinturatos as standard) matched quartz-iodine fog and driving lights complete with very pose-worthy white Volvo covers, two exterior rear vision mirrors, louder horn, alloy-spoked steering wheel, reclining front seats, and a small tachometer. These are all the things most fast drivers regard as essential to their work, but seldom get in one car. What's more, they would be useless if they weren't on a car as beautifully integrated and well-balanced as this one.

With the overdrive comes the 4.56 to 1 final drive ratio which is normally used with the wagon against the 4.1 on the non-overdrive car. A 4.88 ratio is available as a factory competition option. The overdrive has a ratio of 0.756, and at this is a little too tall for the car's frontal area; by the same token it is very good on the open road because the step is wide enough to make it a true fifth gear.

The B18 engine has never been particularly quiet, and we even had to comment on this in the luxury

Left: Too screwdriver, has holder. Boot will stow amount of luggage, with mounted upright for easy loading.

Wheels magazine didn't give a verdict on the 123GT as such, but it did pitch the car against its rivals and it came out looking pretty good.

the test car would not which is th On the oth relaxed and 5000 rpm in only becam hard accele so quickly most of the be done in

The tall o that a lot hills called f the overdriv helped alwa clutch; afte very pleasan snap back to check — su corner to be this contribu high averag picked up al fear of over third gear 70 mph; the we could c mph betwee coast road a

The 123G width as th braced tread shockers hav levels — alr astonishingly understeers l most back to the rear end prodigious o

122S WITH B20B ENGINE (1968–70)

As 122S with B18 engine except:

Engine
Compression ratio:	9.5:1
Maximum power:	118bhp at 4,800rpm
Maximum torque:	123lb ft at 3,500rpm

Weight
Two-door saloon	2,310lb (1,050kg)

Performance (Wheels)
Max speed (top):	100mph (161km/h)
In third:	85mph (137km/h)
In second:	56mph (90km/h)
In first:	37mph (60km/h)
0–60 mph:	10.2 sec
30–50mph in top:	7.5 sec
50–70mph in top:	8.2 sec
Fuel consumption:	28–32mpg (8.8–10.1ltr/100km)

You can do everything in a Volvo with composure and dignity: you can recover from a diabolical wet-road slide with no more effort than the simple ceremony of crossing wrists or stop for an unexpected obstacle while nonchalantly gazing out of your own window – with confidence.

That was the whole point about the 123GT: it wasn't the best in terms of handling or outright speed, but it made everything appear so supremely easy. The magazine continued:

The 123GT isn't spectacular or sensational as a high-performance car – it's simply undramatically efficient. When you toss it at a corner hard enough to tie the boy racer behind in knots, it doesn't scream tyres and hang out on lots of lock. It just leans over on its chassis a bit to take up some of that G load off the suspension and goes round without protest. This is all part of the business of getting a good ride-handling balance.

THE END IS NIGH

The two-door and estate cars continued to be built and in autumn 1968 it was announced that they would be available with the same B20 2.0-litre engine that was offered in the 140 – this was a bored-out version of the B18 powerplant. There was an increase in power to either 90bhp or 118bhp depending on the state of tune, but the real benefit was the greatly improved torque. At the same time the cars were given the dual-circuit braking system that had been fitted to the 140-series from the outset. Joining these added refinements there was now a steering-wheel lock and a higher grade of interior fabrics.

The result of the two-litre engine transplant was a car that outperformed the 144 because of its lighter weight and high power output, and when Australian magazine *Wheels* put a 122S through its paces in 1969, the testers were amazed at just how capable the car still was. Aged it may have been, but with excellent brakes, build quality, ride, refinement and comfort, the Amazon could still give its competitors a run for their money.

By the end of the 1960s the Amazon had become a very familiar sight on the roads, especially in America. The earliest PV444s were two decades old, and many of them were

The Volvo was the only car in the group without an overhead cam engine, but it had long proved its durability even if it wasn't the most refined of the set. Most importantly, though, the Volvo could hold its head high in terms of performance, when it came to taking on three other cars that were all significantly newer designs.

It wasn't all about performance, however: the Volvo was left trailing when it came to handling, with the Lancia feeling much more nimble and fun to drive – the Fulvia was also the only front-wheel drive car in the group.

Where the Volvo left the others trailing was in its level of engineering quality along with comfort for four; it also didn't escape the reviewers just what a safe car the 123GT was, although they thankfully didn't put this to the test.

While *Wheels* was distinctly non-committal when it came to nominating a winner for its four-car group test, *Sports Car World* was prepared to stick its neck out and say that the 123GT was probably the best all-round performance car on sale in Australia in 1967. Suggesting that its tester was speaking from experience, the article ran:

still going strong. Already Volvo, which had been exporting cars for little more than a decade, had fostered a reputation for cars that lasted. To nurture this the company's advertising reinforced the stereotype with such slogans as 'Tougher than dirt' and 'If you're undecided about buying a new Volvo, drive an old one'. The company even went so far as to rubbish its competitors' attempts to facelift their cars every year, stating proudly that its cars hardly changed from one year to another.

In 1969 the Amazon estate was discontinued, superseded by the 145 and leaving just the 122 in production. It was clear that the car wouldn't be built for much longer, so changes for the 1970 model year were very minor, restricted to front-seat headrests and the provision of rear seatbelts. But it was inevitable that Amazon production would stop soon after and sure enough, on 3 July 1970, the last car was built. Bearing chassis number 667,323, the car was put into Volvo's museum.

By the time the final curtain had come down, Volvo had built 234,209 examples of the Amazon four-door saloon along with 359,917 two-door editions and 73,196 estates. Around 60 per cent of these had been sold outside Sweden.

The production of the final Amazon in July 1970 marked the end of an era for Volvo.

CHAPTER FIVE

SELLING THE AMAZON

ADVERTISING THE AMAZON

By the time Volvo launched the Amazon, the marque already had a reputation for reliability and durability. Much motor-sport success with the PV444 and PV544 had also injected a bit of glamour into the brand – and also underlined even further just how tough these Swedish cars were. Throw in a reputation for safety that few rivals could match and you'd think Volvo would have found it incredibly easy to sell the Amazon.

But in the 1960s many new-car buyers were suspicious of imports, while Volvos were usually more expensive than their home-built rivals, which meant the company had to always be inventive when it came to creating its ad campaigns. Unsurprisingly, the facets upon which it focused were those of reliability, toughness and safety – although there were plenty of references to exclusivity too.

Another aspect that was regularly referred to was the lack of built-in obsolescence – something that was especially apt for the US market where the Big Three introduced design updates every year. Not so with Volvo, though, which barely changed the Amazon's styling between its introduction in 1955 and its demise in 1970.

Volvo — the car with built-in safety

The pioneer work carried out by Volvo within the field of car safety is renowned all over the world. A Volvo is a car which satisfies extremely severe demands concerning interior safety

The seating accommodation is as far as possible free from sharp projecting parts which can cause injuries.

The underside of the dashboard is completely smooth. The top is fitted with crash padding. The sun visors are padded. The laminated glass windscreen provides good vision even if shattered by flying gravel.

The seat attachments in the floor are extremely strong. They stand up to the extremely high loading which can occur if the car is run into. The backrests are dimensioned so that they fold backwards if the car is run into from behind. This folding occurs with plastic deformation which happens before the force on the neck becomes too great.

Standard equipment in a Volvo includes three-point safety belts on the front seats and belt attachments for the rear seats.

All the controls, including the handbrake lever, are easy to reach even when wearing the safety belt.

A fresh air thermostat-controlled heater installation provides large quantities of warm air. The temperature in the car rapidly attains a comfortable level.

The passengers in the rear seat are also provided with comfortable warmth in a Volvo. Separate air ducts distribute the heat evenly to the rear seat. A powerful two-speed fan increases the feed of warm or cool air when necessary and also provides excellent defrosting.

Volvo cars are ideal for children but, at the same time, child-proof

Three-point safety belts standard equipment

43

Autocar, 2 November 1962

25

THE MOTOR, January 15 1964

Volvo 121 75 b.h.p. ££47.8.8.
122 96 b.h.p. Disc brakes on
front wheels £1,096.16.8.
Estate Car 75 b.h.p. 65 cu. ft.
luggage capacity £1,207.9.5.
1800S Coupe. New Swedish built—
108 b.h.p. Disc brakes on
front wheels crankshaft
All models have 5 bearing
engines. Prices include purchase tax.
Write for illustrated brochure
and demonstration to:
VOLVO CONCESSIONAIRES LTD
28 Albemarle Street, London, W.1.
Tel: HYDe Park 0051/6
Service & Spares: 46 Gloucester
Ave., N.W.1. Tel: PRImrose 0161
London Distributors:
BROOKLANDS
OF BOND STREET LTD.
108 New Bond Street, W.1.
Tel: MAYfair 2361.

Volvo is a *good car.* Proved reliable in the toughest trials and competitions throughout the world . . . at home in the most sophisticated circles. Performance to delight the enthusiast; *plus* fine roadholding, splendid steering, strong rugged body, laminated windscreen, big wheels, big tyres, big brakes, safety belts, dished steering wheel, padded dash, soft visors and a host of other special safety features. Built for reliability, for performance and . . . for safety.

Be sure...be fast...be safe...

VOLVO

OUTRIGHT WINNERS 1963 R.A.C. RALLY . GUNNAR ANDERSSON DRIVING VOLVO WINNER OF EUROPEAN RALLY CHAMPIONSHIP

for the fortunate few

The dash and élan of a sports car with the smooth quietness of the best in limousines . . . groomed to the finish you expect from the best in Swedish engineering. For shooting the rapids of modern traffic or skimming along new motorways, this is the new VOLVO 122.

Your way is made smooth by the large 15 inch wheels . . . made safe with both disc and drum brakes, no brake fade . . . equally adapted to town and distance driving . . . the best of both worlds. Re-live for yourself that thoroughbred response . . . the elation of driving a car with a really exuberant performance.

VOLVO 122. Whispering Power 90 b.h.p. engine with twin carburetters. Disc brakes on front, front seat safety belts, underbody rust-proofing, mud flaps, and many 'extras' . . . £1,295.10.5 including £355.10.5 purchase tax. Optional overdrive £82.10.0 extra, including £22.13.9 purchase tax.

VOLVO 121 with the new single carburettor engine, developing 75 brake horsepower, is now available costing £1,197.5.5 including £327.5.5 purchase tax. See too, the superb 100 b.h.p. VOLVO P1800 Coupé £1,836.12.9 including £501.12.9 purchase tax.
VOLVO 141 Estate Car £1,198.12.9 including £551.12.9 purchase tax.

VOLVO CONCESSIONAIRES LIMITED
Sales: 28 Albemarle Street, London W.1 Telephone: HYDe Park 0051/6
Service & Spares: 46 Gloucester Avenue N.W.1 Telephone: PRImrose 0161

ENGINEERING   **VOLVO**   122

105

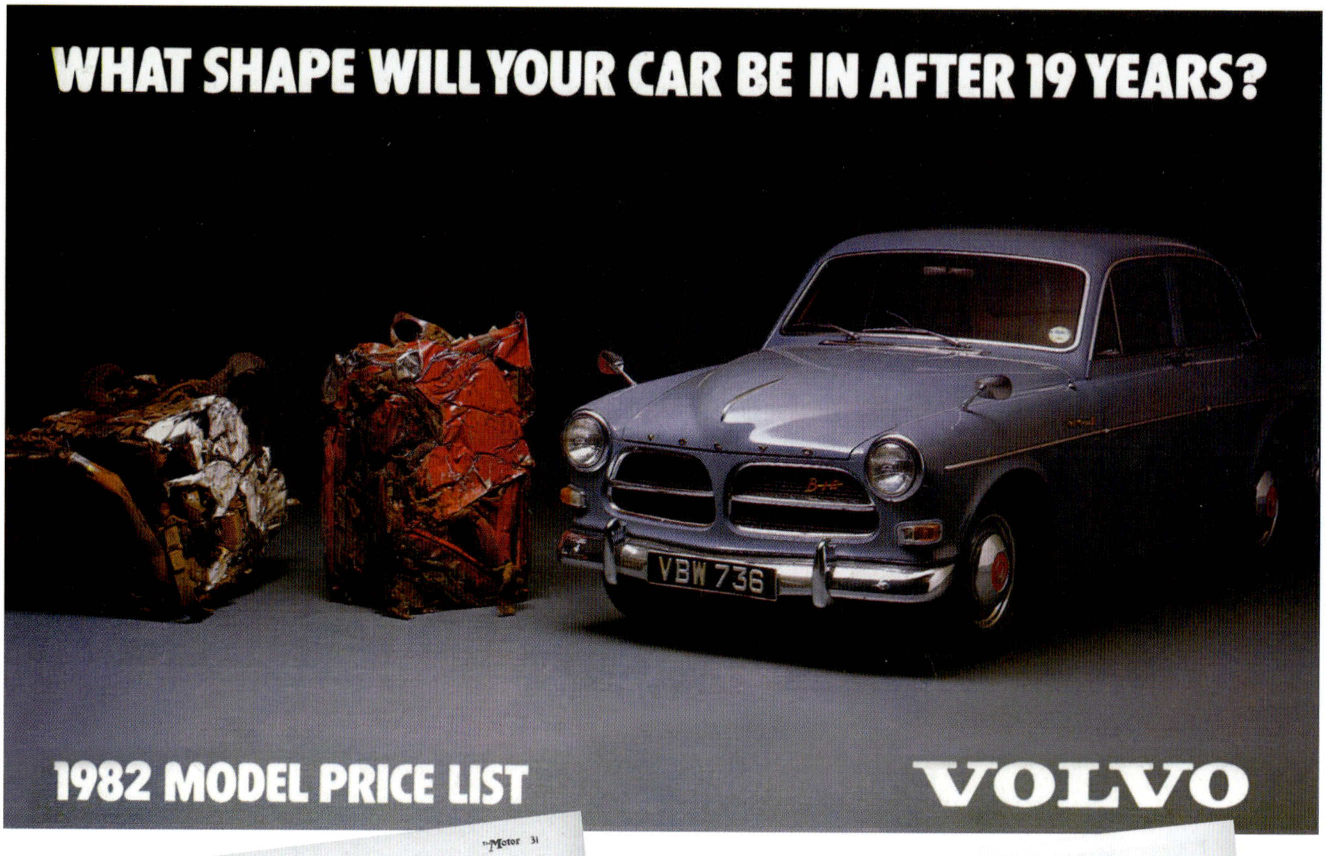
WHAT SHAPE WILL YOUR CAR BE IN AFTER 19 YEARS?
VBW 736
1982 MODEL PRICE LIST
VOLVO

The Motor 31
January 28, 1959
*
The amazing VOLVO 122 S
is now available in this country
Here's what the experts say about the VOLVO:
Mike Hawthorn—"Sunday Express" December 14th, 1958
"The Volvo is a sensation . . . There can be precious few cars of its engine size made anywhere in the world with such performance. It is as fast and vivid as a rocket burst."
John Bolster—"Autosport" June 6th, 1958
"Its roadholding and suspension are of a very high standard and its engine does seem to have more 'punch' than other comparable units. Perhaps the gearbox is the best feature of this very good car, but it is in the comfort of its seats, the correct location of the controls and all the hundreds of little practical touches, that it excels."
Sole Concessionaires in the U.K.
VOLVO
BROOKLANDS MOTOR CO LTD
103 New Bond Street, London W1 MAYfair 8351
DEMONSTRATION CAR — H.P. — PART EXCHANGE — CHOICE OF COLOURS
SPARES AND SERVICE: Old Oak Lane, Willesden NW10 ELGar 5350

NEW
for the fortunate few . . .
Yes new! New with a beauty that is far more than skin deep. Same handsome lines . . . same flawless finish . . . But when you drive it . . . then you know the whispering power of the new engine for yourself . . . the hidden beauty of the new VOLVO. An entirely new engine that produces even more power than its famous predecessor . . . quietly. And, incredible fact, even more economically. Ninety brake horsepower harnessed to give surging sports car performance to a spacious family car. Disciplined by new best-of-both-worlds' brakes—discs at front, drums at the rear. Ninety brake horsepower smoothed by a five bearing crankshaft and—if you wish—aided and abetted by Laycock de Normanville overdrive. This is the new VOLVO . . . your VOLVO.
VOLVO 122S B18. Whispering Power 1780 cc. engine with twin carburettors. Disc Brakes on front, front seat safety belts, 'cold weather start' battery, 12 volt electrical system, more powerful starter motor, improved two-speed heater-demister, two-speed wipers, cigar lighter, radiator blind, chromium wheel trims, underbody rust-proofing, mud-flaps, and many "extras". £1,372.1.5 including £432.1.5 purchase tax.
Optional overdrive £87.10.0 extra, including purchase tax.
Ask your dealer to show you also the 1600 cc. Volvo at £1,240.16.5 including £390.16.5 purchase tax.
VOLVO
PRODUCT OF FINE SWEDISH ENGINEERING
VOLVO
Where to find it:
VOLVO CONCESSIONAIRES LIMITED
Sales: 28 Albemarle Street, London, W.1. Tel: HYDe Park 7980-4248
Service & Spares: 46 Gloucester Avenue, N.W.1. Tel: PRImrose 0161
Second class postage paid at New York, N.Y.

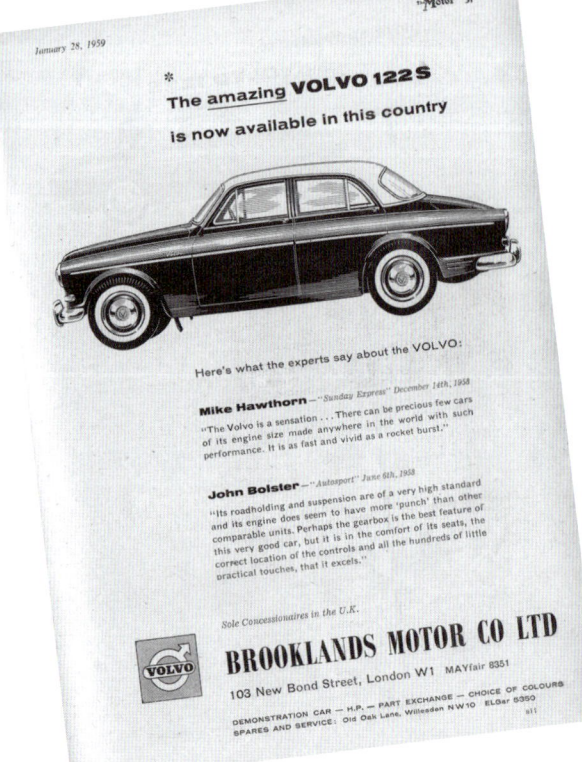

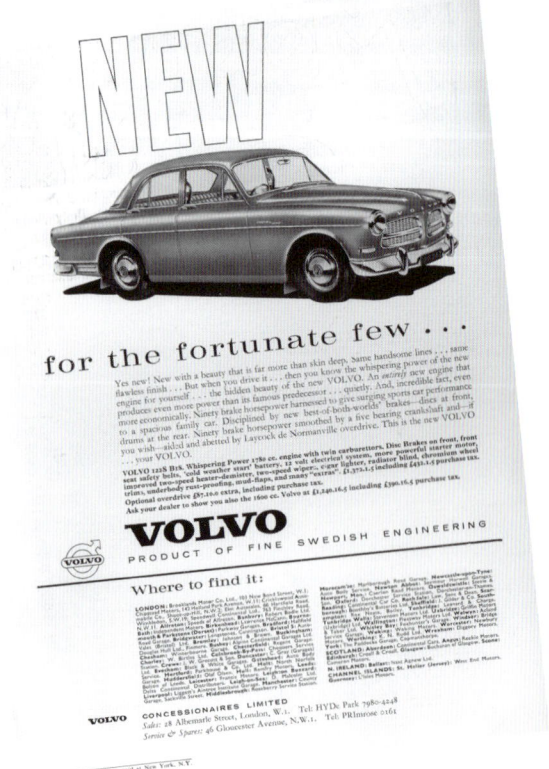

AMAZON SALES BROCHURES

At a time when many car makers were still using drawings of their cars in their sales brochures, Volvo was using photography so there was no distortion of scale. Many rival car makers were guilty of making their tiny cars look like massive limousines thanks to the use of artistic licence – but not Volvo.

What Volvo did do was put its cars into real-world situations to show how brilliantly the Amazon could cope with everyday life. As a result, Amazon brochures were chock full of cars lugging families and luggage around, towing boats and generally being the perfect addition to the family.

Occasionally Volvo would use studio photography to illustrate an Amazon brochure, and it's fair to say that this rather stark imagery doesn't portray the Amazon in a particularly good light – on location is where it really looks at home.

What Volvo wasn't afraid to do was get fairly technical sometimes, with whole pages given over to information about engines and braking systems. Volvo also wasn't afraid to show the Amazon being built – although whether or not anybody ever bought one of these cars because of the way the production line was set up is anybody's guess.

AB VOLVO
Göteborg – Sweden

2-litre engine with exhaust emission control

Triangular-split brake system. Safety body.

A Swedish Beauty

– distinguished
   and representative ...

VOLVO 122 S

The seats are among the best that have ever been designed

– We think it can be seen
– We know it can be felt

Try the driver's seat. Notice the head restraints. They provide extra safety and protection from upper spine injuries should your Volvo be run into from behind. They are, of course, height adjustable. Check the distance to the steering wheel and pedals. Does anything need adjusting? This is easily done. The seat can be moved fore-and-aft. And vertically. The inclination of both the cushion and backrest can be adjusted to your individual requirements. Even the degree of lumbar support is infinitely variable by means of the conveniently located knob on the side of the backrest. Are you sitting comfortably, relaxed, alert? Feel the superb support the seat gives you across the shoulders, across the small of the back and under the thighs. These perfectly contoured bucket seats keep you located—in comfort.

Can anything be more comfortable? Notice the seat attachments in the floor. These very robust anchorages are built to stand up to extreme stress.

A great deal of thought has also been given to the rear seat passengers. The rear seat itself is deep and provides plenty of leg room. This is what makes 121/122 S a pleasure to travel in.

The dashboard has a smooth lower edge without any protrusions. The upper surface is padded with impact-absorbing material. The sun visors are also padded. The laminated glass windscreen of "high-impact" type with a tough intermediary plastic skin retains full vision even when hit by flying stones.

The extremely effective steering wheel lock combined with ignition switch.

All controls are located within convenient reach and the dished steering wheel hub is extra wide in order to spread loading over the greatest possible area in the event of a collision. The antidazzle rearview mirror collapses under impact.

Volvo – a rigid body and thorough rust-proofing make up a safe car

The Volvo 120 series — high class engineering

A car must satisfy many severe demands if it is to be recognized as a product of high class engineering.

Built for Swedish climate and Swedish roads

Sweden, the home of Volvo cars, has a widely varying climate. In addition to this more than 70% of all the roads in the country are narrow, twisting and gravelled. This is one of the reasons why Volvo cars have been built which has

High degree of safety

Volvo has always been one of the pioneers in automotive safety. Volvo cars have bodies which are extremely resistant to torsional stresses and are all delivered with three-point safety belts on the front seats and belt anchorages on the rear seat.

Excellent comfort

Volvo cars are renowned for their comfort. The front seats can be adjusted individually, including a continuously variable lumbar support. Volvo was the first car in the world to incorporate this outstanding feature.

Excellent road-holding

Volvo cars have precision-calculated weight distribution between front and rear. This, together with the special rear suspension and the extremely accurate steering system, ensures perfect course-holding and cornering. This even applies at high speeds.

Strong and ... the stresses of rally ... versatile form of motor com...

Two years in succession – 1963 and ... – Volvo won the World Championship for Car Manufacturers and has also topped prize lists in rallies all over the world.

Outstanding service

Each Volvo car is backed up by a well-developed service and spare parts organization with factory-trained mechanics.

(right column) ...supplied with a wide range of ... and comprehensive under... ... No extra cost is required ... a safe and comfortable car.

... satisfies extremely severe demands and more than justifies the reputation of a top quality car.

This is one of the logical reasons why more and more quality-conscious people are coming to the conclusion that the best car for them is a Volvo.

The Volvo 121/122 S. Technical perfection. Perfectly designed. Carefully tested. Part by part. The leader of its class.

CHAPTER SIX

TUNED AND MODIFIED AMAZONS

Ever since its introduction the Amazon had been seen as a sporting saloon thanks to its predictable handling and sprightly performance. So it's always been a natural contender for the attentions of tuners who wanted to make it go even faster without having to sacrifice the car's usability. Not only that, but a choice of different body styles meant buyers could have a sporting coupé, saloon or even estate without the need to resort to special bodywork. As a result, some British police forces ran tuned Amazons knowing that they'd be reliable while still being able to keep up with villains who were using increasingly fast cars in an attempt to get away.

THE RUDDSPEED AMAZONS

Perhaps the best known of the Amazon tuners was Ken Rudd, who having hung up his racing helmet devoted himself to making cars go faster, especially the Amazon. He offered upgrades for saloons, coupés and estates at a time when estates were seen as nothing other than utilitarian workhorses. By focusing on allowing the cylinder head to breathe better, along with fitting spicier camshafts, uprated valve springs and tweaked carburation, Ken Rudd was able to build Amazons that really flew.

The new camshaft offered increased lift and overlap while the stronger valve springs increased the safe rev limit to around 6,000rpm, which was also where the peak power output of 108bhp was now achieved. To help deliver this there were fresh needles for the twin SU HS6 carburettors fitted by the factory, while a polished cylinder head and a raised compression ratio (now 10.5:1) also did their bit to boost power.

One of the key fitments was an all-new exhaust system, which allowed the five-bearing four-pot to breathe more easily. A Ruddspeed design, there was a tubular steel four-

Ken Rudd was the best known of the Amazon tuners in period; some police forces used cars uprated by his company.

The Ruddspeed 131 was something of an animal; for a four-door family saloon it was indecently quick.

branch manifold that led into a straight-through silencer, which then exited via twin tailpipes. The gearbox and clutch remained untouched, but to cope with the extra power the suspension was heavily revised.

Both the front and rear coil springs were cut down to reduce the ride height by about an inch and a half, while stiffer Koni dampers were fitted to reduce roll in corners at high speed. To round things off (as it were), Pirelli Cinturato tyres were fitted, but the interior was left standard (aside from some extra soundproofing) and so too were the brakes.

It's not known how many Amazons Rudd worked his magic upon, but it's reckoned the figure could be as high as 200, although few seem to survive. Perhaps many later owners didn't know what they had, the discreet badging not being obvious enough; Rudd attached a small yellow logo beside the factory-fitted 121/122S badging along with an identification plate on the cylinder head.

When Patrick McNally tested a Ruddspeed 121 (registered 5 NBP) for *Autosport* in 1964 he was glowing in his praise, claiming it was a truly sporty drive but one that gave away nothing in terms of practicality. The top speed now stood at 107mph (172km/h) while the standing quarter-mile

could be despatched in just under 18 seconds – incredibly quick for a four-door saloon that could carry five adults in comfort. It was affordable too, with its £1,245 price tag. McNally wrote:

> *With perhaps the exception of the Janspeed Mini Cooper S I drove last year I have never driven a car which cornered so quickly with so little fuss. As regards the lack of dramatics when cornering, this can be put down to the absence of body roll and pitch, both of which have been obviated almost completely.*

To summarize, McNally stated:

> *It is difficult to explain why the Volvo was always used in preference to other faster cars at my disposal. Perhaps because journeys were made in identical times with far less effort and considerable saving of bad language. All passengers, whether enthusiasts or elderly people [these are presumably mutually exclusive groups! – Ed.], had good words for the comfort, and the latter were not aware of the speed they were travelling – a great advantage!*

Just in case even this wasn't quick enough for some, Rudd also developed an Amazon with the same mechanical upgrades, but with a pair of Weber carburettors in place of the SUs more usually fitted. Capable of cutting the 0–60mph time to around nine seconds with a standing quarter-mile time below 16 seconds, flexibility was something of an issue compared with the SU-equipped cars, but if ultimate performance was your thing, this was the Amazon for you.

And Estates Too!

Because the Amazon estate was mechanically identical to its saloon sibling, Ken Rudd could also work his magic on it.

And when it came to Q-cars, few were as understated as this one; it looked like a true workhorse yet it could really shift.

Offering 118bhp thanks to a wilder camshaft, twin SU carburettors, a more free-flowing exhaust and a modified cylinder head, the Ruddspeed Amazon estate was able to sprint from rest to 60mph in just 12.2 seconds – a year earlier *Autocar*'s road testers had clocked a standard car at 21.1 seconds. Similarly the 60–80mph time in top gear was slashed from 22.5 seconds to just 10.9 seconds, which meant Ruddspeed was offering something to British car buyers which at the time was probably unique – an affordable and reliable performance estate.

Because at first the estate featured drum brakes all around, Rudd fitted the front discs more usually seen on the 122S saloon – a move that was particularly desirable with the extra weight and power. As with the saloon, there was added soundproofing and stiffer Koni dampers along with Pirelli Cinturato tyres. Amusingly, part of the package was a stick-on strip of metal that gave direct rpm readings in third and top gears from the speedometer. However, with smaller-radius tyres fitted this was woefully inaccurate – at a true 98mph the speedometer was showing 120mph. Not only that, but the odometer also over-read by nearly 18 per cent, so an owner's annual mileage would have quickly racked up.

When *Autocar* tested the Ruddpseed Amazon estate in August 1964, the magazine (unsurprisingly) was rather enthusiastic about it. Its summary ran:

Handling is very much improved, the car feeling firm on corners and barely rolling. When the load included four passengers, two big suitcases

---

·296   AUTOCAR, 7 August 1964

IMPROVING THE PERFORMANCE OF POPULAR CARS—1
Ruddspeed Volvo Estate Car

Apart from the Pirelli Cinturato tyres and very slightly lowered suspension, the Ruddspeed Volvo Estate Car looks normal

ESTATE cars are too often regarded as beasts of burden, used for carting around crates and boxes, ferrying children to school, shopping from the market or moving friends' furniture from place to place. A man with an estate car is never without friends, but a man with a tuned estate car will have even more friends. Recently we have been driving two—the first being the Ruddspeed Volvo estate car.

The standard Volvo estate car is a solid piece of Swedish engineering capable of carrying a lot of luggage and people at reasonably high speeds. It has the single carburettor version of the 1,778 c.c. B18 engine and a lower back axle ratio to give reasonable acceleration when a heavy load is being carried.

Ruddspeed bring the standard engine up to P1800 specification by fitting their own modified cylinder head and S-type camshaft. Twin S.U. carburettors are added, along with a special free-flow exhaust manifold and silencing system. To cope with the extra speed, especially when carrying a load, the front drum brakes are replaced by Girling discs as on the 122S saloons. Koni dampers are also fitted to stiffen the ride and give better handling at speed. As a final touch, the whole car is given the Ruddspeed Silent Ride sound-proofing treatment.

As soon as one drives in the car one can tell that all is not standard under the bonnet. The twin carburettors have no air-cleaners—just bell-mouth ram pipes which create a healthy roar even at quite low engine revs.

The estate car's low overall ratios, combined with the Pirelli Cinturato tyres slightly smaller diameter, give it real sports-car get-away. The standing quarter mile took 18·6sec, while 40 was reached in 6·0sec, 50 in 8·1sec and 60 in

12·2sec. The test car suffered from slight clutch slip, so the times might have been fractionally better with it biting firmly.

Part of the "conversion" includes a stick-on strip of metal which gives direct r.p.m. readings in third and top gears from the speedometer. However, the smaller-radius tyres affect the speedometer so much as to make it almost useless—98 m.p.h. true showing as 120 m.p.h. In addition, the mileage recorder was 17·8 per cent optimistic.

Our best one-way speed was 101·5 m.p.h. and the mean maximum exactly 100 m.p.h. This gives an indication of the low axle ratio used, showing that the engine was running at very near its maximum power output.

The test mileage was 500 miles, most of which was made up of very hard driving and taking the performance figures. The overall fuel consumption worked out at 20 m.p.g., but spot checks during more gentle driving put this up to around the 24 m.p.g. mark. With the 10-to-1 compression ratio, super premium fuel has to be used; one pint of oil was added at the very end of the test to bring the level back to full again.

Handling is very much improved, the car feeling firm on corners and barely rolling. When the load included four passengers, two big suitcases and a large packing case full of books, the ride still remained good and the extra performance made it very easy to keep up with unladen saloon cars of similar capacity. With 118 b.h.p. to order, the Ruddspeed Volvo Estate car is always an interesting way of travelling.

Twin S.U. carburettors and a vacuum servo for the brakes are the external signs of Ruddspeed's conversion

Performance Data

Maximum speeds in gears:		m.p.h.	k.p.h.
Top (mean)	.. .. ..	100·0 (88·3)	161·0 (142·1)
(best)	.. ..	101·5 (89)	163·2 (143·2)
3rd	.. .. ..	82 (71)	132 (114)
2nd	.. .. ..	55 (54)	89 (87)
1st	.. .. ..	36 (36)	58 (58)

Standing quarter-mile 18·6 sec. (22·0 sec.)

From rest through gears to:			
30 m.p.h.	.. ..	3·6 sec.	(5·6 sec)
40 „	.. ..	6·0 „	(9·1 „)
50 „	.. ..	8·1 „	(13·9 „)
60 „	.. ..	12·2 „	(21·4 „)
70 „	.. ..	16·5 „	(29·5 „)
80 „	.. ..	23·6 „	(47·1 „)
90 „	.. ..	33·0 „	(— „)

PRICE: Ruddspeed Volvo Estate Car: £1,399 0s 0d.
Ruddspeed Ltd., The Aerodrome, Ford, Arundel, Sussex.

Figures in brackets are for the Volvo Estate car tested in Autocar of 6 September 1963.

Acceleration Times: Speed range, gear ratios and time in seconds:

m.p.h.	Top	Third	Second	First
10–30	— (—)	7·3 (8·4)	4·1 (5·2)	3·1 (4·5)
20–40	9·7 (11·3)	6·4 (8·0)	4·0 (5·6)	
30–50	9·0 (10·9)	6·0 (8·2)	4·8 (7·3)	
40–60	9·2 (11·9)	6·4 (9·9)		
50–70	10·6 (15·3)	8·0 (15·5)		
60–80	10·9 (22·5)	13·3 (—)		
70–90	15·3 (—)			

Overall fuel consumption for 500 miles: 20·0 m.p.g.; 14·1 litres/100 kms. (29·5 m.p.g.; 9·6 litres/100 km.)

It came as no surprise that Autocar loved the Ruddspeed-tuned Amazon – it did everything the standard car could do, but with even more performance.

and a large packing case full of books, the ride still remained good and the extra performance made it very easy to keep up with unladen saloon cars of a similar capacity. With 118bhp to order, the Ruddspeed Volvo estate car is always an interesting way of travelling.

ROBERT BODLE

It wasn't only Ruddspeed that offered faster Amazons, as Robert Bodle of Oxfordshire-based Dorchester Service Station was also selling them. A modified cylinder head, raised compression ratio, special valve springs that permitted 6,800rpm and re-profiled manifolds produced a car which was capable of 102mph (164km/h). Not only that, but the 0–60mph time was reduced to just 12 seconds while fuel economy improved thanks to the greater efficiency of the tweaked engine.

With the head porting priced at £39 10s – plus another £3 19s for uprated valve springs – the cost wasn't exorbitant, as the 122S was priced at £1,294 (including purchase tax) at the time. That 102mph top speed was even more impressive when you consider that the test car (as driven by John Bolster in *Autosport*) was a fully laden rally car. The fitment of overdrive helped to get beyond the ton and also 'permitted delightfully easy cruising'.

The Bodle-tuned 122S could despatch the standing quarter-mile in just 18.9 seconds along with the 0–30mph sprint in all of 3.5 seconds – with the 0–50mph dash taking 8.3 seconds and 0–60mph an excellent 12.0 seconds. What was even more impressive was the fact that a higher back axle ratio was fitted (now 4.1:1) to enable the car to go beyond 100mph. Yet despite these far quicker times compared with the standard car, fuel consumption was also improved too, thanks to the inherent extra efficiency of the engine – in real-world use a regular 28mpg was possible.

ALCONI AND LAWSON'S CORNER

In South Africa, too, Alconi was busy making Amazons go faster. Better exhausts, ported and polished cylinder heads, larger valves and different carburettor needles gave power outputs of up to 135bhp, while also allowing the powerplant to run more cleanly and economically. With a top speed

of 110mph (177km/h) the cars also benefited from uprated brake pads and stiffer suspension.

The Amazon was popular with South African buyers thanks to its ability to shrug off poor (or non-existent) road surfaces. With some drivers regularly clocking up huge annual mileages, an uprated Amazon was just the ticket for despatching a lengthy journey. That's why, alongside Alconi, Johannesburg-based Lawson's Corner also offered an uprated Amazon.

Best known for its preparation of endurance racers, Lawson's Corner essentially turned the Amazon into a P1800 saloon or estate. By fitting a P1800 camshaft, increasing the compression ratio (from 8.5:1 to 10.0:1) and retuning the carburettors, a healthy 108bhp was coaxed from the B18 powerplant – an extractor manifold and a fresh exhaust silencer were fitted too.

The result of all this jiggery-pokery was a car that now topped out at 98mph (158km/h) (an extra 8mph), could get from a standing start to 60mph in just 13.1 seconds (compared with 17.5 seconds for the standard car); and fuel economy was improved marginally too. As *Car South Africa* wrote when it reviewed a privately owned 122S estate with the Lawson's Corner upgrades:

The Volvo wagon, with Lawson's P1800 kit, pulls, climbs, cruises and tows better than before, by a good margin. This same kit on the lighter and better-geared saloon, should show even more dramatic results.

EVEN VOLVO WAS AT IT...

Perhaps the most intriguing hot-rod Amazon of all was a factory-built machine based on a 1957 car. This dark blue and white saloon was cut down the middle and widened by 120mm so that it could accommodate a Volvo Snabbe V8. The Snabbe was a light truck introduced in 1956 and fitted with a development of the V8 engine seen in the aborted Philip prototype. Despite the wider track, the 3.6-litre V8-powered Amazon, known as the Volvo Brede ('The Wide One'), handled abysmally – although it was decently swift thanks to its 120bhp or so.

JACQUES COUNE'S CABRIOLETS

Although Volvo didn't officially produce anything other than saloon and estate versions of the 120-series, a handful of convertible editions were produced in period and since the Amazon went out of production several owners have opened up their cars with varying degrees of success.

It would have made sense for an open-topped Amazon to be offered by Volvo, even if the work was outsourced to a third party. After all, the Amazon was sold as a semi-premium model in many markets and the car's inherent strength and rigidity would have made the conversion possible, if not straightforward. Volvo also wasn't averse to the idea of selling a convertible (despite the obvious safety considerations) as it had already introduced the unsuccessful P1900 in 1956.

But Volvo opted not to offer an open-topped Amazon so instead it was Belgian coachbuilder Jacques Coune who became best known for chopping the roof off the Amazon.

He built five convertibles, the first of which was shown at the 1963 Brussels *salon*. One car was a two-seater while the other four were four-seaters. Sadly, three of the five cars have disappeared, but two remain, one of which is still to be found in Belgium, where it has been completely restored by its owner.

Based on a two-door saloon, the Coune convertible cost 50 per cent more than the car on which it was based, thanks to a leather retrim, reworked doors and much body strengthening. It took around 100 hours to transform an Amazon into a stylish cabriolet, the interior having to be removed first, so that stronger floorpans could be fitted along with deeper sills. To increase rigidity, the front wings were welded on; they're more usually attached by bolts.

All of this work was relatively straightforward; it was the car's upper body that required the real development time and skill. Rather than have a 'pram-hood' effect, the folding soft-top had to stow away level with the car's rear deck — which necessitated the fabrication of a suitable frame. There

The Jacques Coune-built Amazon convertible looked superb.

Coune built five convertibles, four of which were four-seaters (as here). The other was a two-seater.

also had to be wind-down rear side windows so the roof didn't have to go all the way to the trailing edge of the front side windows. It's in these areas that the home-built drop-tops suffer, as their roofs invariably look hideously amateur-ish when raised.

Predictably, Jacques Coune did a superb job – but at a price. Buyers had to stump up 65,000 Belgian Francs for the conversion – on top of the car's list price of 135,000 Belgian Francs. For that buyers got a beautifully reworked interior with leather trim, but there was no extra power and the conversion added a hefty 85kg to the car's kerb weight. With no amendments to the suspension, the changes didn't do the Amazon's dynamics any favours either.

Although Coune planned to build twenty-five convertible Amazons, after he'd built four of them the orders stopped coming in. Built in 1963, the cars went down a storm with owners and anyone who set eyes on them; the proportions were superb and so too was the quality of workmanship.

For one wealthy US enthusiast, though, a regular four-seat Amazon convertible wasn't exclusive enough – he wanted something unique. To that end he commissioned Coune to build him a two-seater Amazon convertible, which would be based on a regular two-door saloon. As it wasn't shortened, Coune had to be very careful to get the proportions right as there would be a lot of space behind the two occupants.

To this end Coune incorporated a longer rear deck and, because there were no rear seats, there also didn't need to be any wind-down rear side windows. The hood could be noticeably shorter too and that rear deck improved the car's rigidity significantly. Once again there was an expensive retrim in the finest hides while the bodywork was finished in a champagne metallic finish. The car looked superb, but sadly it hasn't been seen for several decades now and has completely disappeared from view. Hopefully one day it will appear once again; after all, who would be crazy enough to scrap such a unique car?

THE SOMMER COUPÉ

Fate can be a cruel mistress, and in the automotive industry it can sometimes be very cruel indeed. Ole Sommer knows all about that, as he decided in 1960 to create his own Volvo coupé using a shortened and lowered Volvo Duett (PV544) chassis along with a handful of Amazon panels.

Sommer was a Danish businessman, and it was inevitable that he'd work with machinery in some way as his father ran a Ford dealership. In the 1940s his father had tried to set up his own car-making business (without success) and later on Ole would go on to successfully sell Jaguars and Volvos in Denmark.

Between 1949 and 1951, Sommer trained with Jaguar then Jowett; from 1952 he furthered his training at Copenhagen Technical University. However, the sudden death of his father in 1952 meant that Sommer had to run the family business, which by now was focusing on Jaguar; by 1957, Volvo had been added to the fold. It wasn't long before Ole Sommer was running Denmark's largest Volvo dealership.

In the thick of all this, Sommer reckoned there was a market for a high-quality coupé, so he set about having one constructed to his own design. Introduced by Sommer in 1960 as the Volvo Special, but known for ever after as the Sommer Coupé, this intriguing machine was built by hand and featured largely bespoke bodywork. The coachbuilding was done by the B. Stesnas Coachworks, the Coupé's front window being borrowed from the rear of an Amazon while the back window was taken from a Jaguar XK150.

The car was largely well received, but by the time it was unveiled Volvo had revealed a sporting coupé of its own – the P1800. Sommer lost interest in the car when it became clear that it was never going to be a viable proposition – although he would later buy it back and hold on to it. It's now on public display in Sommer's private car museum (http://sommersautomobilmuseum.dk); since he retired in 2004 and sold off the various businesses, this is what Sommer now devotes his energy to.

ABOVE: **From this angle the Sommer Coupé looks like little more than a coachbuilt Amazon ...**

LEFT: **... but it was actually much more than that, as only the front end panels were taken from the Amazon – most of the rest was bespoke.**

OFFICIAL VOLVO ACCESSORIES

When the Amazon was launched, it was nothing new for a car maker to offer buyers a range of accessories for their new motor. But the extent of these for many companies was a set of mud flaps and perhaps a choice of driving lights and radios – and possibly a heater for some of the cheaper models.

Not so for Volvo, though, which aimed to offer pretty much anything an Amazon owner could ever want, regardless of where they lived or what they used their car for. Alongside extra lighting (both external and internal), there were various wheel trims, mud flaps and exhaust pipe finishers on offer along with an array of door and rear-view mirrors, roof and ski racks plus all sorts of radio kits.

With reclining seats, car care kits and many cleaning potions also available, Volvo didn't miss a trick when it came to selling products to an Amazon owner once they'd bought their new car.

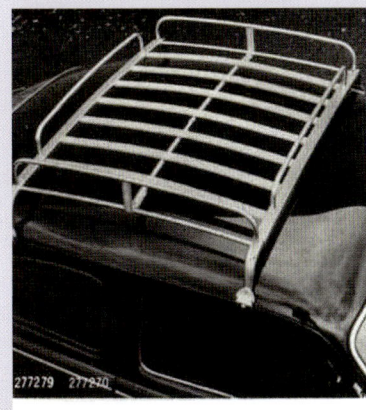

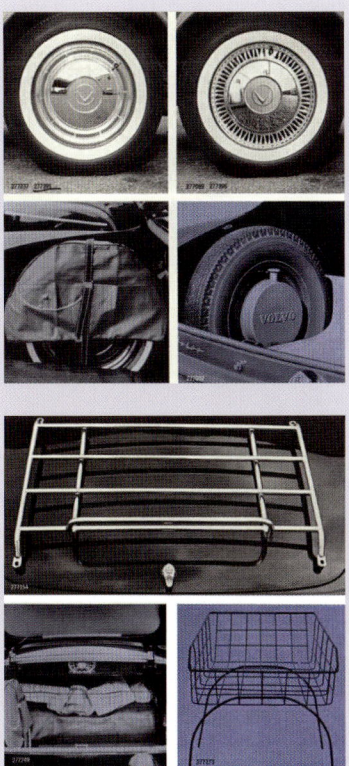

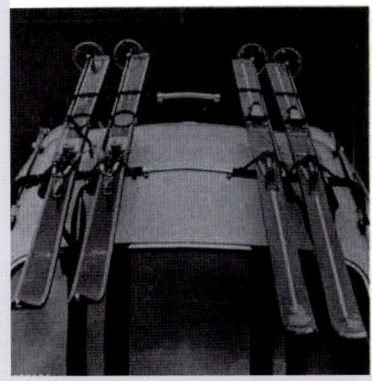

Whether you wanted products to make your Amazon safer, more comfortable, more usable or to keep it in better condition, your Volvo dealer could sell you something from the official accessories catalogue.

CHAPTER SEVEN

THE AMAZON IN MOTORSPORT

Volvo founder Assar Gabrielsson was noted for having pretty good judgement. In business, a steady hand at the tiller is essential, and that's exactly what Gabrielsson provided, so when he stated publicly in 1956 that 'Dog racing does as much for the development of cars as motorsport does', that was a pretty sure sign that factory-backed Volvos weren't likely to be appearing in motorsport any time soon.

Gabrielsson's proclamation came after a hugely successful season for Saab in 1955, which saw its factory team racking up wins in just about every major rally in the calendar. With Saab being Volvo's arch-rival, it would have made perfect sense for Volvo to enter some of its cars into world-class rallying. But it was decided that competition was unnecessary as buyers were already well aware of the strength of the company's cars.

However, despite Gabrielsson's strong views on the worth of motorsport, as early as 1949 a PV444 had been privately entered in that year's Monte Carlo Rally by Hilding Ohlsson, Martin Carstedt and Stig Cederholm. Although they made no great impression, the following year the same team finished 12th overall – a good result for a bunch of privateers.

The turning point came in 1957, after Gunnar Engellau had replaced Assar Gabrielsson as Volvo's boss in 1956. The following year a PV444 was privately entered in the Rally to the Midnight Sun, which was Sweden's qualifying event for the European Rally Championship. In the same year the Norwegian Rally was won by another pair of privateers in their PV444. But this was only the start, as the following year Gunnar Andersson burst onto the scene and got a placing in just about every race he entered. Andersson

A PV544 in the 1960 RAC Rally at the hands of an unknown female driver. It's not Sylvia Österberg or Ewy Rosqvist – so who is it?

had started rallying a Jaguar XK120 in 1953, and in 1957 he bought his first Volvo, a PV444. Junking the factory-fitted engine in favour of an American-spec 75bhp unit, Andersson planned to compete in the Acropolis, Midnight Sun, German and Tulip rallies in 1958 – all with his own money.

On his first outing, in the Acropolis Rally, Andersson achieved third place – Engellau wasted no time asking him if he'd be interested in driving factory-prepared rally cars and continuing his success in the company's name instead of his own. When Andersson accepted, he became Volvo's first works driver in Volvo's brand-new motorsport division.

GUNNAR ANDERSSON

Gunnar Andersson was born in the Swedish province of Dalsland on 17 April 1927 – just three days after the first Volvo car left the factory in Gothenburg. When he was ten the family moved to Gothenburg, and after school he joined the Air Force as a trainee aircraft technician. Meanwhile, he began to repair and sell pre-war cars in a nearby rented garage – he also decided to try his hand at motorsport. The first event he entered, a combined speed and manoeuvre trial, he won. Once bitten, he was smitten. Andersson tried his luck in hill climbs, ice racing, reliability trials and racing, before eventually he focused on rallying.

After trying numerous makes of car, Andersson bought a Volvo PV444 in 1957, with the 85bhp US-spec engine – and immediately he started winning. Within a year Volvo had hired him; 1958 turned out to be a really successful season for Andersson and co-driver Niels-Peter Ellemann-Jacobsen, who had his own Volvo tuning workshop.

During this, his first international rally season, Andersson became European Champion; the following year he won the two-litre class in the Swedish Touring Car Championship, in his PV544, as a privateer. By doing so he beat a very young and keen Tom Trana.

In the same year, 1959, the competition operations were turned into a proper competition department, led by Arthur Wessblad. In 1960 Andersson had the opportunity to participate in the race he'd always considered to be the greatest achievement during his entire career: the Gran Premio de Argentina, a gruelling six-day road race, over 4,650 km (almost 3,000 miles) on narrow and winding Argentinian roads. Gunnar won it outright and five PV544s were among the first eight.

From 1961 Andersson raced less as he became Volvo's

Gunnar Andersson was Volvo's first ever factory-paid racing driver.

competitions manager – but he didn't give up driving altogether; he would go on to claim yet another European Rally Championship for himself and Volvo in 1963.

Volvo withdrew from the international rally scene in 1966, but the competition department was kept running, doing good business through the marketing of tuning kits, accessories and the sale of complete race and rally cars to paying customers. Gunnar would go on to devise the Swedish Volvo Cup, a racing series dedicated solely to 142 and 144 Volvos; the idea was later developed further into the 240 Turbo Cup.

During the second half of the 1970s Volvo returned to motorsport and Andersson came back into the limelight, heading the R-Sport department with an international involvement in rallycross. Five very busy seasons led to both Swedish and European Championship titles. After this hectic period, Andersson switched to the marketing department and became a travelling ambassador for Volvo until his retirement in 1992.

After his retirement, Andersson built his own version of his winning car from 1958, a heavily tuned 1957 PV444 with a double overhead camshaft 16-valve engine with twin Webers. In the early summer of 2009, Andersson died following a short illness.

STRUGGLING FOR ACCEPTANCE

When the Amazon arrived in 1956, it immediately faced an uphill struggle to forge much of a presence in international motorsport – because the PV had such a stranglehold. One of the toughest and most highly respected rally cars of its era, the PV won its class in the Midnight Sun Rally every year between 1957 and 1963 – and for the first two of those years it won the event outright. In the 1959 Monte Carlo Rally there were several Amazons entered, but there were more PVs in the entry lists because the car was so well proven. In comparison, the Amazon was heavier (so less agile) but its suspension was also more fully developed. But, with such an enviable track record, the PV wasn't going to be abandoned too readily.

TOM TRANA

Tom Trana was born in 1937, in the Swedish province of Värmland. It was inevitable that he'd end up doing something with a technical basis; his father was an engineer with marine engine manufacturers Albin Motor, and through motocross a young Trana entered the world of competition.

Trana's first car was a PV444 – which wasn't surprising, as he worked for a small garage called The PV Specialist, which helped him build and maintain the car. Together with childhood friend Gunnar Palm (later on a rally champion himself), Trana practised on the narrow twisting roads surrounding his home town to sort out his car and improve his driving abilities. His debut was in the Kanonloppet ('The Cannon Race') in 1957 on the Gelleråsen circuit and he also took part in the Swedish Car Orienteering Championship in the same year. In 1958 he won the big regional rally, Arvikanatta, with his PV444.

Tom was both a skilled mechanic and a very good driver. Very soon the crowds learned that the black PV with its 'cuckoo' on the roof (a direction indicator) and a white crane painted across the bonnet (trana is Swedish for crane) was always spectacularly driven to the limit, and sometimes beyond.

Trana was a genuine all-rounder and competed in all sorts of events; he was successful in every one of them. In 1959 he was runner-up in the Swedish saloon car racing championship, behind Gunnar Andersson, and he almost won the Midnight Sun Rally, overdoing things slightly at the end by ending up in a ditch while in the lead.

In 1960 he won the Swedish saloon car racing championship and he repeated this victory in 1961. Trana picked up new sponsors and moved to Stockholm to begin a new job and build a new car. In the workshop of his new employer, the large Volvo dealer Ernst Nilson Bil AB, Trana modified a Volvo P1800 to enter it in the 1961 Midnight Sun Rally together with Gunnar Palm. The pairing in the very much lightened and modified 1800 were among the top contenders for most of the distance and were close behind the leader, Carl-Magnus Skogh, who was then a Saab driver, but shortly before the finish the clutch seized and all chances of winning disappeared.

For the 1962 season Trana was hired by BMC but in 1963 Volvo team manager Gunnar Andersson offered him a works contract. Trana showed his gratitude by winning the RAC Rally the same year. Tom Trana, white Volvos and victories became synonymous terms. This, however, did not apply for the Safari Rally in 1964, which turned out a failure for the Volvo team. None of the four cars in the Volvo team reached the finish inside the stipulated time. Tom's crashed PV444 was left in Nairobi, was repaired and went on to win the 1965 Safari Rally in the hands of the Singh brothers.

The 1964 season was Trana's best and his fast-flying white PV544 was again the first car to cross the finishing line in the RAC Rally. He won the Acropolis Rally and the Swedish Rally and finished second in the Finnish 1000 Lakes Rally, which made him European Champion that year. All these successes were achieved in partnership with reliable co-driver Gunnar Thermaenius. Trana's meticulous care of both himself and his cars paid off well. He was always well prepared; he never drank but chewed frenetically on carrots in order to improve his already very good night vision.

During the 1965 season his biggest achievement was winning the Swedish Rally again, but when Volvo withdrew from competition in 1966 Trana found himself unemployed, so he set up his own racing team and bought two Amazons from his former employer. However, life as team manager was not an easy one and to be able to catch up with the fastest works drivers as a private entrant was not as easy either – so he accepted an offer from Saab to become one of their works drivers.

Trana died in 1991, but his name lives on in the Tom Trana Trophy, a kart race held annually at the internationally approved circuit in Gothenburg. Meanwhile, Tom's son Claes Trana would go on to become an endurance racing driver in Volvos, in partnership with Magnus Skogh, the son of his father's old teammate Carl-Magnus Skogh.

SYLVIA ÖSTERBERG

Sylvia Österberg was born in 1934, as Sylvia Eriksson. By the time she was twelve, Österberg was already driving the family car, an Opel Olympia. After she met and married Ingemar Österberg, a young man with a keen interest in motorbikes, Sylvia learned how to work on a motorbike and how to handle a car with a trailer. She also tried her luck on four wheels in some minor events, among them a couple of stock car races with a 1938 Ford V8 Coupé.

One day in the spring of 1960, Ingemar surprised Sylvia by telling her that he'd entered her in the Nordic Rally for Ladies. Although she already had some experience, she had never taken part in a proper rally before. So, with her husband as co-driver, Sylvia started in her first rally, using the family PV444.

Sylvia won her class and finished seventh overall, out of the eighty starters. This was instantly picked up by the press and for the young class winner the result was even better: for her next event, the 1961 Rally around Lake Malaren, she was lent a rally-prepared PV544 by the local Volvo dealer. Sylvia repaid them by winning the ladies' class.

Tom Trana was a skilled mechanic and a brilliant racing driver too; he was successful in any series he tried. Here he's seen with Gunnar Thermaenius on the 1964 Acropolis Rally.

In 1962 Sylvia took part in her first Rally to the Midnight Sun and finished second in the ladies' class, behind Ewy Rosqvist, who had just left Volvo to become a Mercedes works driver. Gunnar Andersson, manager of the Volvo motorsport department, was always on the lookout for new talent and it was not long before he called her and offered her a position as a Volvo works driver; soon after, Sylvia finished second in the ladies' class in the Finnish Jyväskylä Rally.

Sylvia quickly became one of Volvo's top drivers in PV544s, but she rallied Amazons too. By winning the ladies' class in the Midnight Sun Rally, the Jyväskylä Rally, the Polish Rally and the German Rally, Sylvia became European Champion in 1963. After the Volvo days, in the mid-1960s, she continued to perform well with other makes, first Renault and later Opel. Like so many other rally and racing drivers she came back to the sport in later years, as a co-driver. Sylvia öster-berg died on 13 February 2012.

RALLYING SUCCESS

By 1963 Volvo was shouting very loudly about its motorsport successes, using images of what looked like more or

Sylvia Österberg was better known for competing in PV544s, but she also enjoyed success in an array of Amazons.

**An Amazon prepares to set off on
the 1959 Monte Carlo Rally.**

they would be buying from the Swedish company would be equally durable in everyday use.

Between 1950 and 1964, the major Swedish long-distance rally had been the Rally to the Midnight Sun. In 1965, the name was changed to the KAK Rally (Kungliga Automobil Klubben, the Royal Swedish Automobile Club) and it was no longer run during the summer but in the winter. Tom Trana and co-driver Gunnar Thermaenius won and showed the rally world that they were just as comfortable on snow and ice as on any other surface.

In the Acropolis Rally, however, a white Amazon Sport won, with Carl-Magnus Skogh behind the wheel and Lennart Berggren as co-driver. Tom Trana also competed there, driving the same PV as he did in the KAK Rally, and this was actually the last major event in which a works PV544 was entered.

In the autumn of 1965, tragedy struck the Volvo team during the British Gulf London Rally (formerly the RAC Rally). In his specially built Group 4 Amazon, with a bodywork partly made of glassfibre, Tom Trana collided with a private car during a transport stage and his co-driver Gunnar Thermaenius was killed. Volvo withdrew all its cars at once. Trana was found to be blameless but the tragic episode resulted in no competition activities whatsoever for several months.

For the 1966 season, Volvo was back again and Trana was second in the season opener, the KAK Rally. Unfortunately, tragedy struck once more during the Acropolis Rally in the middle of the summer. Two service mechanics from Volvo were killed when their car was involved in a crash with a truck. After this, Volvo withdrew completely from all competition activities.

With the factory no longer funding any motorsport endeavours, Tom Trana bought an Amazon and continued as a privateer. He became Swedish Group 2 champion and came third in the English Rally, but he really wanted works support. In the spring of 1967 he left Volvo and Carl-Magnus Skogh became a travelling safety ambassador for Volvo, promoting the 144 when it was launched in 1966. Team manager Gunnar Andersson continued to run his special department but on a different scale, concentrating on producing tuning kits and accessories for private Volvo drivers.

Although Volvo officially withdrew from rallying and racing, the interest and enthusiasm of private teams and drivers kept Volvo on top. During the rest of the 1960s hordes of PVs and Amazons were to be seen on racing circuits, on rally roads and in hill climbs both in Sweden and in most other countries.

less standard Amazons being campaigned in rallies. Volvo works drivers Tom Trana, Sylvia Österberg and Gunnar Andersson were all notching up one victory after another during the 1963 and 1964 rallying seasons in both Amazons and PV544s. By this stage Volvo was running adverts that didn't even talk about road cars – merely its cars' successes in rallying, track racing and even economy runs throughout the world.

There were even short biographies of the works drivers included in these advertisements – the company had finally realized that by entering cars which, to the outside world, were essentially the same as those found in its showrooms, buyers would very quickly latch on to the fact that the cars

READY TO RACE

Motorsport was incredibly important to Volvo. It demonstrated the reliability of its cars and helped to inject some glamour into the brand. While factory-supported cars competed in motorsport there was a limit to what the company could achieve with limited resources, so it made sense to encourage as many privateers as possible to don their crash helmets and get competing.

Instead of doing this at a factory level though, Volvo encouraged its importers to offer packages that made it easier for privateers to get into motorsport. Perhaps the importer that tried the hardest was Volvo's German importer, based in Frankfurt, which offered a race-ready Amazon known as the 122SR.

Launched in 1962, the 122SR was one of those under-the-counter specials that wasn't really promoted as such – it was more a case of being in

Almost there; an Amazon on one of the last hairpin bends before it arrives in Monaco on the Monte Carlo Rally.

An Amazon blasts through the Alps on its way to Monte Carlo.

CARL-MAGNUS SKOGH

Carl-Magnus Skogh was born in 1925 in the Swedish province of Dalsland. He wasn't the most spectacular driver but drove efficiently and always chose the fastest line – he had a reputation for looking after his cars and bringing them home in one piece. Between 1963 and 1966 he was a works driver for Volvo; he started as a test driver in 1963 – and was equally at home on a circuit as in the forest.

When Volvo recruited Skogh, he was already a famous and successful driver with many victories under his belt. During these intensive years Skogh won, among others, the prestigious six and twelve-hour races for saloon cars at the Nürburgring in 1964 and the Acropolis Rally in 1965. In the unsuccessful Volvo effort in the 1964 Safari Rally, Skogh was the only driver of the four-strong team who brought his car to the finish, unfortunately outside the time limit.

The Amazon 122S was really Carl-Magnus's car but he also used the PV544 a lot. When Volvo officially withdrew from

Carl-Magnus Skogh enjoyed a long and varied career, racing Volvos from the PV544 right through to a heavily modified 340.

racing and rallying in 1966, Skogh did the same and instead concentrated on the new 144 project, which he helped to market.

In 1969, however, he was talked into making a rally comeback in the Finnish Hankiralli when visiting Finland on business. He used his own company car, a lightly-tuned 145, complete with roof rack and skis. He was still the fastest, and won his class. In 1978 Carl-Magnus Skogh drove his own much-modified Volvo 340, called the XD-1, with a plastic body and a tuned diesel engine in a record attempt, setting a new land speed record for diesel cars with maximum two-litre engine capacity by reaching a measured speed of 209.18km/h (129.9 mph) over the flying kilometre.

the know if you wanted to secure one. Listed officially in the price lists only very briefly – but actually available for several years – the 122SR carried a premium of around 50 per cent over a regular 122S.

Although the 122SR didn't come with a roll cage – one could be fitted of course – it did come with everything that a serious race or rally entrant would want. Alongside a limited-slip differential and stiffer suspension there was a brake servo, while a Plexiglas rear window helped reduce the weight.

Meanwhile, to boost power the engine's compression ratio was raised to 9.5:1 with a slightly spicier camshaft; the result was 90bhp at 5,500rpm and 105lb ft of torque at 3,500rpm. To improve reliability there were stronger big-end bearings and an additional external oil filter plus an oil cooler.

To give the 122SR a sportier look on the outside there were twin spotlamps while on the inside a rev counter was added to the instrumentation along with a Halda Speedpilot.

There was also a fire extinguisher and extra interior lighting, and if the buyer wanted to spend some extra cash there was also the option of thinly padded bucket seats.

The 122SR proved popular with German privateers keen to get into racing or rallying, but by 1965 it had become the less inspiring Limited Edition, robbed of its Halda, limited-slip diff and (bizarrely) the bucket seat option too. Instead the brakes and clutch featured stronger linings and the engine was beefed up significantly to produce a heady 128bhp at 6,000rpm.

To squeeze these extra horses from the 1.8-litre engine, the compression ratio was increased to 11:1, there were bigger valves, and a hotter camshaft was fitted too. With a ported and polished head also included, peak torque was raised to 115lb ft at 4,300rpm – enough to give 0–62mph in just 10.5 seconds and a top speed of 115mph (185km/h). Even better, the Special Edition cost significantly less than the 122SR had done, so it's no wonder the model proved popular, although it's not known how many such cars were sold.

CHAPTER EIGHT

AFTER THE AMAZON

History can be seriously unkind sometimes. In the twenty-first century, there are many who look back on the Volvo 140/160-series and 240/260-series with derision because of their boxy looks. How could Volvo replace something as beautifully designed as the Amazon with something so squared-off?

When it was unveiled on 17 August 1966 Volvo CEO Gunnar Engellau stressed that the 144 was to continue in the same direction as its predecessors, with an emphasis on safety, quality and economy. A great deal of attention had particularly been paid to make the new car a very safe one. Just like Volvos had been first with standard-fitted three-point safety belts, the new 144 was the first car to feature a unique dual-circuit brake system.

The straight body sides provided a roomy and spacious interior. The large glass areas enhanced this impression, besides giving an excellent all-round view. Large parts of the body, like the doors, wheel arches and the glass and roof were carried over to the 240-series and, with only small modifications, were to be kept all through its life to the end in

1993. The interior followed the simplicity of the exterior with uncluttered surfaces, no protruding details, safety padding in places which could be hazardous in a crash and a deeply recessed steering-wheel centre.

The body and chassis had been designed with safety in mind, too, with a safety cage around the passengers and with crumple zones front and rear. The steering column was split and collapsible while four-wheel disc brakes provided ample stopping power.

As with the Amazon, the 144 (internally designated the P1400) was available only as a four-door saloon initially, but in 1967 a two-door version, the 142, was added. The year after, an estate version, the 145, was also introduced. The 140-series was the first Volvo to use the new three-digit designation system. The first digit was for the series, the

The straight-edged 144 came as a rude shock to many, after the curvy Amazon – but it was objectively a much better car.

As with the Amazon, there would be two- and four-door
saloons in the 140 range, along with a five-door estate.

Whereas there had never been a 6-cylinder Amazon,
there was a straight-six option in the 164.

second stood for the number of cylinders in the engine and the third indicated the number of doors. Clear and simple.

However, safe and durable as the 140-series may have been, many people were put off driving something that looked like a tank. By the early 1970s Volvo was clearly sensitive to this. The company even went so far as to put together an advert which stood a 144 next to an M48 tank and then compared the two, using the heading: 'The execution is different, but the concept is basically the same.' It was good to see that Volvo's advertising agency had a sense of humour. But although the advertising department didn't mind some self-deprecation, when it was inflicted by others the marketing department was rather more sober. When *Car* magazine in the UK splashed the 140-series across its front cover in 1972, with the cover line 'The car as an appliance', Volvo was not amused. Advertising was pulled from the publication for a decade and the company's cars continued to be the butt of *Car*'s – and other magazines' – jokes for years to come.

Throughout the 1970s and 1980s and well into the 1990s Volvo was in a styling wilderness. But, to be fair, when the 140 arrived in 1966 it was modern and its styling was crisp. Few of its competitors were especially stylish and the car's build quality certainly put it above pretty much anything else. But over the next twenty years many of Volvo's competitors moved on to more adventurous styling and the company was gradually left further and further behind.

Considering Volvo had built its name on 6-cylinder cars during the pre-war years, such models were notable by their absence from the company's range after the Second World War. In August 1968 this was remedied with the announcement of the 164, effectively a 6-cylinder version of the 144. But it wasn't quite as simple as that, as the 164 had an extended wheelbase to allow for an engine bay long enough to house the longer engine block.

It was a true executive express, and when Autosport tested a 164 in December 1969 it claimed that the 'new Volvo 164 is in the chauffeur-driven class, but with the kind of performance to attract the master to the wheel'. Things got even better in September 1973, with the adoption of fuel injection as standard.

THE 240-SERIES ARRIVES

Production of the 140-series ended in 1974 with the 164 going out of production the following year. The cars were replaced by the 240-series and 264 respectively, with the introduction of the latter paving the way for a whole new range of 6-cylinder cars that would replace the 164. Looking like a cross between the 140/160-series and the VESC (Volvo Experimental Safety Car) of 1972, the 240/260-series

The 240-series was clearly an evolution of the 140 that came before, but
it was even safer, more refined and more efficient too.

Ever since the Duett had been launched, no Volvo range was complete without an estate for middle-class suburbia – in this case, the 245.

was immediately identifiable as a Volvo – square, slabby lines and the look of great weight with little in the way of grace. But it seemed that buyers didn't especially care, because this was a car which built on the selling points of Volvo's earlier cars – safety, comfort and reliability.

Generous crumple zones replaced the particularly ungainly bumpers that had been fitted to the last of the 140/160-series and, although the B20 engine that had been fitted to earlier Volvos was still available, there was a new engine on offer in the 240 in the shape of the B21 overhead cam unit, an engine that was able to meet the increasingly tough emissions standards set by the North American market. Perhaps more importantly, there was a whole range of cars available from the outset because two-, four- and five-door versions of the 140-series had been developed, and the 240 was merely a development of the 140 rather than an all-new model.

Aft of the A-pillars there were relatively few changes, although from the windscreen forward most of the metalwork was new so that MacPherson struts could be adopted along with more progressive crumple zones to make the car safer in the event of a collision. Rack-and-pinion steering also made an appearance, and was much sharper than the cam-and-roller set-up with which the 140 had been equipped. The front and rear ends were now wrapped in thick black rubber-faced bumpers, to comply with tougher US crash regulations, and it was these that gave the car such an exces-

sive appearance. Boxy – and to some eyes bland – styling was one thing, but such obtrusive bumpers really defaced the car in the view of many commentators.

Although the B20 engine was still available in the entry-level 240, the principal power unit was the new B21, now available in either carburetted or fuel-injected forms. Displacing 2127cc, this new powerplant shared much – at least on paper – with the B20 engine that had been fitted to Volvos for so many years. But the really big news was the 260, which featured a completely new engine – the 2.7-litre 'Douvrin' 90-degree V6 unit that resulted from an alliance with Peugeot and Renault. This powerplant, badged the B27, was available with fuel injection or twin carburettors and featured twin chain-driven overhead camshafts. Something that was especially significant about the B27 engine was that it was no longer than Volvo's 4-cylinder units, which meant that if a 4-cylinder car needed to be uprated to 6-cylinder specification, the front of the car – or at least the engine bay – no longer had to be completely re-engineered to accept the larger powerplant.

Throughout the 1970s and 1980s the 240- and 260-series would do sterling work for Volvo, bolstered by the smaller 340- and 360-series models that had arrived in 1975. Along the way (in 1979), Volvo had launched its first production diesel car. Developed in conjunction with Volkswagen, the D24 engine was the world's first 6-cylinder diesel powerplant for use in a passenger car. Displacing 2383cc, this

MERGERS AND ACQUISITIONS

As early as the late 1960s, Volvo had been eyeing up the Dutch manufacturer DAF with a view to a merger. With both companies producing heavy commercial vehicles in the same sector, it made sense to share resources rather than compete with each other, but DAF had other ideas. It wasn't its truck division that it wanted to share with Volvo, but its car manufacturing facility. In 1969 the Van Doorne family which headed DAF approached Volvo with a view to taking over their car-building business. At that time Håkan Frisinger was president of the Volvo Car Corporation and after a year of studying DAF's car-making business he concluded that Volvo would be better off not getting involved.

But within a year everything had changed. Volvo had a new president in Pehr Gyllenhammar and DAF had made some changes to its 55 model, which had become the 66. Sales had increased and the DAF operation was now profitable. Gyllenhammar was keen to expand Volvo and acquiring DAF was a quick way of achieving that, so on 1 January 1973 Volvo become the owner of one third of DAF. At first the cars retained DAF badging, while their quality was improved to Volvo levels – the first DAFs built after the Volvo takeover were

Turning a DAF into a Volvo required plenty of effort; safety levels and build quality both needed to be improved radically.

still pretty shoddily built and damaging the reputation of the parent company would have been a real possibility if Volvo badges had been used instead.

The result was some rapid re-engineering of the car, and in summer 1975 the DAF name gave way to Volvo's, with the 66 looking like a Swedish product rather than a Dutch one from then on. The name change coincided with the acquisition of 75 per cent of DAF by Volvo, along with the car production facility at Born in the Netherlands.

To free up some capital so that its newly launched 343 could be developed, Volvo reduced its stake in DAF from 75 per cent to 55 per cent in 1978. Initially the Van Doorne family retained an interest in the company, but when Volvo reduced its interest it was the Dutch government that bought all the extra shares. So Volvo retained a controlling stake in DAF but the Dutch government, which held the other 45 per cent of the shares, was able to inject some much-needed cash into the company so that the 300-series could be developed properly.

While the 343 was a Volvo confection, it took some financial jiggery-pokery with its DAF shares to be able to fund the car's development properly.

overhead cam unit featured an aluminium cylinder head and was basically a 6-cylinder version of the VW/Audi five-cylinder unit.

From the end of 1982 the 242, 244 and 245 badges gave way to a straightforward 240-series tag, the range being offered with a choice of three engines and manual or automatic transmissions. Car reviewers may have avoided them (there was little press coverage of the 240 range after 1981) but it made no difference – sales continued to boom, which is why Volvo just couldn't pull the plug. But time was finally called on 5 May 1993 when the last 240 was built.

VOLVO PUSHES UPMARKET

As far back as the mid-1970s the management of Volvo had realized that if they didn't start some major product develop-

ment soon, the company would be in trouble. Even if they'd begun developing a new car there and then it would be well into the 1980s before the fruits of their labours would be seen, so something had to be done, and fast. As a result Jan Wilsgaard started to put some proposals together, and before long he had around fifty sketches of cars which could conceivably become Volvo's all-new car to be launched in the early 1980s. Although the car was to have dimensions very similar to those of the 240, there would be much more interior space.

Twenty of these designs progressed to full-size drawings, which was then reduced to eight full-scale clay models. Of these a pair of designs was chosen for further development with mock-up interiors being created, and there was a major input from technical and marketing staff. The car was so important to Volvo that it did a huge amount of consultation before committing anything from this project to production.

It may have been spectacularly safe and surprisingly efficient, but many were put off the 740 and 760 by its angular design.

THE MERGERS THAT DIDN'T HAPPEN: SAAB

The 1970s was a very unstable decade for Volvo, just as it was for most other car manufacturers. As a result the company was always looking at opportunities to share resources and expand its operations.

In May 1977 the boards of Volvo and Saab announced they were to merge, to form a new company called Volvo-Saab-Scania AB which would be headed by Pehr Gyllenhammar, CEO of Volvo. The overcapacity that ran throughout the car manufacturing industry during the 1970s, along with the erratic economic fortunes of the developed world, made such a proposition attractive.

By pooling resources it was estimated that billions of kronor could be saved – platforms could be shared, parts could be bought in or manufactured in greater quantities, and instead of investing in two models for the same sector it would be possible to develop just one.

But it quickly became clear to the directors of Saab that Volvo would be the dominant partner (despite the agreement being that it would be a merger rather than a takeover), and less than three months later it was announced that the deal was off, the management of Volvo having decided that they could wait no longer for the members of the executive board of Saab-Scania to make their minds up.

But Pehr Gyllenhammar was still keen to expand, and he set up talks with the Norwegian government to see if they would be keen on financing the company. In May 1978 the talks were made public when it was announced that, in return for SKr750m, Norway would get a 40 per cent share of Volvo. The deal was signed in December 1978 but within weeks the company's shareholders were expressing their fury about the proposals and were insistent that such a deal should never happen. They got their way and the deal was called off.

The result was the 760, shown publicly for the first time in February 1982. The initial reaction was mixed, with many commentators deciding very quickly that the styling was already very dated. As well as finding its square lines off-putting, many people thought it was too big, although it was actually the same size as the 240, albeit with a significantly longer wheelbase – 109 inches (2,768mm) against 104 inches (2,641mm) – while also being shorter, lower and lighter than the 260.

Most people who reviewed the 760 reckoned that the styling wasn't nearly imaginative enough, but at least the car was good to drive. American magazine *Car & Driver* reckoned the 760's styling would always be much more palatable to transatlantic buyers than to European ones. But *Road & Track* was kinder, claiming that although it wasn't attractive, the 760 was good to drive. They even singled out the live rear axle as being better than many independent systems because Volvo had taken the time to engineer it properly so that the roadholding and handling were as good as the ride. When *Car* magazine evaluated one it was unequivocal with its verdict – this was a damn good car that was let down by its looks. It handled well, was spacious, comfortable and well equipped, and was blessed with good performance.

Car's report also mentioned that the 240-series would be pensioned off within two years, but in fact it soldiered on for more than a decade, and because the 760 cost significantly

more than the 240 it made sense to introduce something between the two. The result was the 740, which arrived in the spring of 1984. Prices were lower because equipment levels were rather less generous.

Any doubts about the success of the 700-series, either during the development process or since the launch, had been dispelled by the end of 1984. In 1983, the car's first full year of sales, the 760 accounted for 12 per cent of cars sold by Volvo. This rose much further the following year and it was clear that offering owners of the most expensive 240s and 260s an alternative to a Mercedes or BMW was just what had been needed. Despite their satisfaction with Volvo's products, when they wanted to upgrade to something more luxurious and exclusive they had no alternative but to switch allegiances – now they could stay with Volvo.

ENTER THE 940 AND 960

Production of the 740 and 760 range ended in 1990, when the cars were replaced by the 940 and 960 respectively. But these weren't all-new cars – they were based heavily on their predecessors and featured few significant changes. The most obvious improvement was in the styling, which had been softened at both ends so that the car looked more contemporary. But once more – as has so often been the case with Volvos – the biggest change, at least for the 960, was under the bonnet. This brought the option of a 2922cc 6-cylinder powerplant, which was not only the most powerful engine ever produced by Volvo for any of its cars, but also signalled the demise of the PRV engine in Volvo's line-up, which had been developed in partnership with Peugeot and Renault in the 1970s.

The 900-series was in production for eight years, from 1990 until 1998. In that time there was almost no development of the car, the most significant change being the adoption of Volvo's patented SIPS (Side Impact Protection System) at the end of 1991. For some inexplicable reason the 960 was renamed in 1996 but not the 940: 960 saloons became known as the S90 while estate versions carried V90 badges. But the 900-series' going out of production was a significant step for Volvo, because it marked the end of the big, boxy saloon for which the company had become famous. Instead a new generation of luxury cars would arrive, bringing softer lines and excellent dynamics while retaining all the marque's safety credentials. At last, drivers would no longer have to justify their ownership of a Volvo.

THE RENAULT PARTNERSHIP

By the end of the 1970s it was clear to Volvo that it couldn't afford to continue to develop its cars without some outside financial assistance. The answer proved to be an alliance with Renault, which was announced on 19 December 1979. Under the terms of the deal Renault would acquire 10 per cent of Volvo for SKr330m, with the option of increasing its shareholding to first 15 and then 20 per cent.

In the event Renault exercised its option to increase its stake to 15 per cent in 1981, but once things had started to pick up for Volvo the decision was made to buy back all but 9.4 per cent of the shares in 1983, with the rest of the shares being purchased the following year.

But this wasn't the end for Renault and Volvo in terms of a partnership, as on 23 February 1990 the announcement was made that the two companies were to merge. This was the biggest news story ever to hit the Swedish motor industry and it was clear that Volvo's shareholders weren't going to take it lying down. Initially Volvo's shares increased in value as the news was greeted positively, but this very quickly changed once it became obvious that Volvo was really being swallowed up by the French car manufacturer. Volvo claimed it could save SKr25 billion over the next decade, but nothing happened until September 1993.

Since the announcement had first been made that the two companies were to form an alliance, Volvo had done badly while Renault had done well in the marketplace. Volvo had been forced to enter into a round of cost-cutting measures because of major losses – the company posted its first loss since 1929, just two years after it had first been formed. Declining sales and falling exchange rates led to enforced early retirements, redundancies and other measures that would hopefully shore up Volvo's finances. Meanwhile Renault's sales remained fairly buoyant and by 2 December 1993 things came to a head, and a board meeting was called that would settle the matter for good. It was clear that not only were most of the Volvo shareholders against a merger, but so were most of the company's top managers. The result was the mass resignation of Volvo President Pehr Gyllenhammar and the entire board.

Teaming up with Renault meant Volvo could use the French company's parts bin for its own cars, which is why many Volvos of the 1990s featured Renault power – such as this 480ES.

The 960 was the first sign of Volvo's design softening – although it was hardly what you could call curvy.

THE 850: A NEW TYPE OF VOLVO

Although the introduction of the 850 in 1992 didn't appear especially significant to the casual observer, it marked a new path for Volvo. Not only was it the first of a new generation of more rounded models, but great attention had been paid to the car's dynamics, with completely new delta-link rear suspension endowing the car with handling equal to the best of its competitors. It also featured front-wheel drive, which was not only unusual for a Volvo (although the 400-series had offered this since 1985) but was also very unusual for the class. High power outputs were common in this size of car, and the best end to channel lots of power through isn't necessarily the front.

By the time the 850 T5-R made its appearance in 1994 it was putting 250bhp through the front wheels, something that didn't do its tyres any favours. It was the 850GLT that

single-handedly began to turn round the image of Volvo, because although it was still pretty boxy by anybody's standards, this was the model that showed dynamics were no longer unimportant to the company. Indeed the marketing campaign constructed around the 850 focused on dynamics ahead of everything else – including safety. Yet while any seriously powerful car would always have rear-wheel drive, here was an executive performance car that was rapid, surefooted and handled well.

The result of all this effort on the part of Volvo certainly paid dividends. As *Autocar* wrote of the 2.5-litre 850:

> *Anyone who doesn't know by now that Volvo has produced a real driver's car in the 850 must live on another planet. The arrival of this well-built, spacious, front-drive five-cylinder saloon with zestful performance and rewarding handling has been one of the most encouraging automotive stories of 1992.*

The last of the truly boxy designs, the 850 was revolutionary for Volvo in that it was a car that was genuinely great to drive.

THE MITSUBISHI PARTNERSHIP

In the early 1990s Volvo found itself looking for a company with which it could develop a new small car to replace the 400-series. That company turned out to be Mitsubishi, and in conjunction with the Dutch government a factory was set up in Born, in the Netherlands, to build a new range of small cars for the two companies. Volvo already had an alliance with the Dutch government going back to the late 1970s when Volvo had bought DAF. The introduction of Mitsubishi into the plan meant there was more capital available to develop a car, and the Nedcar name was chosen for the company that would facilitate this.

Nedcar would develop and build cars for both Volvo and Mitsubishi while the two car makers would retain their own separate sales and marketing groups. By 1995 Volvo was producing its S40 alongside Mitsubishi's Carisma and by October 1997 a deal was in place for Volvo to market Mitsubishi's Canter light truck.

When Mitsubishi introduced its GDI (Gasoline Direct Injection) engine in 1997 the cooperation expanded with the fitting of the powerplant to the V40 and S40 from the following year. When the Nedcar project had been set up the agreement had always been for the Dutch government to sell its stake in 1998, and, as planned, Mitsubishi and Volvo bought the government's shareholding – at about the same time as Ford was looking at buying Volvo.

Things progressed from there with the companies taking a stake in each other, and the intention was to develop trucks and buses together. But there was a fly in the ointment, because Volvo's largest competitor, DaimlerChrysler, acquired a majority shareholding in Mitsubishi at the start of 2001. As a result Volvo was obliged to sell its interest in Mitsubishi to DaimlerChrysler in April 2001 and cut its ties with the Japanese company.

Mitsubishi had the Carisma while Volvo had the S40 and V40 – all of which were as mediocre as each other.

The next major step for Volvo was the introduction of its first four-wheel-drive production car. Launched at the 1995 Geneva Motor Show, the 4WD 850 estate wasn't intended to be an off-roader – instead it marked Volvo's attempt at making the car even safer by offering greater traction when driving conditions were less than ideal. It wouldn't go into production until the spring of the following year, with the North American market the main focus for sales.

A NEW SMALL CAR – AND A COUPÉ

The four-wheel-drive 850 could never be seen as anything more than just a niche model; the really significant introduction for Volvo in 1995 was that of the S40. Launched at the Paris motor show, this was the car that would replace the 400-series, although those cars continued to be built alongside the S40 in the Netherlands until the end of the following year. Under the skin the car shared much with Mitsubishi's new Carisma, and between them the S40, Carisma and V40 – introduced at the end of the year – would underwhelm the motoring press with their completely unexceptional dynamics.

Altogether more palatable was the introduction of the C70, which marked a welcome return for Volvo to the sports coupé market. First shown at the 1996 Paris motor show, the C70 was developed jointly by Volvo and Tom Walkinshaw Racing. Since the demise of the P1900 in 1957, Volvo hadn't offered a convertible in its range; that was remedied with the launch at the 1997 Detroit Motor Show of the rag-top C70. The choice of venue for the launch signalled very clearly that the North American market was the one for which the car had been developed, and once more the work had been done by TWR. In the event the convertible version of the C70 would outlive the closed car, with the latter version being taken out of production at the end of 2002 to focus on the more glamorous open-topped derivative.

For consistency across the range the big saloons and estates were renamed in 1996 (for the 1997 model year), when they became the S70 and V70 respectively. With 'S' standing for Saloon and 'V' for Versatility, the main changes to the cars were cosmetic, with a new front end and revisions to the saloon's rear-end styling. By the time these cars were taken out of production in 2000 they were looking desperately long in the tooth, descended in their styling as they were from the 700-series, which had been launched in 1982 – and which had been developed at the end of the

After years of building sensible cars that were worthy but often a bit dull, the C70 showed that Volvo could do aspirational. This was also the first convertible the company had offered since the ill-fated P1900 of the 1950s.

1970s. So the arrival of the S80 saloon in the summer of 1998 was just the ticket; an estate – confusingly retaining the V70 name – made its debut at the 2000 Detroit Motor Show.

The launch of this new executive contender from Volvo was the start of a new design direction – Peter Horbury's design team was moving away from straight lines to softer, more flowing curves. The results were instant – as soon as the new car was shown the company was viewed in a different light. As *Autocar* commented:

> *This is one good-looking car. And it's a Volvo. Let the ramifications of that sink in and it's hard not to believe that the new S80 is perhaps the most revolutionary Volvo ever – a real mould-breaker.*

And it was, because suddenly drivers were no longer embarrassed to admit that the keys in their pocket were for a Volvo.

VOLVO EMBRACES THE TWENTY-FIRST CENTURY

By autumn 2000 the final gap in the Volvo range had been filled. With extra-large and medium estates and saloons available, all that was needed was something in between. For some reason Volvo decided that a mid-range estate wasn't something that it wanted to offer, so in the event just a four-door saloon arrived, wearing the S60 badge and slotting into the range below the S80.

Although the arrival of the S60 seemed to give Volvo a complete range, market trends meant the portfolio had a significant gap in it for as long as an off-roader, or SUV (Sport Utility Vehicle) wasn't offered. The ACC (Adventure Concept Car), which was first unveiled at the 2001 Detroit show gave a taster of what was to come a full two years before the car was available in production form, as the XC90. As soon as it was launched the Volvo received an overwhelmingly positive reception, things helped by the fact that it was the first SUV to offer seven seats – although the cramped third row was strictly for children only.

Despite its huge popularity, the XC90 didn't usher in a change of fortunes or reputation for Volvo. Most buyers continued to see it as a quirky Swedish company that produced rather staid designs that weren't quite as good as those produced by rivals – especially German rivals. A sort of Swedish Jaguar, which also sat in Ford's Premier Automotive Group.

Over the next few years there would be a raft of new models launched, including the compact V50 estate in 2004, an all-new S60 (this time with an accompanying V60 estate) in 2010 and a compact SUV to sit below the XC90 – the XC60 of 2008. There would also be an all-new C70, this time a coupé-cabriolet, launched in 2006. Perhaps most important to the company, though, was the all-new V40, first sold in 2012. As the company's most popular car in many key markets, Volvo's smallest car was also key to maintaining sales and aiding cashflow as a result.

At the time of writing (2015) Volvo appears to have an exciting future, with an all-new XC90 just hitting the market and an all-new platform (dubbed SPA) created, ready to underpin all of the company's models for the next few years. Designed to carry Volvo's new range of petrol and diesel engines along with an array of hybrid powertrains, it's fair to say that Volvo has come a long way since the OV4 and PV4 of 1927!

Volvo has never done trendy, but SUVs were all the rage when the XC90 was launched in 2003. Volvo couldn't build the XC90 fast enough, such was demand. This is the second-generation car, launched in 2015.

VOLVO LOSES ITS INDEPENDENCE

Volvo's acquisition by an American company in 1999 was a move that had nearly happened seventy years before. In 1929 Volvo had yet to make a profit and its owner, SKF, was on the verge of giving up hope. The SKF President, Björn Prytz, had begun talks with Charles Nash, head of America's giant Nash Corporation, with a view to selling the Swedish company. Charles Nash had already set sail to sign the deal when Assar Gabrielsson persuaded Prytz not to sell – Gabrielsson had to put forward 220,000 kronor of his own money to secure the company's future.

The gamble paid off, as by September 1929 Volvo was operating at a profit. A slip into the red the following month was a blip and from November onwards the company stayed resolutely in the black – a position that would have been rather more appealing to Ford than the mass of red ink on the balance sheets when Nash had been approached seven decades earlier.

On 28 January 1999 it was announced that Volvo Cars would be bought by the Ford Motor Company, leaving the rest of the Volvo Group to manufacture trucks and buses. The cost of the sale was SKr50 billion ($6bn), a price that reflected Volvo's healthy, profit-making status. But, despite this profitability, Volvo had become too small to be able to compete with the big manufacturers as it didn't enjoy their economies of scale.

A shareholders' meeting on 8 March 1999 approved the takeover and that paved the way for Volvo to become one of the marques in Ford's Premier Automotive Group – along with Aston Martin, Jaguar, Lincoln and Land Rover. As part of PAG, Volvo's range expanded significantly – but Ford still couldn't make any money out of it. After Ford sold Jaguar Land Rover to Tata in 2008, the company initially decided to keep Volvo, the plan being to push it further upmarket.

But by December 2008 Volvo was up for sale again, priced at a rumoured US$6 billion. It was also rumoured that Volkswagen would buy the company, but in the end (in December 2009) it was Chinese company Geely Holding Group that took over Volvo, having paid just US$1.5 billion for it. A definitive agreement was signed on 28 March 2010, for $1.8 billion; the deal was closed just over four months later.

**When it was unveiled in 2011, there were many who hoped that the
Universe concept didn't represent the future for Volvo.**

CHAPTER NINE

BUYING AN AMAZON

If only all classics had been engineered to the levels of the Volvo Amazon, thousands more cars would have survived from the 1950s and 1960s. But, as with any car, the Amazon can rust and wear out, so in this chapter we'll consider what you need to look for when buying one of these saloons or estates. Once again big thanks are due to Rob and Emma Henchoz at Amazon Cars, who have offered assistance galore to ensure the information here is accurate.

BODYWORK

Despite all Amazons now being many decades old, serious rust isn't normally too much of a problem. What can turn an Amazon from a great example to a basket case is a leaking front or rear screen, so your first port of call should be the screen surrounds – once water gets in, it'll wreak havoc. The problem lies in the fact that modern sealing techniques aren't much use – old-fashioned mastic needs to be used to ensure the aperture stays watertight.

If the screens have been leaking, the corners of the bulk-head are the first to go – this is best checked from the engine bay. Also vulnerable are the walls of the footwells; to check the condition of these you'll have to remove the cardboard trim panels. A sodden driver's footwell can also be the result of a failed heater valve; replacements were very expensive and are unobtainable at the time of writing, but workarounds are possible.

The first area to corrode is normally the rear wheel arches, although serious rot is unlikely. The thing to look out for is poorly repaired rust, as the wheel arch lip is double-skinned and some repairers don't recreate the seam by the corner of the rear door.

While you're at the back of the car, check the panels below the rear wings, which get covered in road dirt then rot from behind a cheap repair panel. If corrosion has advanced it may have attacked the chassis legs, so it's worth checking from inside the boot just how much rust there is. While you're inspecting inside the boot, look for a rotten spare wheel well as the drain hole can get blocked. Also examine the bottom edge of the boot lid, which is double-skinned and prone to rust.

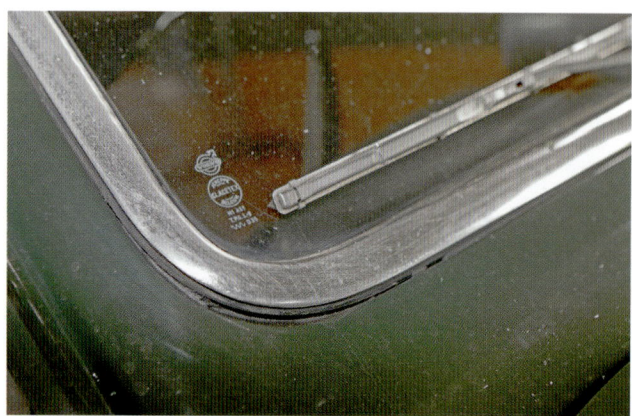

Check the screen surrounds for evidence of them letting water into the cabin.

The spare wheel well collects water if the boot seals are leaking; it'll then rot out.

The bottom of the front wings can corrode along with the lower edges of the doors; while you're on your knees checking these, take a look at the underside of the doors and the inner wings. Also inspect the sills along their entire length as well as the front and rear wheel arches. Not only do the sills get attacked by corrosion that works its way out from inside, but injudicious jacking up of the car can lead to distortion of the sills – sometimes the correct jacking points aren't used.

Amazon estates don't suffer from rotten spare wheel wells as the layout is different, but the split tailgate can corrode badly, so inspect both halves carefully. Condensation can seep under the rear side window seals, so check the metalwork below this seal to make sure it's intact; also take a look at the top of the upper tailgate.

It's unlikely that there will be any corrosion in the roof panel, but there could be some in the rain gutters that run down each side. While these don't usually give problems, if anything has been clamped to them – such as a roof rack – the paint may well have been damaged. Once this has happened, corrosion is bound to follow, with repairs awkward.

On any Amazon you need to check the front inner wings as they're prone to corroding along their top edge, which is reinforced. Repair panels are available, but things are complicated by the fact that the outer wings are bolted to this reinforced top edge, through a rail – which also rusts badly.

The area behind the headlamp bowls gets full of mud, which rots out the bowl itself, along with the wing. New wings are just bolted on and plastic bowls are available, so repairs aren't difficult. The bottom

edge of the bonnet and the seams around the grille can also rust, but major corrosion is unlikely.

The really good news is that all the panels you're likely to need are generally available, and although many are repro they generally fit very well. Even better, most of them are

The wing and door bottoms can corrode, sometimes from the inside out.

The split tailgate of the estate can corrode spectacularly, especially along its lower edge, as here.

Lift the bonnet to check the edge of the front inner wings, as rot here is common.

ABOVE RIGHT: **The rear wheel arches can blister from constant exposure to road debris; if left, they'll end up like this.**

ABOVE LEFT: **The rear quarter panels get bombarded with road debris, then end up rotting away if they're not kept rustproofed.**

BOTTOM LEFT: **The top of the headlamps can rust – although things are rarely as bad as here.**

eminently affordable, apart from front wings, which tend to be very expensive.

ENGINE

Three engines sizes were available in the Amazon, the most common being the 1780cc B18 unit along with the 1990cc B20 that was used for the last of the cars. The earlier 1580cc B16 engine is now very rare; it's the only three-bearing unit as the other two have five main bearings. Parts to rebuild the B18 and B20 engine are easy enough to find, but the 1.6-litre unit costs more to rebuild because parts for it aren't as easy to find – if you can track them down at all.

Because the B20 engine wasn't introduced into the Amazon range until mid-1968, few cars left the factory with this powerplant fitted. With the B16 engine killed off from 1961,

by far the majority of Amazons were built with a B18 power-plant. By now, though, many Amazons have had a B20 engine fitted to replace whatever was already there; with the B20 being just a development of the B18 unit, such transplants are very straightforward.

Both the B18 and B20 engines are durable, racking up 250,000+ miles quite happily as long as they've had regular oil changes. Make sure the oil filter is the correct Volvo item, complete with non-return valve, as anything less will starve the bearings of oil when starting from cold.

If there's a thump like worn big-end bearings at cruising speed it's probably because the timing gears have worn; sometimes it sounds more like a can of nails. This tends to happen from around 90,000 miles, by which point the crankshaft will also be suffering from increased play in the bearings.

Whereas the B18 engine has a forged camshaft, the B20 has a cast item. Predictably, the result is that these later

The **B18 engine** is the most common Amazon powerplant – and it's a tough unit too.

camshafts aren't as durable as their earlier counterparts, with wear almost always occurring first on number four cylinder, leading to a loss of power. What tends to lead to a loss of power more often, however, is broken piston rings, especially where the older engines are concerned.

Oil consumption also shouldn't be especially high, although once an engine has clocked up 60,000 miles it tends to burn a bit more oil. Incredibly, Volvo doesn't specifically recommend a rebuild until an engine is getting through a pint of oil every 200 miles. The problem is that it's easy to assume that an engine is burning oil when in fact it's leaking it.

There's an array of gaskets around the engine that can leak oil, including the cork item for the sump as well as the ones for the fuel pump and the valve cover. If the retaining bolts for the cover are overtightened, the cover will distort so it'll never seal properly. The front and rear crankshaft seals can also leak as they're made of felt so they're not especially tough – but they can be replaced with modern neoprene seals, which are far more effective.

If a lot of oil is escaping from the engine, the chances are it'll find its way onto the engine mountings, which then perish, leading to the engine moving about noticeably. The left-hand mount tends to take the brunt of this and if things are allowed to get really bad the engine may move about enough for the upper radiator support bracket to shear.

Oil pressure should be around 40psi at idle once the engine has warmed up, while 50–55psi should be showing once the car is on the move. Once this drops significantly, assume a rebuild is due – by this point blue exhaust smoke will be evident under acceleration, as oil is burned in the combustion chambers.

Although the engines aren't frugal, especially heavy fuel consumption is probably due to a duff thermostat, allowing the engine to run cool. The other likely reason is because the needles have worn in the carbs if the original Strombergs are still fitted. If there are SUs installed instead, it'll be down to the jets needing to be replaced. Amazons built from 1967 may well have a single Stromberg fitted, while earlier cars had a single Zenith. Cars with twin carbs were always fitted with SU HS6 items, and while there were a couple of factory alternatives, the chances of you seeing such a car are minimal.

Engine ancillaries

If there are any signs of the engine having overheated, it's worth checking what type of water pump is fitted. Some cheap pattern pumps feature pressed-steel impellors, which rust away; a genuine pump will have a cast impellor, which

Although the exhaust system is usually pretty durable, the manifolds have a tendency to crack.

The SU carburettors (seen here) tend to be more reliable than the Zenith and Zenith-Stromberg alternatives.

is far more durable. These will easily last 60,000 miles or more – much more if the fan belt hasn't been overtightened, putting strain on the bearings.

Exhausts can prove to be more short-lived than you'd think, and while most Amazons still have the manifold that was fitted at the factory, few cars will still feature the rest of the original system. However, while exhaust corrosion is easy enough to fix – simply by replacing the system, probably with a set of fit-and-forget stainless-steel pipes – you're surprisingly likely to experience issues with the various manifolds fitted. The B16 exhaust manifold has a tendency to crack, so listen for blowing – the same goes for B18 and B20 manifolds, which are most likely to be damaged between cylinders two and three. However, such occurrences aren't all that common on the B18 and B20 engines.

The Zenith carburettors fitted to Amazons up to 1966 tend to leak as they get older, while the carburettor bodies can get damaged through being installed badly – which makes reliable rebuilds that much trickier. From 1966 there were Zenith-Stromberg carbs fitted, and these usually suffer

from worn jets and needles leading to poor running, high fuel consumption and inflated exhaust emissions. These carbs can be rebuilt; while you're at it, it may be necessary to pay some attention to the butterfly valve spindles too, which also tend to wear after tens of thousands of miles have been racked up.

Sportier Amazons were fitted with twin SUs, the most likely problem with these also being worn butterfly valve spindles. Again, high fuel consumption and exhaust emissions are the result, along with the possibility of uneven running. The spindles can be rebushed; if there's any detectable play in them the job will need to be done. Expect to have to do this every 30,000 miles or so.

TRANSMISSION

Amazon transmissions are amazingly durable, whichever unit is fitted. Although three-speed manual or automatic gearboxes will be found on some cars, the chances are you'll

It's worth seeking out a car with an overdrive gearbox. Converting is possible but expensive.

be looking at a four-speed unit with or without overdrive. It's well worth having overdrive, but even if the car you're looking at doesn't have it, upgrading the gearbox isn't difficult – but it will cost a fair chunk of cash.

You can expect to get at least 150,000 miles out of any Amazon gearbox, as long as the fluid levels are maintained. The top cover of manual gearboxes tends to wear from this mileage, thanks to the long gear lever constantly rubbing against it – your best bet is to find a decent used replacement.

If the gearbox doesn't seem very secure it's probably moving about because its rear mounting has sheared. This happens after it's been soaked in gearbox oil, which has escaped via a failed seal at the tail of the box. Alternatively it could be that the rear output shaft seal has failed.

Driveshafts, rear axles and propshafts are all strong, but the rubber centre bearing of the latter wears eventually. Replacements are available, but bear in mind that three designs of propshaft were fitted. The B16 and early B18 fea-

As with any old car, the universal joints in the propshaft wear out leading to clonks as drive is taken up.

Rear axles are very strong, but all sorts of ratios were offered so you need to ensure the correct one is fitted.

tured one type, the later B18 another and the B20 a different spec again, although the latter two are very similar – to the point of being interchangeable.

Differentials are another potential minefield as there were all sorts of ratios available depending on the car's original engine and gearbox. All Spicer diffs are bomb-proof though, and while the ENV units aren't as strong, wear is unlikely to be an issue on well-maintained cars.

Clutches tend to last very well, and all parts are available to keep on top of things. Amazons with a single-circuit braking system have a hydraulically operated clutch while dual-circuit cars have a cable-operated clutch. As a result you need to check for leaks with the former and poor adjustment with the latter. If a cable-operated clutch is overtightened it'll lead to the clutch being very stiff and the cable – or more likely the operating arm at the bellhousing – is also likely to break prematurely.

STEERING AND SUSPENSION

With no power assistance to complicate things, the Amazon's steering system is tough and shouldn't give any cause for concern. However, on cars built up to spring 1967 there's a universal joint fibre disc in the steering column, which can

wear – although it's unlikely to fail altogether, even if it's worn. Later cars have a two-piece collapsible column that doesn't need any checking or maintenance.

The front suspension is straightforward, being of a double-wishbone design that requires little in the way of maintenance. The key thing to check is the state of each bush in the wishbone bushes where they're attached to the front crossmember. While these rubber bushes age and perish as a result, the ageing process can be accelerated by oil dripping onto them from a leaking front crankshaft seal. It's best to fit polyurethane replacements as they're more durable but still very cheap; it's easy to do the work yourself.

Earlier Amazons featured track rod ends with grease nipples, while until 1965 there was also a nipple in the upper ball joints – until 1968, the steering arm also needed to be lubricated regularly. As long as these items are maintained properly they won't wear, but not all owners cherish their Amazons as much as they should, which is why it's worth checking for wear. Also make sure the springs are intact; cars on their original coils can snap at the bottom, but replacements are available and easy to fit.

The rear suspension is equally problem-free on post-1966 cars, which used a twin-trailing-arm design. But earlier Amazons featured a single radius arm of uncharacteristically

The Amazon featured a steering box rather than a rack-and-pinion set-up.

Pre-1966 Amazons feature a weak rear suspension design, but later cars are stronger.

poor design. Being of pressed steel they rust badly, although most cars have had replacements fitted by now.

Estates have a problem of their own with the rear suspension, as their much more heavyweight 140-style radius arms contain very large rubber and aluminium bushes. Because of the higher potential loadings on these cars due to the greater weight, the arms can crack under the strain – although such occurrences are rare. What's more likely to be an issue is the big bush breaking up when the bolts seize in the alloy tubes, creating lots of loose suspension knocks.

WHEELS AND BRAKES

Cars built up to 1964 were fitted with solid steel disc wheels, while later models featured vented items. Problems are unlikely but it's still worth checking for heavy corrosion, especially within any seams. Early Amazons came with chrome-plated steel hubcaps, which tend to rust badly, but replacements are available. Incidentally, estates and 123GTs

featured 4.5J wheels, and saloons had 4J items, but some Amazons now sport repro 5J wheels; they allow modern rubber to be fitted more easily.

All Amazons came with pressed-steel wheels as standard, but many owners have turned to alloy wheels so they can fit wider tyres.

The Amazon's braking system can be trouble-free on cars that are maintained properly, but there are issues that can crop up – especially on the single-circuit cars that were built up to 1968. Until 1964 most Amazons featured drum brakes all round; until 1961 none of the various versions had front discs, and even then it was only the sports models. It's possible to convert to front discs but not really necessary as the parts are all available to maintain the drum system and they're up to the job if properly maintained.

The optional remote Girling servo on the B16 and B18 can suffer from a perished diaphragm, leading to the brake fluid being sucked into the engine – a drop in the brake fluid level will soon be obvious, and potentially catastrophic if you don't stay on top of the situation. Rebuild kits are available but you're better off buying a replacement Lockheed servo instead.

Not all Amazons had a servo, though; the single-circuit system didn't get one as standard until 1967. It was made by Girling, and if there isn't a servo fitted some owners reckon it's worth installing one. But don't assume this is an essential move; Rob Henchoz doesn't agree, as he thinks the brakes are plenty strong enough without any assistance. The B20 got one as standard, however, along with dual-circuit brakes; earlier cars featured a single-circuit design.

Where this single-circuit system is installed, the front calipers feature three pistons; dual-circuit calipers have four pistons. The seals for these single-circuit pistons tend not to be very durable, and once they've perished they'll let in water and dirt, leading to the pistons seizing. It's easy enough to rebuild the calipers, however – it's just a question of spotting that there's a problem that needs to be fixed.

The rear brakes aren't always immune from problems either. The best thing you can do is to stay on top of the rear brake adjusters in terms of keeping things lubricated and free to move. The steel adjuster runs in an aluminium housing, so electrolytic corrosion is guaranteed as soon as any moisture gets in. Once this has happened, it all seizes solid and if left for too long the only way of effectively fixing things is to replace everything.

The braking system changed significantly over the years, with some set-ups more reliable than others.

Not all Amazons got a brake servo; there's some debate about whether such a fitment is essential or not.

The dual-circuit braking system tends to be much more reliable, except for the self-adjusters at the rear: replace these with the earlier Girling adjusters if necessary. This potential issue apart, it's just a question of checking that the system hasn't worn out. Scored or corroded discs and tired pads are the most likely issues you'll have to contend with, but it's all fixed easily enough as all of the parts are available.

TRIM AND ELECTRICS

Although most of the exterior trim is either stainless steel or anodized aluminium, and hence immune to corrosion, the front and rear bumpers are heavy, chrome-plated affairs, which are very expensive to repair or replace. Each unit consists of three parts plus the irons, each of which is of thick steel, so if bent they're not easy to straighten out.

The rest of the brightwork doesn't give any problems, although replacing the aluminium strips at the base of the C-pillar is difficult because they're secured by fastenings behind the headlining. Even the mazak parts, which on most cars pit badly, don't corrode much on the Amazon because they're much higher quality than is usual. The grilles fitted to B16s and pre-1964 B18s are extinct (they're different designs from each other), and so is the boot handle of early B18s.

If any of the brightwork is missing, you should be able to replace it with decent second-hand parts, but it can be difficult establishing exactly which are the correct parts. There were lots of different badges and bits of trim fitted over the years, and there's a good chance that even if there appears to be a full complement of trim pieces, some of them probably won't be what was fitted when the car left the factory.

The electrics give few problems, although the 30-amp fuse in the engine bay can fail. The rear light reflectors can go dull, but re-silvering is possible and replacements can be bought too. The instruments and switchgear are very reliable; if there are any problems, replacements can be sourced easily enough. Incidentally, until 1961 the (B16) Amazon featured a six-volt electrical system, but there are few of these cars left, so it's unlikely that you'll be buying anything other than a twelve-volt car.

Most of the Amazon's brightwork lasts well, but if repairs or replacement parts are needed, the costs can quickly add up.

CHAPTER TEN

UPGRADING THE AMAZON

In the late 1990s, Rob and Emma Henchoz were working in the oil industry, travelling the globe. Meanwhile, somewhere in deepest rural Suffolk, Nik Yandell was busy running Amazon Cars (www.amazoncars.co.uk), a workshop set up in the 1970s, dedicated to the preservation of overhead-valve Volvos. At the time it didn't seem possible that these two worlds could collide, but when Emma and Rob decided they quite fancied a Volvo Amazon, the lines started to converge.

Ultimately they did a lot more than merely converge, because in 2000, after a couple of years of Amazon ownership, Rob and Emma decided to buy Yandell's business and settle down nearby. The pair had been bitten by the historic rallying bug; in 2001 Emma won the Newcomer's Cup in the Historic Rally Car Register Road Rally, in a completely unmodified Amazon, and she was keen to go much further. Says Emma:

In the early days of Amazon ownership we bought the parts from Nik and worked on the cars ourselves, so we quickly learned how they're put together. Once we'd taken over the business, we focused initially on selling used parts, but customers kept asking for help with maintenance and upgrades. Rob's passion is the mechanical side, so within two or three years we had a busy workshop offering items such as engine and gearbox rebuilds along with general maintenance.

Amazon Cars continued to work on all overhead-valve models – the PV, Amazon, 1800, 140-series and 164. As Emma puts it, the firm's philosophy is that for all these models, she and Rob 'make sure they can stop, go round corners and go faster – in that order'.

When it comes to tuning and upgrades, Emma and Rob Henchoz have been there, done it and got the T-shirt.

To get the most out of these Volvos, Emma and Rob have developed a whole raft of modifications. Nothing tells you about a car's weak spots like historic rallying; over more than a decade of rallying, Rob and Emma have developed an array of upgrades to help keep the Amazon moving in even the most arduous of conditions.

Typical of the attention to detail at Amazon Cars is the long-distance fuel tank, developed in-house. These foam-filled tanks were designed by Rob and they're made beautifully out of aluminium. Designed to fit over the rear axle in a specially fabricated frame, there's still space for a couple of spare wheels in the boot. As well as these tanks, Amazon Cars also produces its own coil springs and upgraded brake pads.

Rob finishes by saying:

We drive these cars every day, and we rally them, so we know what they're like to drive, what goes wrong and what breaks. This allows us to find the most effective fixes to make the cars as reliable as possible, whether that's for road use or the rally stage.

So when it came to writing this chapter, it was pretty clear who I needed to speak to. As a result, these words of wisdom on tuning Amazons and preparing them for rallying come from Rob and Emma – and if you need your Amazon pepped up a bit, you know who to turn to.

You don't have to stick with a Volvo engine to power your Amazon; V8s can be fitted or, in the case of this relatively tame conversion, a Ford Granada V6 unit.

TUNING AND MODIFYING

Amazons are easy to upgrade, with mechanical improvements often both cheap and straightforward. The solid build of an Amazon also means durability isn't compromised, and while the standard cars are surprisingly sporty, there's plenty you can do to make an Amazon even perkier. The great thing about the Amazon is that it's generally over-engineered, so you can turn up the wick in numerous ways without compromising reliability.

With B16-engined Amazons now very rare, and parts to rebuild these early powerplants now hard to come by, the assumption from the outset is that you won't be working on any engine other than a B18 or B20, both of which are well served by specialists. These larger-capacity engines also feature a stronger five-bearing block than was fitted to the three-bearing B16. This helps no end with reliability when revving above 6,000rpm.

Before you get carried away buying and fitting a raft of performance parts, though, it's worth sticking to the basics

if you're going to completely overhaul the engine anyway. Even without opting for hotter camshafts or a reworked cylinder head, significant extra power can be coaxed from the B18 and B20 engines.

While blueprinting will achieve the best results, you don't have to go that far. For example, compared with many mainstream rivals, piston and con rod weights are surprisingly well balanced. However, lightening and balancing the crankshaft, flywheel, con rods and clutch will reap rewards. The same goes for matched pistons, steel timing gears and a stronger oil pump. Doing all these things will increase power over the quoted figure for a standard engine, and if you're embarking on more involved modifications they'll provide an essential platform if you want a reliable engine. Which presumably you do…

ENGINE TUNING

The rule is that a 121 has a single SU carburettor while a 122

FACTORY TUNING

In period, Volvo was keen to make it easier for Amazon owners to tune their cars, without compromising reliability. As a result, it offered tuning kits throughout the 1960s and 1970s. Provided by Volvo Tuning Services, the B18 kit was capable of providing a very healthy 128bhp thanks to the fitment of a reworked cylinder head with larger inlet valves, revised carburettor needles and springs plus an array of further minor tweaks.

Most of the kits supplied, however, were for the B20 engine. Until 1978 there were four kits available to give four stages of tune; after 1978 this dropped to three choices. Even the Stage I kit could coax around 140bhp from the B20 engine, through the fitment of a cylinder head with enlarged tracts, radial valve seats, 44mm inlet valves, 35mm exhausts, a 10.5:1 compression ratio (a 1.2mm-thick head gasket was employed) plus a pair of Solex twin-choke 45 ADDHE carburettors. To complete things there was also a 4-2-1 exhaust manifold and a high-capacity mechanical fuel pump.

The Stage I kit was the only one available for road cars; the Stage II and Stage III kits were offered exclusively to those building an Amazon for racing. While the Stage II kit was capable of generating 165bhp from a 2.0-litre engine, the Stage III package upped this to 170bhp – or a very healthy 180bhp if the unit was taken out to 2.2 litres.

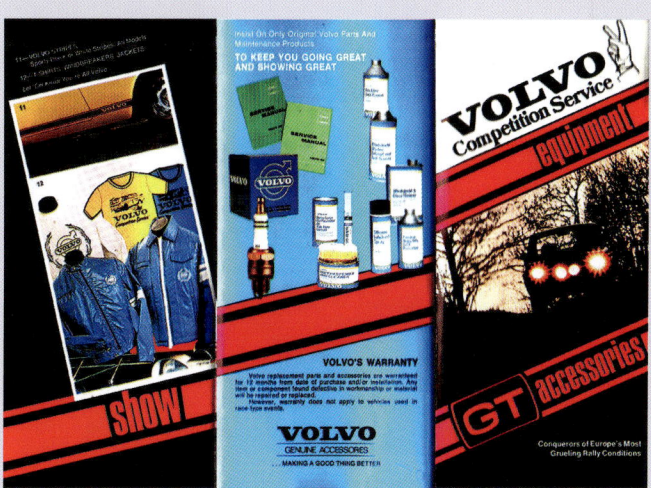

Volvo initially offered tuning parts through its Tuning Services division, but later on it was possible to buy parts through its Competition Service arm instead.

or a 123 has a pair. So if you've got a 121 the easiest thing to do is to fit a pair of SUs along with a standard 122 manifold and camshaft to see an increase in power from 85bhp to around 100bhp.

To help the engine breathe more freely it's worth fitting a more free-flowing exhaust manifold – a four-branch (or even a 4-2-1 item), and a two-inch system in place of the rather restricted standard set-up. Don't fall into the trap of thinking that fitting an 1800E cylinder head (which was also fitted to the last of the 140s) will allow a B20 engine to breathe more easily. While early B20 powerplants featured a small-valve head, and later B20 units got a big-valve item, fitting a B20 head to a B18 block will lower the compression ratio, reducing the power dramatically. Incidentally, the later big-valve head can be recognized by the machined bosses for the injectors.

CAMSHAFTS

Once you've improved the engine's breathing, it's worth investing in a slightly less tame camshaft, especially if you're working on a single-carburettor car. These were equipped with an A-specification camshaft, while those fitted to the twin-carb cars featured a C-specification item. Neither of these is as good as the D-specification item with which the GT was equipped, but there are some who reckon that for the ultimate in hot (standard) camshafts, the K-Type is where it's at. Fitted to the fuel-injected B20 engine, this camshaft provides a good spread of torque across the rev range, whereas the D-Type can be rather peaky – it doesn't really come on-song until 3,600 revs are on the dial. While the D-Type camshaft ultimately provides more top-end power, it's not very tractable as it's all rather hit and miss below 1,800rpm. However, Rob Henchoz isn't persuaded by this school of thought:

> I'm not convinced that there's any significant difference between K-Type and D-Type camshafts. The D-Type possibly provides more bottom-end torque, but I wouldn't say the difference is as clear-cut as some people think.

Whichever you opt for, fitting one of these hotter camshafts will see the power output rise to 110–125bhp without sacrificing tractability or reliability. In fact at this stage the

There are all sorts of easy engine upgrades you can make, from extra carburation and improved filtration to a bigger powerplant (such as a B20).

engine is so far from its limits that durability isn't remotely compromised.

If you're not so bothered about tractability and you want the ultimate in power, it's the F-Type or R-Type cams you should be aiming for. Alternatively there's the S-Type camshaft, which also has a 300-degree overlap. Any of these camshafts are capable of producing 140–150bhp with the correct fuelling and exhaust modifications too – but they're only really suitable for competition cars as the power delivery is just too peaky.

There's a big caveat, though, as Rob explains:

> We've always found R-Type and S-Type cams to be a nightmare, and nothing like as powerful or tractable as modern designs. The key is to buy a really well-made camshaft; we use Isky and nothing else (www.iskycams.com) because we've had so many problems with other brands – even well-known ones that should be so much better than they are.
>
> Some of these big-name brands suffer from appalling lobe accuracy, to the point where you don't really know what the spec is because the reality is so different from the on-paper figures. For the best balance of power and tractability you should be looking at camshafts with 300 and 287 degrees of overlap, although we use a 310-degree cam on Emma's road and rally car, and it's lovely with a single DCOE.

If you want an engine that'll rev to more than 6,200rpm, you'll need to lighten the followers. For high-lift cams, switch to the twin-spring set-up with its associated follower and pushrod to the valves. This will allow you to routinely run to 7,000rpm, and Amazon Cars has built engines using this set-up that can rev reliably to over 7,500rpm.

CYLINDER HEAD

If you want to liberate more horses reliably, you'll need to tweak the cylinder head too. It's a specialist job, though, so don't get too carried away or you might regret it. Your best start point is with a head from a late B20-engined 140, but you'll be doing well to find one as they're now ultra-rare. Built between 1973 and 1975, these have the largest valves (44mm for the inlet and 35mm for the exhaust valves). The B18 engines have 40mm inlet valves and 35mm exhaust. It's

the same for the earlier B20 head, which had 42mm inlets; it was from 1972 that the inlet valves grew to 44mm.

It's possible to go as far as 47mm inlet valves and 38.5mm exhaust, but this is right on the limit and if you do go this far there's a good chance you'll be compromising reliability, with cracks likely between the valves. That's why restricting yourself to no more than 44mm (inlet) and 37mm (exhaust) is a good idea.

Rob Henchoz comments:

> Going oversize on the valves gets horribly close to the chamber wall, shrouding the valve opening and effectively giving poorer gas flow. The way Volvo tuning expert Flok Boer overcomes this is by 'grooving' the chamber at the valve proximity to permit some gas flow.

Raising the compression ratio is worthwhile, but you can't go beyond 11.5:1 or reliability will be compromised. At this point the cylinder head will be down to 84.6mm thick, compared with the original 88mm. If you want to stick with the factory-supplied head gasket you'll need to take the combustion chambers out to 91mm – although if you want to go for those 44mm inlet valves and 37mm exhaust, you'll need to go all the way to 92.3mm if you're not to go beyond that 11.5:1 compression ratio. However, this isn't something Amazon Cars has ever needed to consider.

On this note, it's possible to increase the B20 engine's displacement to 2.1 litres using B21 flat-top pistons and the 1974 crankshaft. That's if you want an easy life and you don't want to compromise reliability. If you want more power and torque, though, and you don't mind compromising durability, it's possible to go as far as 2.4 litres. However, this involves eccentric grinding of the crankshaft journals, which weakens them, and gives a practical red line of around 6,500rpm at best.

Of course you don't have to go to all of this hassle and expense if you want a more powerful Amazon than the factory ever supplied. All you need to do is slot a later B20 engine into the engine bay, complete with fuel injection. You're looking for a B20E or B20F unit, which in standard (injected) form will push out 124bhp or 115bhp respectively. Originally fitted to the 140 GLE, these engines can be bored out to 2.1 litres and with standard tuning mods including the fitment of a pair of SU or Weber carburettors it's possible to coax 180bhp from the unit – although it's far from easy.

As Rob Henchoz points out:

> *We've got one of Flok Boer's most powerful motors,*
> *which is rated at 190bhp, but that's the most power-*
> *ful option he offers with everything thrown at it – so*
> *180bhp isn't that easy to get. But it is possible to get*
> *a clean and true 240bhp by fitting a 16-valve cylinder*
> *head. It's a delight to drive whatever the conditions –*
> *from going to the supermarket to full-on competition.*
> *It's a fabulous conversion, but it's costly.*

COOLING

It doesn't matter how much money you pour into the
rebuilding and upgrading of your engine – if you don't also
pay attention to detail with the cooling system it'll all be
for nothing. It would be easy to assume that you'd need
to upgrade the cooling system to cope with the rigours of
competition, especially if in hot climes, but you don't actually
need to. In fact, some 'upgrades' can cause more problems
than they solve, as Rob Henchoz confirms:

> *We've found that SuperX (three-core) radiators give*
> *no improvement in cooling, even though they allow*
> *more volume over the standard two-core units. That's*
> *because large-bore cores reduce cooling due to the*
> *speed of flow being too high. These days we will fit a*
> *SuperX radiator only if forced, but we'd always prefer*
> *a standard rebuilt unit.*

For the best, most consistent and most reliable cooling, fit
a five-blade engine-driven asymmetric fan. If you're seeking
ultimate power (or expecting deep and long fording), opt
instead for an electric system, with a thermostatic switch
mounted in the radiator; avoid at all costs the alternative
option of a capillary stuffed into the top hose.

The engine-driven fan fitted by the factory runs as long as
the engine is turning, and as a result it can be guilty of over-
cooling. By fitting a thermostatically controlled electric fan,
the engine will be cooled only once it's up to temperature,
so efficiency is improved along with fuel consumption, while
noise levels are also reduced. Kenlowe is perhaps the best
known supplier of aftermarket cooling fans, but there are
others available.

Once an Amazon engine is run at high revs for a pro-
longed period, it's likely that the oil temperature will climb

to a point where the engine suffers permanent damage.
That's why fitting an oil cooler is essential; it should make
the difference between your engine breaking or continuing
to work, so it's a pretty fundamental modification. There
are various proprietary oil coolers on the market; whatever
you fit, one way of splicing it into the system is to use a 240
Turbo adapter plate, which fits between the engine block
and oil filter. You'll be doing well to find one of these, though,
as they're so hard to come by, which is why you'll almost
certainly have to take the aftermarket route. Some of these
aftermarket systems feature an integral thermostat while
others don't. Take the 240 Turbo route and you'll automatically get one, so the cooler isn't brought into play until the
oil is up to 75 degrees Celsius.

TRANSMISSION

While the Amazon's gearbox is pretty tough, if you crank
up the power too much you're just asking for trouble. The
easiest way of upgrading the transmission is simply to fit
something stronger, with the M40 K10 gearbox fitted to
later 140s the easiest and cheapest route. The M40 gearbox
was also fitted to the Amazon, though, and in this application
its output flange may be a different diameter, but this can be
changed easily enough.

Where the M40 and M41 gearboxes are extremely
strong, the M400 and M410 are outrageously tough – these
transmissions were fitted to some examples of the P1800E
and P1800ES. And just in case you were thinking of slotting
in a 164 gearbox, the bellhousing won't fit the B18 or B20
engines.

If you want an overdrive or five-speed gearbox there's an
array of options, starting with the D-Type overdriven transmission fitted to the Amazon and carburetted P1800. It's not
very strong, though, so if you're fitting it to a car that's got
significantly more power than standard it'll benefit from the
oil pump and clutch lining being uprated. Otherwise, with
a safe limit of no more than 100bhp, you're just asking for
durability issues.

Alternatively, you could opt for a gearbox with a J-Type
overdrive, as fitted to the 1800E and 140. Take this route
and you've got a transmission that'll cope with 180bhp. Just
bear in mind that the M41 gearbox was available with both
D-Type and J-Type overdrives, but, depending on which
overdrive was fitted, the gearbox specification differed as
the output shafts are different for the two types.

The alternative to these overdrive transmissions is a five-speed Ford Type 9 gearbox. It's a recognized conversion that's pretty straightforward; specialists such as Amazon Cars keep the bits in stock. Ford's first five-speed manual gearbox for rear-wheel drive cars, the Type 9 was fitted to models such as the Capri and Sierra, including 2.8-litre V6 variants. With a safe torque limit of around 200lb ft, the Type 9 is plenty strong enough to cope with the torque of an Amazon engine, even if it's been uprated.

Another alternative to all of these transmissions is the four-speed close-ratio M40 gearbox that Volvo offered in period. You're unlikely to find one, however, as they've been unavailable for so long; and if you do manage to find one, it'll cost you plenty. Volvo also offered a limited-slip differential, but as with the close-ratio gearbox, these are now very scarce and valuable. There is an alternative, though: in place of the factory-supplied axle it's possible to slot in a Quaife ATB unit, which works brilliantly for road use.

If acceleration is key, Volvo offered lower-ratio rear axles (4.88:1 or 5.38:1), and these are still readily available. The 4.88:1 axle is the perfect motorsport choice, or for road use with overdrive; the 5.38:1 can also be sourced easily enough.

IGNITION AND FUELLING

Next stop is the ignition system, which benefits from being converted to an electronic set-up in place of the standard points and condenser. There are various routes to this, the first being the fitment of an aftermarket set-up – there are plenty available and they're incredibly easy to fit while usually being completely reliable. But these will only give a strong spark in the wrong place, as they depend upon perfect mechanical advance and the use of leaded fuel. Use unleaded petrol instead, and everything is thrown out.

The 123 by Albertronic (www.123ignition.nl) has ECU-based advance curves to match all the originals. Get a unit that's correctly supplied with an unleaded fuel curve (only available from Amazon Cars), and you'll see a big difference in the bottom and mid ranges.

For the ultimate in ignition systems you could instead invest in a unit that's PC programmable, which allows you to create the curve that precisely suits your engine. You'll have to invest some time in setting things up, though, as there's an element of trial and error in getting the best out of such systems.

If you don't want to take any of these routes, the alterna-

Dispensing with the original points and condenser, and fitting an electronic ignition instead, is one of the easiest ways of improving reliability.

tive is to fit the Bosch system from a post-1975 240, complete with distributor, control box, coil, ballast resistor and wiring harness. Fitting this set-up is easy and, as with the aftermarket systems, if you do it properly you should be able to expect complete reliability. The biggest problem will be finding a suitable set of parts, as they're all now very scarce.

When it comes to fuelling, if reliability is paramount it's worth fitting a 1¾-inch SU in place of the normally preferred twin SUs. This means you don't have to worry about keeping the carburettors balanced but it doesn't sacrifice too much power and it'll boost torque into the bargain.

Choosing which carbs to fit can be a pain as there are so many factors to juggle. If you want to keep things simple, a pair of SU HS6s is suitable for anything up to a 300-degree cam, while HIFs are also a good choice. Amazon Cars have found that Strombergs have a nasty failure mode as the bimetallic goes haywire, causing you to stop without warning, so they're best avoided.

If you're going for a spicier cam (such as a 310-degree item), sticking with SUs will probably lead to problems with the carbs throwing out fuel at idle, which is why you're better off going for a single 45DCOE or pair of 40DCOEs. Below 160bhp the latter is the preferable option as the mid-range is so much stronger, although the red line power is identical.

If you want the ultimate, though, you could always go for the full-blown fuel injection option, complete with throttle bodies and distributorless ignition – it's a superb set-up. Amazon Cars uses an Emerald ECU because of its user-friendly front-end programming.

SUSPENSION

Having upped the power, the next step is to improve the Amazon's handling by fitting better dampers. The preferred option is generally Bilstein units, which give excellent handling and last pretty much for ever – it's not unknown for a quarter of a million miles to be racked up on a set. Koni dampers are also very highly regarded; it's generally reckoned that these, in conjunction with the factory-fitted springs, will provide the best ride/handling balance. However, those who take the Koni route tend not to take the time to set everything up correctly; they're often set too hard, which produces results inferior to the softer dampers fitted as standard. That's why it's the Bilsteins that are generally regarded as the ones to fit.

If comfort is less of an issue, while the dampers are being replaced it's also worth swapping the original coil springs with units that are an inch shorter. These allow the car to sit a little bit lower and also sharpen up the handling thanks to the slightly lower centre of gravity. Beware of some cheap European-made springs, though, which give a nasty nose-down stance; make sure you buy from a well-regarded supplier.

Also keep an eye out for one of the thicker anti-roll bars that Volvo offered until 1981 (part number 659866). You can still buy kits that consist of both front and rear anti-roll-bar kits. It's worth fitting one of these as the Amazon's cornering abilities are noticeably improved with one of these fitted – at least in smooth and dry conditions. If things are rough or slippery, you're definitely better off without the anti-roll bars.

Having gone to all this trouble setting up your Amazon's suspension, it's worth replacing the original Metalastik bushes with polyurethane ones, which are less prone to perishing and which also

Bilstein dampers, such as those fitted here, are reckoned to be the best units you can fit if you want comfort, handling and reliability.

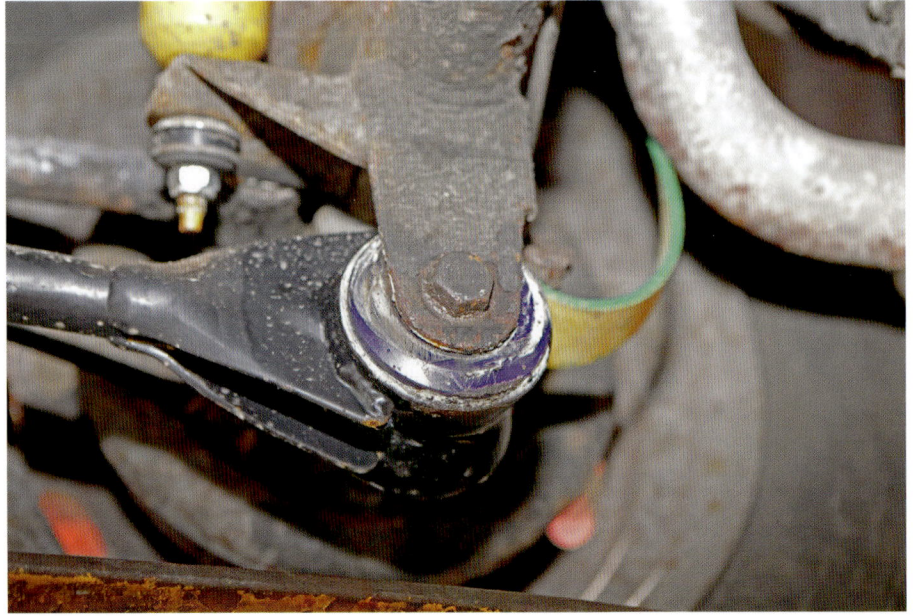

If you're going to replace the suspension bushes, don't bother with rubber – go for polyurethane instead, as they last much longer.

give a slightly firmer ride. Beware of cheap ones, however, generally those made in the USA, as they're just too harsh and produce a distinctly uncomfortable ride.

WHEELS AND BRAKES

Because the standard Amazon brakes are pretty good, there isn't much required to help them cope with the extra power. Until 1965 some Amazons were fitted with drum brakes at the front, so fitting the disc system that was installed from that year is a worthwhile and easy option.

Harder pads are useful, a common recommendation being Mintex 1155 units – although these need heating up to be at their best. That's why you're better off going for Mintex 1144 items, which will work from cold, while they also have excellent hot performance too. If the car is going to be driven really hard the dust shields can be removed to help dissipate the heat.

There's not that much you can do with the rear brakes, although they're not bad anyway. Riveted instead of bonded shoes are a good idea just to make sure that if things get really hot the shoes aren't going to start falling apart. A servo is also a worthwhile fitment, because many Amazons weren't equipped with one. This won't make the brakes any more effective, but it will help you to pull the car up more easily thanks to lower pedal pressures.

There are all sorts of aftermarket wheels available to fit the Amazon. Whatever you fit, make sure it suits the looks of this very pretty car.

One of the most popular modifications that owners make to their Amazons is the fitment of 5½-inch wheels in place of the standard 4½-inch units. This in turn allows the fitment of 195/70 tyres to improve grip and roadholding. Bear in mind, though, that exceeding 195-section tyres will make the handling dead and heavy, and you're guaranteed to lose the balanced handling that makes the Amazon such a delight to drive.

CHAPTER ELEVEN

COMPETITION PREPARATION

Thanks to its toughness, the Amazon is a cornerstone of the historic rallying scene, whether it's stage rallies or long-distance endurance events. In this section we take a look at what you need to do to make your Amazon competitive in these events. In the last chapter we looked at suitable modifications that assume you're after reliable power for fast road use and perhaps the odd excursion onto the track. If the car is being prepared for rallying there are extra steps available to make the car more reliable, and, once again, Rob and Emma Henchoz are our guides.

Whether your start point is a two-door Amazon or one with four doors, it won't make much difference as they both have the same strength and weigh much the same too. That's why you should choose your bodyshell based on its condition, although it's worth remembering that two-door cars have more period charm. However, four-door Amazons are better suited to transcontinental rallies as they offer better access to the spare wheels that are normally stored behind the front seats.

Rob begins:

> If you're going to make your car faster and hence more competitive the key is to cut weight as much as possible. It's pretty much always easier to reduce the car's mass than to increase its power; ultimately it's the power-to-weight ratio that matters. This will be beneficial when it comes to braking, acceleration, top speed and agility; boosting power helps only with acceleration and top speed.

The thing is, while in rallying weight is king, reliability is key too. So you don't want to remove too much weight and find that you've compromised the car's strength. But while removing weight can be very labour-intensive, you can make big gains by tackling the basics such as soundproofing and interior trim. If you've got the time and expertise, though, it's possible to remove as much as 15kg of metal from certain areas such

as by drilling the door hinges, removing the bonnet springs and drilling holes in the interior panels. Before you embark on any of these things, however, make sure you check the scrutineer's regulations as you could shave kilos from your Amazon's kerb weight, only to find it's no longer eligible.

LIGHTING

Start by swapping the standard seven-inch sealed-beam headlamps for H4 halogen items. These are cheap, readily available off the shelf and there are plenty of brands to choose from. Stick with reputable brands such as Wipac, Lucas or Cibie; the last of these are among the most durable and they give a good beam pattern too.

It's also worth fitting 80/100-watt bulbs, which aren't legal in some countries but you're unlikely to be spotted because compared with modern lighting – especially xenon – these uprated bulbs won't seem especially dazzling. However, in case you are spotted, it's worth carrying some legal replacement (55/60w) bulbs as well.

You might feel inclined to fit an array of auxiliary lamps at the front, but there's generally not much need to. If you do feel the need, some Cibie Oscars are a nice period touch that will prove very effective too. If you're driving on public roads all this extra lighting can cause something of a PR issue, with disgruntled locals upset that their local thoroughfares are being used as a race track; cars with standard lighting are less likely to give this impression.

A decent reversing light will prove hugely beneficial as well; if you want to keep things period, seek out a Lucas WFT 576 fog (rather than spot) lamp. If your priority is efficiency rather than period charm, the way to go now is LED reversing lights; they're brighter, more compact, use less power and they're more reliable too.

When it comes to other lighting, don't be afraid to fit lamps so that effectively the whole of the car's interior can

Before you fit a rack of extra lights, start by upgrading the lighting that's already fitted.

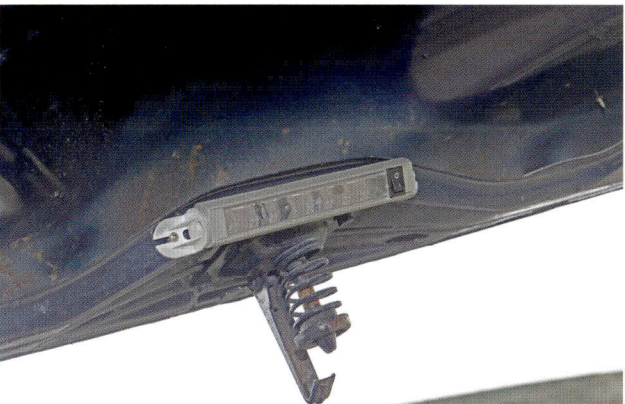

ABOVE LEFT: **When you're manoeuvring at night, you need to illuminate your way as effectively as possible with a powerful reversing light.**

ABOVE RIGHT: **If you suffer an engine malady after dark, you don't want to be messing about with torches; fit an under-bonnet light in preparation.**

BOTTOM RIGHT: **LED strip lights are efficient, compact and cheap, so they're perfect for cabin illumination.**

Amazon Cars builds these bespoke fuel tanks, which allow two spare wheels to be carried in the boot.

FUEL TANK

Keep the Amazon's fuel tank where Volvo fitted it and it'll be highly vulnerable to damage when tackling rally stages. It's no wonder Volvo lifted its factory-supported Amazons by a couple of inches then fitted a guard underneath the tank. Without these measures the tank's pick-up pipe gets clouted and damaged, leading to fuel starvation.

Rather than raise the tank and fit a guard, it's easier to mount the tank in the boot, where you'll also have room for two spare wheels. While you can fit a standard tank with the right bracketry, the ultimate solution is to fit a bespoke foam-filled aluminium tank, along the lines of those fitted by Amazon Cars. Developed by Rob Henchoz to offer the greatest possible capacity (it'll store 80 litres instead of the regular tank's 45 litres), there's also enough space left over for two spare wheels. Stronger, better protected (the filler is in the boot) and with an FIA rollover valve incorporated too, safety levels also get a major boost.

be illuminated at night. This means fitting lighting to the boot, under the bonnet, above the navigator and also to the rear of the car's interior. Self-adhesive LED strip lights are generally the best way to go here; they can be attached easily to the underside of the bonnet, boot and roll cage to give a pure white light using the minimum of current.

BODYSHELL STRENGTHENING

Because of the Amazon's design it's not possible to fit a strut brace, but to stiffen the bodyshell you can strengthen the

A roll cage is mandatory in many race series – even when it isn't, you should have one fitted anyway.

It's vital that you're held in place securely when campaigning your Amazon, which is why bucket seats like these are essential.

front crossmember by seam welding it entirely and adding a couple of triangular stiffeners on each side to stop the turrets curling in. It's also worth welding in an extra heavy washer on the upper damper mounting to stop it cracking, although you need to do this from underneath, rather than on top. When strengthening the chassis, also think about adding a couple of box sections between the inner wing and the front bulkhead – it's easy enough to do.

Even if you don't modify the bodyshell in any significant way, you shouldn't be looking at competing in an Amazon without fitting a roll cage – it'll be mandatory a lot of the time anyway. Not only does a roll cage protect you in the event of things going belly up, but it also stiffens up the bodyshell significantly. For maximum effectiveness, the cage needs to be bolted to the A, B and C pillars; it attaches to the floorpan in six different places. When choosing your roll cage, make sure you go for a harness bar so you've got somewhere you can easily attach your safety harnesses. Some of the best roll cages are made by Safety Devices. They're made in sections and bolt into place.

SEATS

It's crucial that you fit seats that are comfortable for long distances and which support you in even the most arduous of conditions. While you can fit costly new seats from the likes of Sparco, Corbeau and Recaro, often the best option is to find some decent used chairs from something old and sporting. These might be an old hot hatch or something more luxurious – although the latter often doesn't provide the necessary side support.

For example, Rob and Emma Henchoz use Saab 9000 seats, which are wonderfully comfy, but which don't offer enough side support when things get really hectic. Don't forget that you should really have some kind of head restraint too; most new seats will come with this as standard, but some older ones don't.

ELECTRICS

Reliability is paramount when rallying, and if there's one area that lets many cars down it's their electrics. Tackling a challenging set of bends and having your lighting fail is something you really don't want to experience, which is why major electrical system upgrades are par for the course for most rally cars. Not the Amazon, though, which has a brilliantly reliable electrical system straight out of the box. Despite the fact that the last Amazon was built in 1970, poor connections and fragile looms are still not an issue.

As a result, you should stick with the original wiring as

You don't need to replace the Amazon's electrical system wholesale, but you do need to upgrade it carefully.

much as possible, adding to it – rather than replacing it – as necessary. It's worth replacing the factory-fitted fusebox with a standard four-blade alternative. The lack of relays isn't ideal, though, which is why you should add one to the horn circuit.

Swapping the original foot dip switch is worthwhile too; your best bet is to convert to a 140 indicator/flash column stalk. You'll also need a clock; most competitors favour a Brantz item with an appropriate tripmeter. However, digital clocks are now allowed universally; take this route and

You'll need to fit some kind of fire extinguisher, but you don't need to go overboard.

it's worth going for Monit product. And don't forget to fit another stopwatch for the driver so they can also calculate the average speed, allowing the navigator to get on with plotting the route.

FIRE EXTINGUISHER

You'd have to bonkers to compete in any car not fitted with some kind of fire-extinguishing system. Regulations mean you must have a hand-held two-litre extinguisher within reach of both the driver and navigator once strapped in. You may be able to just about get away with the extinguisher being located under the navigator's knees or on the transmission tunnel, but whatever you do, don't take chances.

What isn't required is a full-on plumbed-in extinguishing system unless you're taking part in stage rallies; the key is to fit whatever suits your pocket. There are mechanical as well as electrical systems available; if you avoid these and go for a simple hand-held item, make sure that it can't come loose in the event of the car being rolled. The best solution is to lock wire any extinguisher(s) in position so they can't come free; if they start flying about in the event of a roll, serious injuries can easily result.

BRAKES

Being mounted next to the door jamb, the handbrake is far from ideally located if you need it to execute a tight turn. That's why it's a good idea to relocate the handbrake lever to the transmission tunnel, ideally using Peugeot 205 parts as these fit pretty well. Obviously the key is to mount everything in the right place; it's easy to get things wrong here, but get it right and it'll make a big difference to the car's manoeuvrability.

If you're not anticipating using the handbrake much, it's fine to keep things as standard. If you are planning to use it a lot, go for woven, sintered brake linings at the back. Whether or not you'll be using the handbrake a lot, it's worth fitting Mintex M1144 linings to the brake pads, while at the back you should go for Ferodo linings. You shouldn't expect any difference in terms of brake feel or effectiveness, but these alternative linings have a better heat tolerance so they're less liable to fade.

Cars with twin-circuit brakes are fitted with a self-adjustment system that doesn't work well enough for competition use, which is why you need to convert to the earlier Girling manually adjusted set-up. However, this in itself presents problems because the Girling adjusters tend to twist and rip through the back plate, which is why you need to reinforce everything with a massive washer, which will keep everything working smoothly.

SUSPENSION

It's easy to get carried away as there are all sorts of things you can do to tweak and/or uprate the Amazon's suspension. In the main, though, keeping things simple is the best solution. So don't go for adjustable dampers, as many people do, because they take ages to set up – then you have to do it all again for the next run because the conditions will be different.

You can also opt for dampers with an external reservoir, but these are expensive and generally banned in most branches of rallying – so just stick with a decent set of gas Bilsteins. With these in place it's just a question of working out which springs you require; you'll need to pick the length and stiffness depending on the terrain you'll be covering.

There are four different spring set-ups available, starting with the standard offering. These are fine if you're not covering seriously challenging terrain and you're in no hurry. But in competition you're always in a hurry, which is why you're

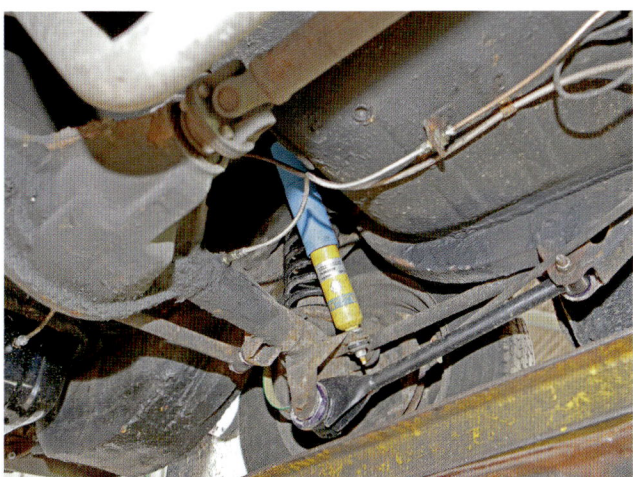

You're spoiled for choice when it comes to suspension options; what your car will be used for makes a big difference as to which route you should take.

more likely to want a set of fast road springs. Lowered by 20mm, these have a huge effect on cornering and they're ideal for road rallies.

If you're going to be tackling really challenging terrain, you'll need to fit Africa springs. These give the same ride height as the standard items but they're stiffer so the car can be yumped without fear of bottoming out. Essentially, the front springs are designed for the car to cope with yumping, while those at the rear are designed to cope with the extra weight of a long-range fuel tank, roll cage, twin spare wheels and so forth.

The final option is one created for UK road and/or night rallying. These are essentially Africa spec at the front while at the rear they're fast road.

While you're setting up the suspension, fit a set of high-quality polyurethane bushes. Fit cheap or poorly made ones and they won't last long, plus the ride may well be compromised. But a decent brand such as SuperFlex will last for years and won't destroy comfort levels.

Steering Geometry

A touch of negative camber (−0.75 degrees) and the book caster is the perfect set-up for most conditions. If the steering feels heavy, check that caster angle (and the top and bottom balljoints). Never overtighten the steering box adjustment; there is supposed to be 'slop' off centre, but dead ahead should just be free of play.

AIR FILTER

Fit a Volvo 2-litre air filter, so you'll be able to cope with deep standing water. With pretty much any aftermarket filter you'll find the water gets sucked in and it'll take 100 metres to clear, with the engine coughing and spluttering for all of that time – just what you don't need. Stick with a Volvo filter and you'll be able to go through pretty much any depth of water at any speed and your engine won't miss a beat – and all the while the Volvo item provides the best filtration into the bargain.

As Rob Henchoz comments:

Unless the car is being used in hot conditions for endurance rallying, we tend to delete the closed-circuit breather fitted to later cars – this connects

There's no need for fancy aftermarket air filtration – just stick with a Volvo 2-litre set-up instead, from the 140.

Cooling can be a big issue in competition situations, so ensuring the radiator is in tip-top condition is key.

Fuel vaporization can be a problem too, so fitting rubber spacers between the carburettors and manifold can make all the difference.

the crankcase breather to the manifold. The filler cap and crankcase breather breathes to the atmosphere, and as long as you're not going to go through lots of dust for long periods, this is more effective – that's how the early B18 was set up. However, on transcontinental rallies you have to live with a slightly strangled breathing system by fitting the correct closed-circuit system.

TYRES

Don't go overboard with your tyre sizes; the widest items you should fit are 195-section items. However, you're better off sticking with 185/65 15 as they're easy to get at a good price for the most highly regarded brands. By sticking with these tyres you can also stay with standard pressed-steel wheels. In theory, 185-section tyres shouldn't fit on a 4½-inch wide wheel, but they do. As a result you can fit 185/65 15 tyres to any of the original factory-supplied wheels, but if you want something beefier you can also easily source 5.5J wheels that'll just slot straight on.

TRANSMISSION

Fitting a decent limited-slip diff can make more of a difference in rallying than uprating the engine. That's because an LSD will allow you to make the most of the power you have, and when the going gets slippery that counts for a huge amount. There were genuine Volvo LSDs offered in period but these are now hard to find and very costly, which is why you're better off fitting a Quaife ATB unit instead. One of these will make a massive difference when competing in snow and ice, as it cuts tramping enormously. However, the Quaife ATBs aren't as good as the Volvo items as they can be unpredictable on the limit, such as when taking part in forest stages.

COOLING

When driving in extreme conditions it's normal for a large amount of heat build-up around the carburettors, potentially leading to fuel vaporization. As a result, it's worth speeding up the heat dissipation process by letting some louvres into the bonnet. To reduce the amount of cooling that's needed, also think about getting the exhaust manifold ceramic coated; stick with a decent product such as Zircotec though, or it's not worthwhile. Don't take the cheaper route of wrapping the exhaust manifold, though; if the carbs leak the wrap will get soaked in petrol, which will then ignite.

UNDERBODY PROTECTION

Your car's underside tends to get bashed about rather a lot when rallying, which is why it's essential that you fit some kind of protection to key parts if they're to survive. The exhaust is especially vulnerable, so instead of relying on regular, rather flimsy exhaust pipe mounts, use engine mounts instead. Far more substantial, they'll last much longer – mount one just ahead of the rear axle and another one to hold the rear box in place. There's no need to protect the exhaust itself; on big rallies, your best bet is to fit skid plates for the length of the car.

Guards for the sump and steering box are essential, however. The sump guard doesn't need to be especially wide; use 8mm thick aluminium between the gearbox member and the front crossmember. And because the steering gear is very vulnerable, you'll need to fit a similar guard from the front crossmember to the radiator crossmember.

WHAT YOU DON'T NEED TO DO...

For years, twin coils were an essential part of the rally driver's armoury, but modern coils are so reliable (Amazon Cars has never had one fail in 15 years) that it's just not necessary. Fit a Bosch coil and the chances of problems are minimal. If you're not convinced and you do decide you need to carry that second coil, don't just stick it in the boot – make sure it's in the engine bay, where you can quickly swap the dead outgoing item for the new one.

Because the Amazon has a two-piece propshaft, the joint between the two sections could be seen as something of a weak spot. As a result, some people assume when preparing their Amazon for rallying that they should eliminate this joint by fitting a single-piece shaft. However, not only does the two-piece item not cause any problems in terms of durability, but the single-piece option will cause far more hassle because it's not possible to fit something with the necessary rigidity, even with 80mm tubing.

Fitting a back-up coil won't cause any problems – but the chances are that you won't need it if your main coil is of a decent quality.

OTHER FEATURES WORTH ADDING TO YOUR AMAZON RALLY CAR

There's a whole raft of things you can do to make your Amazon more comfortable, more reliable or easier to live with when you're campaigning it. These include:

A foot rest for your co-driver, so they can brace themselves when the going gets tough.

A bonnet quick release is more reliable than the original pull cord.

An oddments bag strapped to the roll cage will allow you to keep small items safe so they don't get thrown around the car.

Extra gauges will help you keep on top of the engine's condition.

An electronic rev counter reduces the likelihood of you over-revving the engine.

A quick release on the boot is also worthwhile, in case of lock failure.

You shouldn't travel without a spare drive belt on your road car – and it's the same with your Amazon racer.

AMAZON SPOTTER'S GUIDE

121 (B16A, 1957–61): The first production model, with a 60bhp 1582cc single-carb engine, four doors and three-speed manual gearbox.

122S (B16B, 1958–61): Produced for export, with an 85bhp twin-carb 1582cc engine and four-speed gearbox.

121 (B18A, 1961–68): Still just one carb, but a new cylinder head and 1778cc means there's 75bhp (85bhp from 1966). There are two- or four-door saloons or a five-door estate. The four-door saloon was dropped in 1967.

122S (B18D, 1961–68): A twin-carb 121. There was a two-door from 1963, with the last four-door built in 1967. Power outputs were 90bhp (1961–65), 95bhp (1966), 100bhp (1967) or 115bhp (1968).

221/222 (B18A, B18B, B18D, 1962–69): Amazon estate with a 1778cc engine. Sometimes referred to as the 121 or 221 Combi or estate. Fitted with 4.5J wheels borrowed from the 1800.

121 (B20A, 1968–70): Two-door with the B20A 1998cc engine of the 140-series. 90bhp gives 100mph.

123GT (B18B, 1966–68): Two-door with 115bhp high-compression version of P1800 engine. Also fitted with 4.5J wheels.

122S (B20B, 1968–70): The most powerful Amazon, with the 118bhp 1998cc powerplant of the 140-series. Offered as a two-door only, it can manage over 100mph. Fitted with either twin SUs or Strombergs.

131 (B18D, 1965–70): Two-door entry-level Amazon with single-carb 75bhp engine.

THE DIFFERENT SERIES OF AMAZON

A-series (from January 1957)
* 60bhp B16A engine
* Four-door saloon only
* Two-tone paintwork

B-series (from spring 1958)
* B16B engine
* Four-speed M40 gearbox

C-series (from August 1958)
* Standard front seatbelts for all cars
* Amazon Sport for Swedish market
* A new type of brake servo (known as the duo-servo)
* Improvements to the heating system

D-series (from August 1960)

- New three- and four-speed gearboxes (all-synchronized)
- Introduction of overdrive option for the 3-speed gearbox
- New seats

E-series (A-series for P130 and P220, from August 1961)

- 12-volt electrical system
- B18 engine
- Asymmetrical headlights
- New grille
- Two-tone paint option ditched
- Stronger front suspension is reinforced and heavier
- Girling front disc brakes for sportier models
- Two-door saloon introduced

F-series (B-series for P130 and P220, from August 1962)

- Rear axle strengthened
- New rear lights (now incorporating reversing lights)
- Improved rustproofing

G-series (D-series for P130 and P220, from August 1963)

- Borg-Warner BW35 automatic gearbox now offered
- Redesigned boot handle now incorporates the number plate lighting
- New headlining design

K-series (E-series for P130 and P220, from August 1964)

- Front disc brakes now standard for all models
- The estate gets a brake servo
- New radiator grille
- New wheels and hubcaps
- New emblems on the sides
- Rear seat passengers now get their own heating duct
- There's now a rear armrest for all Amazons
- The front seat passenger gets a handle on the dashboard
- The radiator blind is no longer fitted
- The estate gets a gas strut for the upper tailgate
- New, ergonomically designed seats

L-series (F-series for P130 and P220, from August 1965)

- New compression ratio for B18 (by fitting thinner head gasket)
- New camshaft
- Sealed front suspension and propshaft
- Rear wheels now have a valve to help prevent locking when braking
- Amazon Favorit economy special introduced (with no chrome around the windows, black or white paint only, two-door bodyshell and an M30 three-speed gearbox)

M-series (from August 1966)

- New grille
- Redesigned seatbelts
- 123GT introduced
- Extra power for all engines (thanks to Stromberg carburation)
- Sealed cooling system with new radiator
- P120-series discontinued for most markets

P-series (from August 1967)

- Collapsible steering column
- New steering wheel
- Brake servo for all models
- Four-door production ceases (replaced by the 144)

S-series (from August 1968)

- B20 engine
- Dual-circuit brakes
- Brake servo

T-series (from August 1969)

- Estate production ends
- Only the B20 engine is now offered
- Standard seatbelts for the rear seats
- Adjustable front headrests

AMAZON PRODUCTION FIGURES

Amazon two-door saloon

Year	Cars built
1961–62	10,500
1962–63	29,500
1963–64	44,600
1964–65	59,800
1965–66	72,550
1966–67	62,950
1967–68	32,600
1968–69	27,500
1969–70	19,918
Total	**359,918**

Amazon four-door saloon

Year	Cars built
1956–58	5,184
1958–60	49,214
1960–61	29,900
1961–62	28,500
1962–63	27,200
1963–64	26,400
1964–65	27,400
1965–66	31,250
1966–67	9,160
Total	**234,208**

Amazon Estate

Year	Cars built
1962	1,400
1962–63	6,875
1963–64	9,675
1964–65	11,450
1965–66	15,200
1966–67	17,200
1967–68	8,500
1968–69	2,897
Total	**73,197**

Total Amazon production = 667,323

INDEX